Nirupama Rao, former Indian Foreign Secretary, and author of
The Fractured Himalaya: India, Tibet, China, 1949–1962

'At last, an accessible, accurate and up-to-date account of the India–China border.
Steeped in Joshi's deep knowledge and long experience, this timely and topical book
places the India–China border within the larger context of relations between the two
countries, and of Asian and global politics. Coming when India–China relations are poised
at the crossroads and could go either way, this book is an essential read.'

Shivshankar Menon, former National Security Adviser, Foreign Secretary and
Ambassador to China, and author of *Indian and Asian Geopolitics: The Past, Present*

'In a field already crowded with several works on the India–China border issue, this finely
crafted book stands out for its meticulous research, sharp analysis and outstanding
insights. Joshi has skilfully used the prism of the border issue to explore the possible
trajectory of India–China relations in a vastly altered geopolitical landscape, lending to
the book's contemporary relevance.'

Shyam Saran, former Indian Foreign Secretary,
Prime Minister's Special Envoy on Nuclear Affairs and Climate Change and author of
How India Sees the World: Kautilya to the 21st century

'The territorial dispute between China and India is one of the world's largest and most
consequential. In clear, lucid and engaging prose, Joshi offers an accessible and definitive
account of the dispute's complex history and how the stability created along the border
in the early 1990s has steadily eroded. A terrific accomplishment and must-read for
anyone interested in the past, present and future of India–China relations.'

M. Taylor Fravel, Arthur and Ruth Sloan Professor of Political Science, and Director,
Security Studies Program, Massachusetts Institute of Technology

'Having covered India's unsuccessful struggle to resolve the boundary dispute with China
over the last three decades and more—as a reporter, editor, analyst and scholar—Joshi
offers deep insights into the tragic tale of unaligned interests and unrealisable expectations
of each other in Delhi and Beijing.'

C. Raja Mohan, Visiting Research Professor, Institute of South Asian Studies,
National University of Singapore

UNDERSTANDING THE INDIA–CHINA BORDER

MANOJ JOSHI

Understanding the India–China Border

The Enduring Threat of War in High Himalaya

HURST & COMPANY, LONDON

First published in the United Kingdom in 2022 by
C. Hurst & Co. (Publishers) Ltd.
New Wing, Somerset House, Strand,
London, WC2R 1LA
© Manoj Joshi, 2022
All rights reserved.
Printed in Great Britain by Bell and Bain Ltd, Glasgow

Distributed in the United States, Canada and Latin America by
Oxford University Press, 198 Madison Avenue, New York, NY 10016,
United States of America.

The right of Manoj Joshi to be identified as the author of
this publication is asserted by him in accordance with the
Copyright, Designs and Patents Act, 1988.

A Cataloguing-in-Publication data record for this book
is available from the British Library.

ISBN: 9781787385405

This book is printed using paper from registered sustainable
and managed sources.

www.hurstpublishers.com

All maps by Spatial Technologies, Faridabad

CONTENTS

For the one person who matters more to me than anyone else, Mandira Mitra

ACKNOWLEDGEMENTS

This book is the outcome of three decades of reporting, writing and commenting on China and the India–China border in particular. I would like to thank Hurst for giving me the opportunity to put it all together in what, I hope, is a useful and coherent narrative. Michael Dwyer has played the role of a publisher as well as editor, and this has been to my benefit. Here I would also like to express my thanks to Daisy Leitch, the Production Director at Hurst, who has helped see the book from the first proofs to its production. This is not an academic study of the Sino–Indian border problem, but rather the work of a journalist aimed at both scholars and the interested reader.

Over the years, given the remoteness of the border and the official nature of the Sino–Indian discourse, I have relied almost exclusively on official sources and contacts and on news reports. In the past many officials took time to explain the arcana of the border dispute to me. They cannot be named, but I would like to express my appreciation to them. Truth be told, I would not have been able to complete this book in the time I did were it not for the COVID restrictions that have blocked all travel. Working from home was the norm at the Observer Research Foundation (ORF), where I work as a Distinguished Fellow, as well. This also meant a limited access to libraries. Fortunately, my personal collection of documents and books as well as the resources available online proved useful here.

I owe Ambassador Ranjit Singh Kalha, who passed away some years ago, a debt of gratitude. He was the early interlocutor who got me interested in the Sino–Indian border dispute in the mid-1980s when he was Joint Secretary (East Asia), at the Ministry for External Affairs, the

ACKNOWLEDGEMENTS

point man for India's relations with China. I have cited his book, *India–China Boundary Dispute*, extensively in mine.

I also owe a debt of gratitude to Pushpindar Singh (Pushy) Chopra, who sadly passed away in 2021 during the second and deadly wave of COVID-19. I can now disclose that I had obtained the manuscript copies of the official war histories of India because of him. Most scholars assume that those being cited are official publications, but that is incorrect: they remain in ready-to-publish form only. Since then, the 1965 and 1971 war histories have been published. Peculiarly, the Ministry of Defence has asserted its copyright, but the editors, now retired from service, have said in the respective Introductions that as such the book 'does not reflect the view of either the Indian Armed Forces or the Government of India in any manner.' However, and this is germane from our point of view, the 1962 war history remains unpublished and available for anyone to view on the internet. Thanks to Pushy.

My interest in China has intensified in the past seven years that I have worked at the Observer Research Foundation (ORF). The Foundation has been generous in allowing me the time and freedom to explore my areas of interest. The ORF has meanwhile transformed itself into a global think tank and I have found that the value of its platform in putting across ideas has been enhanced manifold. I wish to express my thanks to the two drivers of this process: the Chairman of ORF, Sunjoy Joshi, and its President, Samir Saran. I would also like to express my appreciation to all my ORF colleagues for providing the collegial atmosphere that has shaped the writing of this book and to offer special thanks to the Foundation's librarian, Ms Nisha Verma, for providing me with all the assistance she could, despite the COVID-19 lockdown.

Two experienced China hands—former Foreign Secretary and National Security Adviser Shivshankar Menon, and former Foreign Secretary and Special Envoy of the Prime Minister, Shyam Saran—did me a huge favour by going through an earlier version of my manuscript. I am grateful to them for being kind enough to look at what was then still a very rough draft. Their suggestions have improved the book immensely, but needless to say, they cannot be held to account for any inaccuracies or gaps that may remain. Those are entirely my responsibility. Menon, my senior in college and longtime friend, was kind enough

ACKNOWLEDGEMENTS

to review my final conclusions and as a result of his advice I re-wrote portions of it. That is a heavy debt. Thanks so much, Shivshankar.

Finally, I would like to express my gratitude to my daughters Saba and Manya, as well as my sons-in-law Daniel and Amit for providing the warm family atmosphere which is essential for a project like this. But a really big hug goes out to my 3-year-old granddaughter Lila who visited while I was finalising the manuscript and tried her best to help by periodically hopping on to my lap and thumping the computer keys at my work station. Her efforts provided that special stimulus that I needed. Between the time this manuscript was submitted and finalized, Manya gave birth to Farhan and I was doubly blessed as a grandparent.

Finally, I would like to express my deepest appreciation to my wife and partner, Mandira Mitra, to whom this book is dedicated. She has sustained me with her affection, love and companionship for nearly half a century.

New Delhi, December 2021

Map 1: The outline map of Ladakh

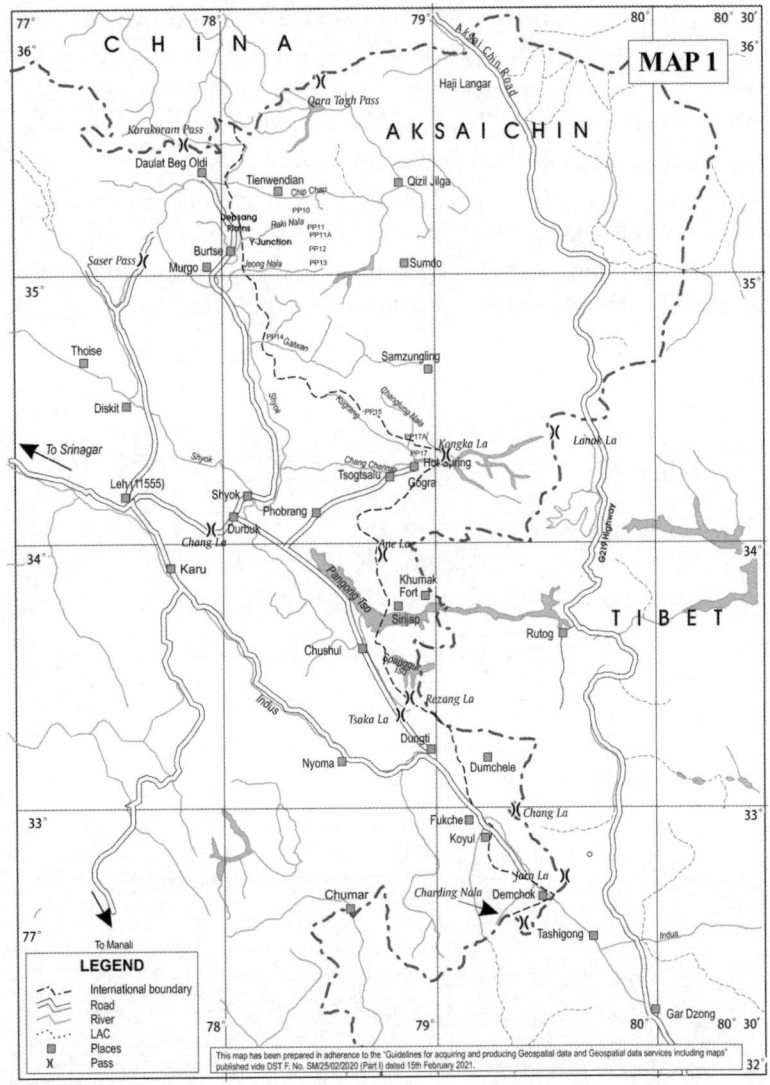

This map has all the principal places in Ladakh related to the China-India encounter of 2020.

Map 2: The Pangong Tso and Spanggur Tso

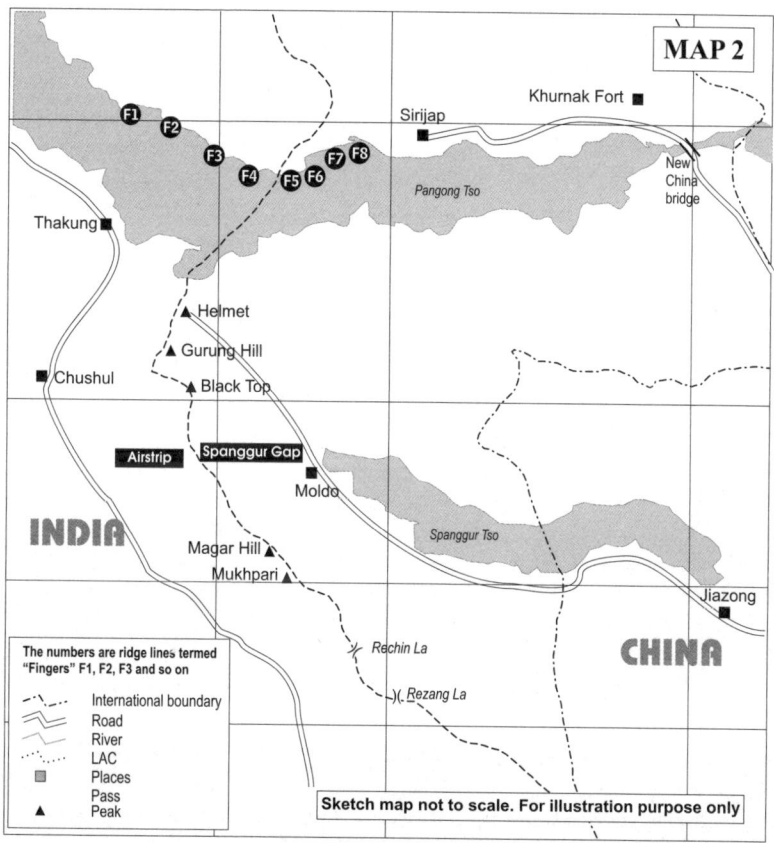

This is a region through which an important trade route from Leh to Gartok in Tibet passes. This was recognized by Tibet and Ladakh as a border region, but just where the border points lay was not clear. This area was the scene of heavy fighting in 1962.

Map 3: The Kugrang river valley, Gogra and Hot Spring

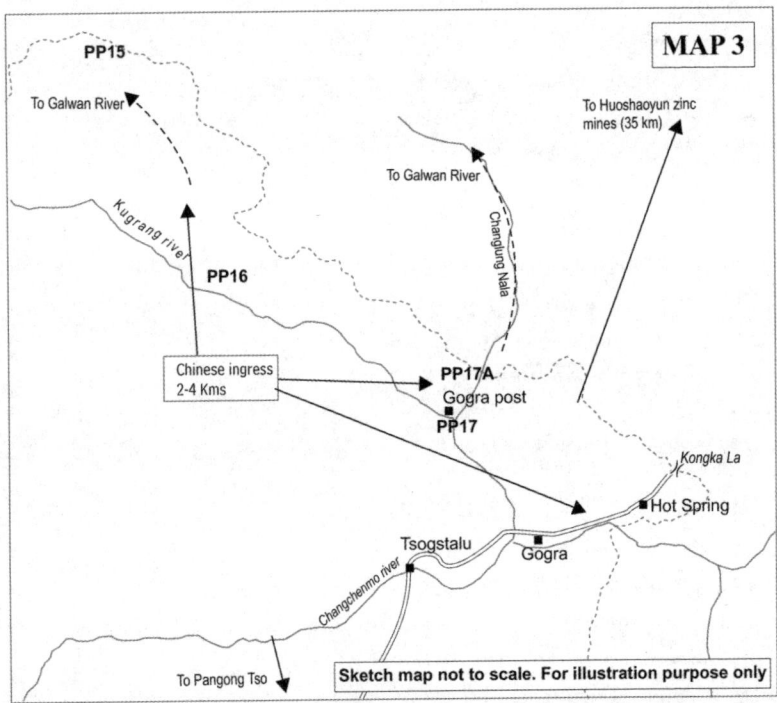

The Chinese ingress here has not been acknowledged clearly by the Indian side. The Chinese themselves had accepted the watershed between the Kugrang and Changlung as the border but now seem to want to revise it.

Map 4: The Depsang Problem

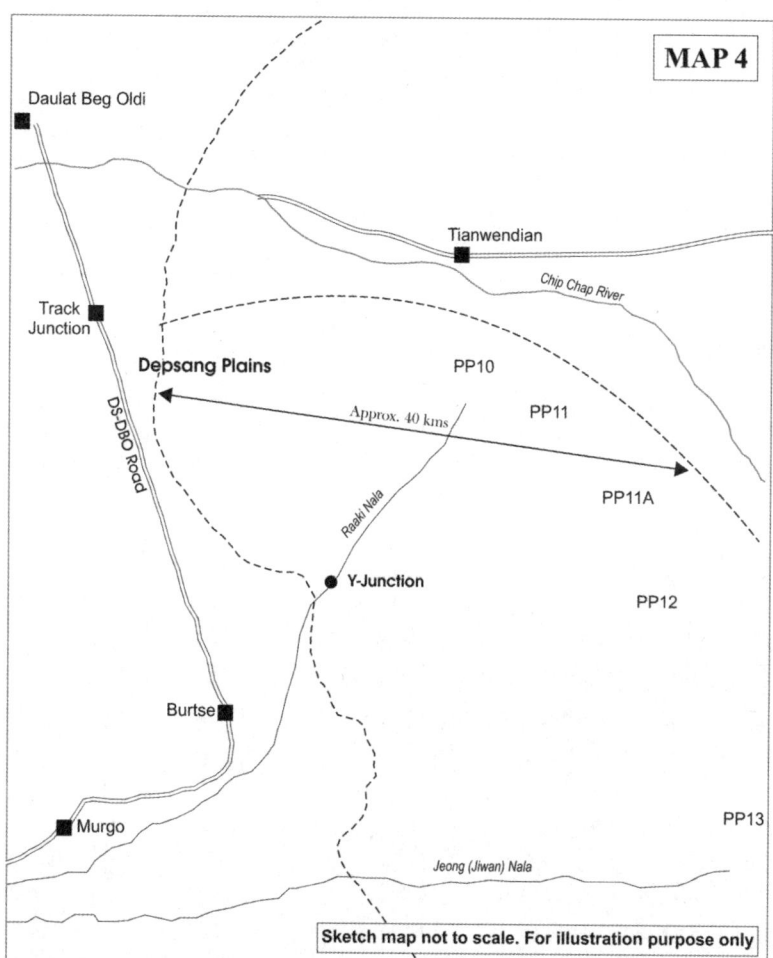

The Chinese blockade at Y-Junction is preventing India from patrolling a vast, high altitude desert area marked by its Patrolling Points (PP) 10-13. This was the scene of a 2013 face-off as well. Again, the Indian side has been quiet about this area claiming that this to be a "legacy" issue.

Map 5: The entire China-India border

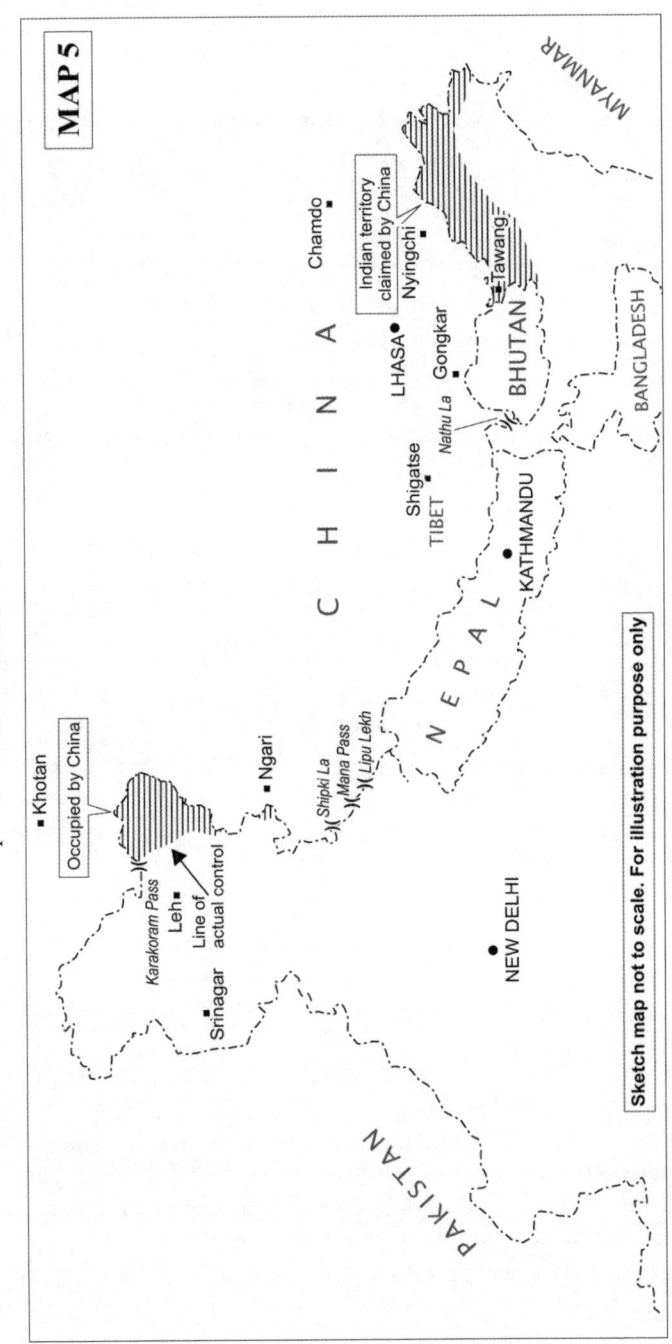

MAP 5

Khotan

Occupied by China

Karakoram Pass
Leh
Line of
actual control

Srinagar

Ngari

Shipki La
Mana Pass
Lipu Lekh

NEW DELHI

PAKISTAN

NEPAL

KATHMANDU

TIBET

Shigatse

Nathu La

Gongkar

BHUTAN

LHASA

C H I N A

Chamdo

Nyingchi

Indian territory
claimed by China

Tawang

MYANMAR

BANGLADESH

Sketch map not to scale. For illustration purpose only

The Chinese say it is 2000 kms in length, which is about half of the Indian estimate. The difference relates to the way the claims are expressed.

Map 6: The Sumdorong Chu/Wangdung region

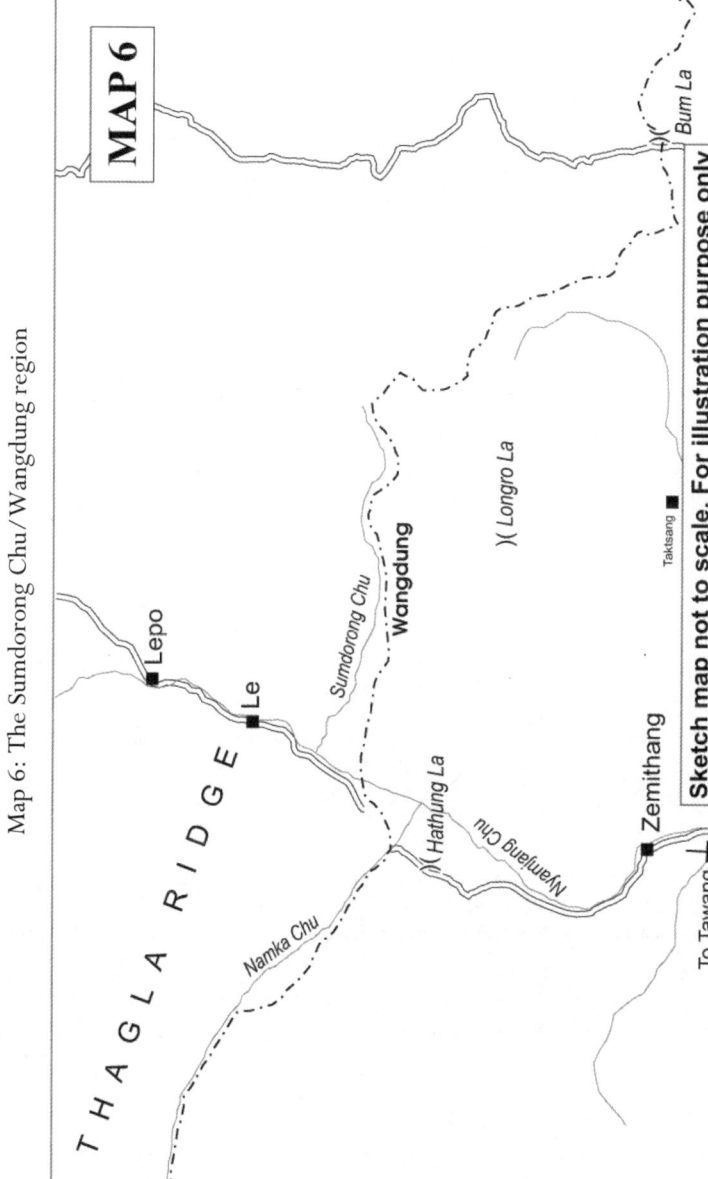

This is where the 1962 war between India and China began. It was the site of another confrontation in 1986–87.

Map 7: Doklam and its environs

The Chinese claim to this Bhutanese region depends on an 1890 convention with Britain, to which Bhutan was not a party.

Map 8: Doklam and the Siliguri Corridor

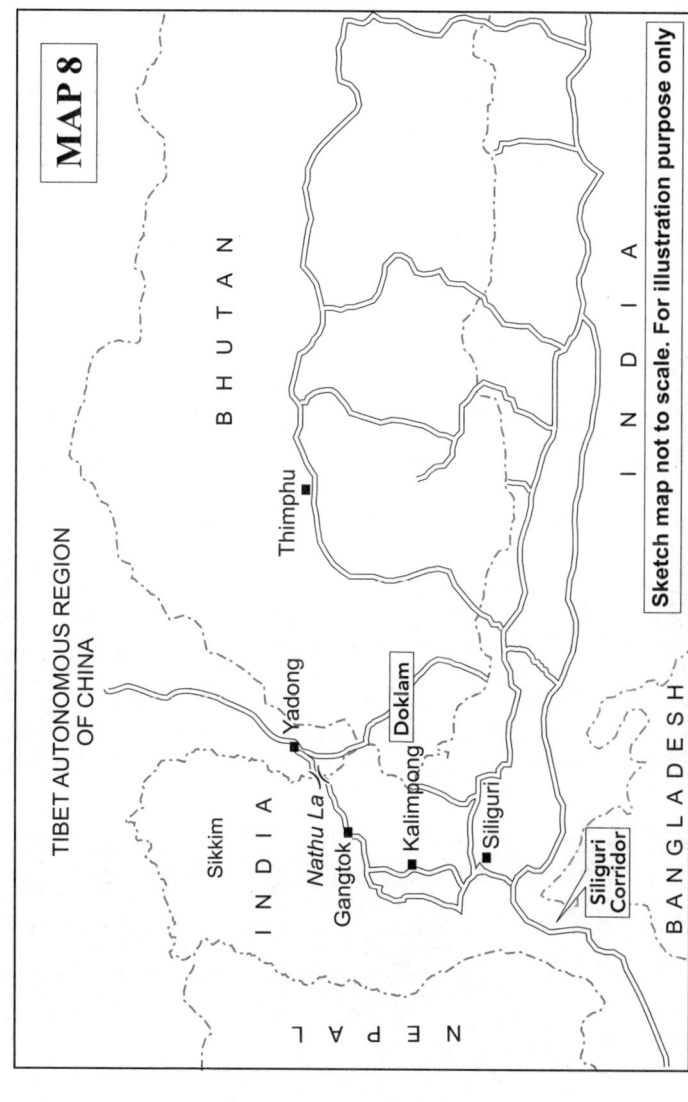

The proximity of the Chinese to this "chicken's neck" is viewed as a grave national security vulnerability by India.

Map 9: Bhutan

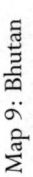

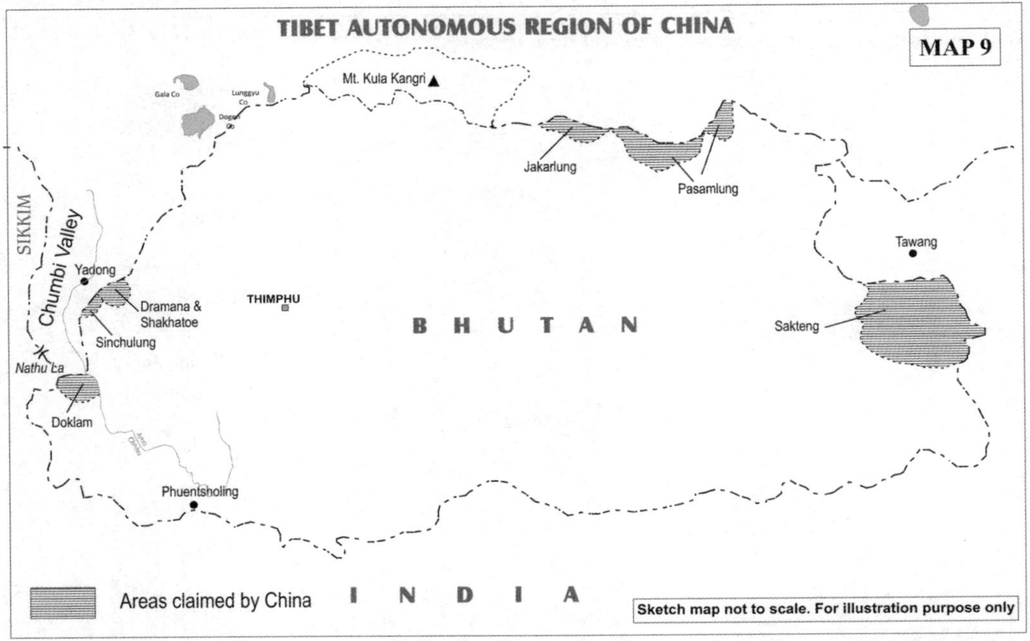

The Chinese tried to swap their northern claims with the western ones, but now they seem to be in the process of simply occupying these areas. The claim to Sakteng has suddenly emerged in 2020. As can be seen this could be very sensitive considering its location south of Tawang.

INTRODUCTION

During one long summer night of mid-June 2020, Indian and Chinese troops clashed on the Galwan river valley in Ladakh in north-western India. Using fists, stones and improvised clubs, they slugged it out in the dark at an oxygen-deficient altitude of 14,000 ft (4,250 m), in sub-zero temperatures next to a swift-flowing river. By the time senior officers brought the situation under control next morning, twenty Indian and four Chinese soldiers were dead; they included the Indian commanding officer, while his Chinese counterpart was seriously wounded. Scores had been wounded and taken captive. Both sides accused the other of starting the fight by crossing into the other's territory.

This should have come as no surprise, yet it did. Since April, even as the COVID-19 pandemic spread, there were signs that things were not normal in this north-western part of the Sino–Indian border. In Ladakh, India's northernmost territory, China has, since the 1950s, occupied Aksai Chin which India considers its territory; while in the east, India controls the state of Arunachal Pradesh which is claimed by China. After having fought a short war in 1962 over the border, the two sides worked out a series of confidence-building measures in the 1990s to keep peace. But since the border is defined by a Line of Actual Control that has never been delineated on a map, both sides had routinely charged each other with transgressions and incursions.

The one incident that had stood out in recent times, the Sino–Indian confrontation at Doklam, was really in a disputed part of the Bhutan–China boundary, but there had been no casualties. Proverbially, not a shot had been fired across the Line of Actual Control, which is patrolled by the respective Chinese and Indian border guards backed by their respective armies.

The incident in Galwan was the culmination of an unprecedented development around the third week of April 2020, when an estimated 50,000 Chinese troops with tanks, armoured personnel carriers and artillery took up positions near the border. At the same time, Chinese border guards began to push into the Indian side at five points simultaneously—Depsang, Galwan, Pangong Tso, the Kugrang river valley, and the Charding Nala near Demchok. (See Map 1)

Since the Chinese advanced into what were essentially unheld areas, the Indians were taken by surprise. Fortunately the Chinese action was not intended as a military invasion, but was rather a complex operation aimed at strategic coercion, accompanied by a move to occupy some areas of the Indian Union Territory of Ladakh, which is marked by what the two countries term a Line of Actual Control (LAC) of some 900 km. Both sides have their own versions of the LAC and there are some points of dispute along it which, by common agreement, were hitherto patrolled by both sides. Militarily, the Chinese intrusions may have been minor, but with the huge clash of June 15, along with the resulting deaths and injuries, they became politically extremely significant for both New Delhi and Beijing.

Initially taken by surprise, India reacted fast and conducted a counter-deployment. But it was aimed only at checking further Chinese advances. New Delhi decided that it did not have the wherewithal to force the Chinese to restore the *status quo ante* as of April 2020. This was clearly a failure of India's border management strategy as well as a statement of its inability to deter the Chinese military action on its frontier.

The Sino–Indian border problem is *sui generis* in many ways. For one, the two countries are not agreed over the length of the boundary that they dispute in its entirety, in its western, central and eastern sectors. The Indians variously say it is 4,057 and 3,488 km long, the Chinese say it is 2,000 km only. Note that India claims the boundary from the Afghanistan-Xinjiang-Kashmir trijunction, while the Chinese begin counting only from the Karakoram Pass. The two have, on occasion, sought to exercise their claims militarily and fought a short war over the border in 1962 that did not go well for India.

The region where the Sino–Indian border lies is mountainous, mostly uninhabited, and subject to extremely cold weather for six months of the year. Through history, the notion of a border only had a meaning at certain points along the terrain through which there was cross-border trade, carried by sheep and yaks along vertiginous mountain trails. There were no border guards, yet people who traversed the border knew at which point they left their own frontier and entered that of the other. And then there were pastures which were used commonly by shepherds from both sides.

Articulating a modern boundary for the area was always going to be a source of tension, and it certainly became one, once other geopolitical interests intruded. Currently, even as India and China continue their long-running efforts to settle their dispute, their border is marked by a Line of Actual Control. This is a notional line, linking a number of points over which each side claims to exercise effective control. In the east, the LAC runs along the Himalayan watershed, although the Chinese claim 90,000 sq. km of north-eastern India, comprising largely of what used to be the North East Frontier Agency (NEFA) but which has since become the state of Arunachal Pradesh, that runs down to the Assam plains. In the west, on which this book will focus, the LAC leaves in the hands of the Chinese some 38,000 sq. km, claimed by India as being part of the Union Territory of Ladakh. Till 2019, Ladakh was part of the state of Jammu & Kashmir, which is itself disputed between India and Pakistan. (See Map 5)

Across this vast terrain, actual military posts are sited in relatively few places, so that the border on a mountain ridge, an escarpment, a fast-flowing river or a high mountain pass, is often a "Line of Perception" rather than one showing "actual control." Parts of it are simply inaccessible; other parts are "marked" mainly in the summer months, by sending out routine patrols to the points where one side perceives lie the limits of its LAC. But there are places where the perceptions overlap and, in the past, border sentinels deliberately left behind tell-tale debris—empty cigarette packets, cans of food, newspapers, wrappers of biscuit packets and so on—to show possession, as it were.

The Indians say they have accurately mapped the LAC and ensure their patrols do not transgress it. The Chinese say the same. But since the two sides have not yet worked out a commonly delineated map, this is a ready-made recipe for trouble. Yet, until 2020, barring a clash in the eastern region of Sikkim in 1967, the vast and inhospitable border had been peaceful. Indeed, the last significant incident took place in 1975 when four Indian soldiers were killed in an ambush in an area north of Tawang in north-eastern India.[1]

Through agreements in 1993 and 1996, the two sides had agreed to "strictly respect and observe the LAC between the two sides" pending the final resolution of their boundary dispute. They had also agreed to clarify the status of some of the places where the claims of the two sides overlapped, in other words address the perceptional issue.

Through common agreement, at least till 2020, both sides patrolled up to the limit of their claim at the twenty or so points along the LAC where their claims overlapped. Since this is a notional line, as it were, it is not surprising that as their logistics improved, both sides began to bump into each other. When through this book we will talk of "intrusions" or "transgressions" they are really perceptional categories; the Indians view Chinese actions to patrol up to their claim as a "transgression" or "intrusion", and vice versa. In 2014 an official of India's Union Home Ministry explained the difference to a reporter this way: An "intrusion" is when Chinese troops entered and stayed put in an area for a while, while in the case of a "transgression" they entered Indian territory, but returned to their own side without establishing a camp.[2]

With the clash on the Galwan river, a long process of maintaining peace and tranquility on the LAC abruptly ended. By this time both sides had brought up substantial additional forces, weapons and equipment, which were at some points, eyeball-to-eyeball with each other. For a while, it looked like the two big powers were headed for a larger skirmish, if not war. But the habits of the decades of maintaining peace prevailed, as the two sides continued a dialogue at multiple levels to restore the situation. But, as of December 2021, they have done so only partially.

This book uses the events in summer 2020 as a prism to provide an overview to Sino–Indian relations in the past thirty years or so. Looking at the incident itself you may wonder why two of the largest armies in the world clashed the way they did—with clubs and stones—in a region as inhospitable as north-eastern Ladakh. You would want to know why two republics founded within months of each other in 1949 and 1950 have a border that has yet to be delineated, let alone demarcated.

The answers lie, as they often do, in politics, but also in the world-views of the two Asian neighbours. China from the outset was a "national security state" which felt it was besieged by "imperialists" and whose policies had to, first and foremost, deal with the issue of national security. India, on the other hand, saw development and democracy as its primary goal and began to focus on "national security" only in the 1980s.

The universal franchise in India came with the Republic in 1950 and the compulsions of development persuaded its leaders to progressively whittle down its military spending, just as challenges to its security were growing. The Communist Party of China (CPC) saw the mission of the state it had established, the People's Republic of China (PRC), as to reinstate China's "traditional" boundaries; in essence, those set by the Qing Empire. That meant re-asserting Chinese authority over Xinjiang and Tibet. India having been divided into two states—India and Pakistan—saw itself as a successor state to the British Raj in South Asia and claimed the boundaries set by the Empire.

Almost immediately, it came into contact with the newly founded People's Republic, determined to end the "Century of Humiliation" the country had suffered at the hands of western imperial powers. It was led by insular Marxist-Leninists who had come to power through the force of arms. Their armed wing, the People's Liberation Army (PLA), comprised battle-hardened cadres who had been fighting for a generation.

There could not have been a greater contrast between the urbane leadership of India with its sprinkling of western educated lawyers and professionals and the hard-as-nails veterans of the CPC, more a military organization than an orthodox political party, which slaughtered an estimated 2 million class enemies as soon as it came to power.[3]

For independent India's Prime Minister, Jawaharlal Nehru, influenced by Gandhi's non-violence and Fabian socialism, friendship with a fellow Asian country like China was pre-destined. But as Jagat Mehta, a former foreign secretary of India put it, "just as China never bothered to understand the workings of democracy, India never followed carefully the impact of the domestic debate inside China."[4] It would not have been easy, even if India had tried. While its own society was open, with its internal debates widely reported in the media, China's were closed, just as they remain today.

Being part of what was probably the world's greatest empire, left the Republic of India with a substantial burden. Colonialism did not just impact the economy and culture, but even the notion of national

5

boundaries and borders. Maps of the Republic inherited from the British showed the northern borders in the west and central parts of the country with merely a flat-wash, an even band of colour on the paper. The British had an active culture of surveying, exploring and mapping, but some of the regions they ruled, or were adjacent to, were truly difficult to access. Yet, ever alert to geopolitical challenges, the British worked assiduously to shape the boundaries of their Indian empire. Their biggest worry was Tsarist, and later, Communist Russia. To take care of this, they bolstered Qing authority to the extent of accepting its "suzerainty" over Tibet and Xinjiang.

They managed to force the Afghans to accept a boundary with India and the Kashmir state, and also created the Wakhan Corridor to separate the British from the Russian Empire. However, efforts to persuade the Chinese to accept a boundary line between Jammu and Kashmir and Xinjiang failed. In 1914, a Simla Convention was worked out to shape the border in the eastern part of India through the McMahon Line. The line was never spelt out in the text of the convention itself, but was put down on an agreed map of a scale 1 inch to 8 miles "by a thick pen dipped in red ink." The Tibetan plenipotentiary appointed by the Dalai Lama, Lonchen Shatra, signed the convention and it was initialled by the Chinese central government plenipotentiary, Ivan Chen. However, the Chinese later introduced a certain ambiguity about its status, even though at this time, Tibet, which had formally declared independence in 1911, was a sovereign state which it remained till 1951.[5]

Actually, nature, custom and tradition shaped much of the Tibetan boundary with India. In the nineteenth century there had been little or no Chinese official presence near the borders in any case. There was an Amban (Chinese Resident) in Lhasa and some official representatives in Kashghar, but that was about it. There were issues with Tibetans at various places, but they were minor.

Former foreign secretary, Shyam Saran, has pointed out, "In terms of historical evidence, the Chinese never exercised any jurisdiction south of the Kunlun mountains, even when their empire was at its most extensive under the Qing dynasty (1644–1911)." The Chinese called the Kunlun the Nan Shan or the southern mountains.[6] Indeed, it was the British who, wanting to keep the Russians out, encouraged the Chinese to extend their jurisdiction south and offered them part of Aksai Chin, or all of it at various points of time in the late nineteenth century.

The rise of the People's Republic of China and its military occupation of Tibet in 1951, notwithstanding commitments to giving the area autonomy, changed things. From the outset, New Delhi took the not entirely unreasonable position that there was a traditional and customary boundary which had actually been fixed as much by nature as by usage and agreements. Unbeknownst to India, China occupied the eastern segment of Aksai Chin and, in the early 1950s began to build a road there as part of its project to consolidate its hold on Tibet. Though Indians claimed they were aware of this, they did not react till the road was complete.

Later, a *post-facto* justification was created to say that the remote region of Aksai Chin was important for China because a vital track linking Xinjiang with Tibet ran through it. But at the time, in the early 1950s, conditions in Xinjiang weren't such that it could be used as a logistical corridor as was subsequently claimed, and neither was the road through it ready till 1958 when the Chinese had already been in control of Tibet for eight years and had several alternative roads into Tibet.

Just how disturbed things were in the region comes out through an incredible side-story of how a group of Cossacks, who were part of the Kuomintang (KMT) forces in Xinjiang, fought their last battle against the PLA in Rudok, near Pangong Tso lake in 1951. Indian border guards refused to let them into Indian territory, and they were hard pressed as the PLA stepped up its attack. Fortuitously, Nehru was visiting Jammu & Kashmir and the Ladakh garrison commander, Brigadier K. Bag Singh, met him at the Srinagar airfield and got permission to give them asylum. Subsequently, over the protests of the Chinese all the Cossacks were allowed to come into Indian territory. Where they went thereafter is unknown.[7]

The Indians extended a claim on Aksai Chin based on history and periodic exercise of administrative jurisdiction. Actually, neither the Indian, nor the Chinese claim was iron-clad. Till the Chinese began to think of annexing Tibet, they had little use for the area; likewise it had no strategic or economic value for India. In some ways it was a vast uninhabited no-man's land, but modern boundaries do not cater for such things. So Aksai Chin became the point where two different notions of border-making clashed—one based on national security, and the other on historico-legal claims.

As for the McMahon Line that defined the Sino–Indian border in the east, the PRC refused to accept its validity, but promised to respect it, and, indeed, did so till the mid-1980s. In 1962 they captured all the North East Frontier Agency (NEFA), but went back north of the McMahon Line after the ceasefire. While the Dalai Lama in Lhasa may have exercised ecclesiastical authority over Tawang monastery, there is no evidence that he had exercised administrative jurisdiction there, or in the vast tracts of NEFA. This region was administered directly by New Delhi till 1987 when it was constituted into the state of Arunachal Pradesh.

As modern states, India and China could hardly depend on the concept of traditional and customary boundaries in a region which was so remote and largely uninhabited. Their challenge was to sit down together, negotiate and establish a boundary that could be delineated on a common map and thereafter demarcated on the ground. Jawaharlal Nehru took the unconscionable position that India's boundaries were fixed and India knew where they were and hence there was no question of negotiation.

Nehru's handling of the border issue was somewhat over-subtle and he was outplayed by his wily counterpart Premier Zhou Enlai. The Indians did not raise the issue of the boundaries in the mid-1950s, and the Chinese brushed aside questions relating to their maps, saying that they were from the older Kuomintang era. It was only after their Aksai Chin road was ready that, in 1959, the Chinese sprang the surprise that in their view the entire border needed to be negotiated afresh and that the older maps were not really inaccurate.

The Tibetan revolt of 1959 and the flight of the Dalai Lama and over 60,000 Tibetans to India changed the context of the dispute and the Sino–Indian relationship. Ostensibly, the 1962 war was occasioned by the border dispute but in reality it was about Chinese insecurities in Tibet, triggered by the 1959 revolt. New Delhi was soundly defeated but, having captured all of Arunachal Pradesh, the Chinese retreated back to the north of the McMahon Line. In Ladakh, however, they moved to their self-defined border, and retained some of the areas they had captured from India.

It is worth speculating why the Chinese withdrew from Arunachal Pradesh after capturing it. Was it because their supply lines were extended? Were they afraid of US intervention? Or was it the fact that they were not too serious about their eastern claim?

Over time there have been three kinds of proposals to resolve the boundary dispute. The first is a "package" deal made in 1960 through which each side keeps what it was holding—Arunachal Pradesh in the case of India and the Aksai Chin for China. The package offer was revived by Deng Xiaoping in the early 1980s. Around that time, India raised a demand that the Chinese, in addition to accepting Arunachal as being part of India, return territory they had captured in Aksai Chin in the 1962 war. This "LAC Plus" offer did not fly either. Any of these were doable, but India could not get over the feeling that one piece of Indian territory was being traded for another, even if there was enough evidence that Aksai Chin had really been a huge no-man's land.

Beginning 1985, China withdrew the package and now said that since the area of the largest dispute was in the east, India needed to make "meaningful concessions" there and only then would China make concessions in the west, though it was never clear as to what they would be. In 1987, when India upped the ante by declaring that Arunachal Pradesh would become a state of the Indian Union, China, too, followed suit by now specifically demanding the Tawang tract as an irreducible minimal concession by India.

Saran, who has accessed Chinese scholarship and the archival material on the issue has concluded that the Chinese only raised the McMahon Line issue, after India formally protested in 1958 that China had violated Indian territorial integrity by building the road through Aksai Chin. He says that the eastern claims were a bargaining chip to acquire the western territory, noting that "had China been convinced of its claim in the west there would have been no reason to suggest this trade-off."[8]

* * *

In 1993, China and India decided to set aside the efforts to resolve their boundary dispute and get on with normal relations in other areas. To that end, they agreed to maintain a *status quo* on the Line of Actual Control that marked their existing border. But what they needed and did through a succession of agreements in the next two decades, was to establish a set of protocols and rules to ensure that the LAC, which we noted was often merely a Line of Perception, remained peaceful.

A major reason for this was that neither side needed to assert their maximal claims; they already held most of what they considered important—the Chinese had Aksai Chin and India Arunachal Pradesh. A subsidiary factor was that the primary security concerns of both sides lay in other directions—India towards Pakistan, and China towards Taiwan—and so they felt their interests were best served by maintaining peace along the LAC.

The problem was, for reasons we will elucidate, that China changed her behaviour and India, which earlier lacked the wherewithal, responded to this in ways that Beijing was not comfortable with. Along most of its length, there were no differences as to where the LAC lay, but over time, as we noted, some eighteen to twenty places had emerged where there was an overlap of claims, usually never more than of a dozen or so kilometres, mostly less. Though the two sides were committed through agreement to look at these areas and fix them, it never happened because the Chinese backed out. Yet, through the 1990s and till the mid-2000s, there was peace along the LAC. But then things began to change.

The locations where claims overlapped became points of contention. As per the protocols, both sides patrolled them, and they even evolved elaborate rules as to what to do if they met face to face. But that did not entirely do away with friction. As both sides improved their infrastructure along the mountainous border, they met more frequently. In some places there was a breakdown of rules and a few physical scrimmages. Yet, the rule that no guns were to be used prevailed, again, until 2020.

From the mid-2000s Beijing began to complain about the Indian efforts to build up its border infrastructure. Considering India was only playing catch up, this was a bit strange unless you understood that the Chinese did not want India's new roads, airfields and other facilities to undermine the dominance that the PLA was exercising along the Line of Actual Control by virtue of its superior infrastructure in Tibet. In this sense, it viewed Indian behaviour as destabilizing, which it probably was.

In the early 2000s after the Chinese walked away from the process of fixing the points of difference on the location of the LAC, an ambitious parallel process was begun to set aside old disputations and contentions and strike a political bargain to settle the boundary dispute once and for all. Two top officials were designated Special Representatives to deal with the issue. This was a time when both India and China were growing rapidly and were already being spoken of as leading powers of the emerging era. The Indians saw the process as one which would largely legitimize the existing Line of Actual Control with minor adjustments here and there. But the Chinese have insistently pressed their demand for "eastern concessions" by which they mean the monastery town of Tawang and its adjoining region. Since there is no way India can sell such a concession domestically, this process has also run dry, at least as of 2021.

The 2008 global financial crisis helped China to pull away decisively from India in terms of what the Chinese call "comprehensive national power." In both economic and military terms, China surged where India, after a significant rise, stumbled.

Therein probably lies the root cause of the current crisis: China has stopped viewing India as an equal. In 1990, when the two sides began the process of normalizing their relations, the size of the Indian and Chinese economies were roughly the same and India's military forces, if anything, probably had an edge on China. Thirty years later, with an economy five times as large as India's and spending three times more on its military, China is a Great Power. This asymmetry that has developed affects its attitude towards the border management agreements it had signed with India when it viewed itself as some kind of an equal.

In an article last year, a prominent Chinese scholar Ye Hallin noted that China's main worries on the economic and security fronts emanate from the US: "China has never regarded India as its main concern. Whether it is a partner or opponent, it is a secondary level." He went on to add that even in South Asia, China did not recognize India's pre-eminence, "not out of hostility" but through a "judgment of the geopolitical structure of the Indian subcontinent and the Indian Ocean." And, he was candid enough to add, the problem was that "China's conclusion is precisely what India cannot accept."[9]

US scholar Yun Sun put it another way in early 2020, before the outbreak of the crisis: "China believes in power politics and its own natural superiority. Beijing's vision for Asia is strictly hierarchical—

with China at the top—and does not consider India an equal." In her view despite their respective public postures, "distrust and hostility" between them run deep.[10]

In response as it were, to redress the balance of power that has been shifting against it, New Delhi had begun to inch closer to Washington. This process has not taken place overnight, and is also the product of other factors beyond China. After all, till at least 2017, the US policy of engagement with China was running full throttle, though the Obama administration had begun talking of the "rebalance" to Asia. And it is not as though India was walking away from China. Indeed, in 2018 and 2019, the two countries initiated the process of informal summits between their leaders to deal with the issue of mistrust and lack of communications between them. These agenda-less meetings gave them ample time to range over a number of issues of bilateral and international concern.

India and China had been fellow-members of BRICS, New Delhi is a shareholder in the Beijing-promoted Asian Infrastructure Investment Bank (AIIB), as well as the Shanghai Cooperation Organisation (SCO) and other multilateral and plurilateral bodies like the ASEAN Regional Forum, the East Asia Summit, and so on. Yet, beginning 2016, India had become the lead country in resisting China's signature Belt & Road Initiative (BRI). Though articulated as a plaint against Chinese activity in what India considered Pakistan Occupied Kashmir, it soon became the basis of a wider attack on Beijing on account of its alleged lack of transparency and the predatory practices of the BRI. During the Trump administration, the US adopted and popularized several points of the Indian critique of the BRI. Then, at the end of 2019, India decided to stay away from the Regional Economic Cooperation Partnership (RCEP), again blaming China for its decision. It appeared that even if India was no competition for China in terms of its economy and military power, it still had considerable capacity to play the role of a spoiler.

Another development was the Indian intervention in Doklam on behalf of Bhutan in 2017. This was a wake-up call for China which has since undertaken a crash upgradation of its infrastructure, civilian and military in Tibet. In July 2021, Xi Jinping became the first general secretary in recent times to visit Tibet and inaugurate a high-speed rail system to a town just 15 km from the Indian border. The Chinese have been able to ride out the last major Tibetan uprising, of 2008–2009, for which they blamed Tibetan exiles in India. But they are now seeking to consolidate their grip by a surge of investments to promote development and simultaneously Sinicise Tibetan Buddhism.

A combination of these factors probably pushed Beijing into some muscle flexing in Ladakh to show India its place in the scheme of things, thereby upsetting the thirty-year-old process of maintaining peace and tranquility on the disputed border. Where in 2018 the US had begun a process to decouple with China, suddenly India took the lead. It banned over 300 Chinese apps, virtually blacklisted the operations of various Chinese companies, and slowed down Chinese imports. Yet, the irony is that China remains the principal source of India's imports and, in 2021, trade has grown sharply.

So, the two countries are at a situation where they need to work out a new *modus vivendi*. Beginning in the second half of 2020, the military leaders of the two sides have held successive rounds of meetings alternately at Chushul and Moldo which are near the Pangong Lake. Though they had managed to disengage from the site of the Galwan Valley clash in July 2020, and in the Pangong Tso area, there remain several important places where there has been no change. Further, the troops and combat equipment of the two sides remain massed in areas close to the Line of Actual Control.

Both sides have been talking of "disengagement followed by de-escalation" but their end point is different. The Indian side wants a restoration of the *status quo* as of April 2020. The Chinese want a withdrawal of both sides marked from their new positions followed by a buffer or no-patrol zone, which would naturally be mostly on the Indian side of the erstwhile LAC.

Clearly it will be difficult to rely on the old protocols to manage the disputed border: there will be need for a new set of confidence building measures. The next clash will not be with clubs and rods, but guns. Both India and China have stepped up their border deployment significantly, as well as their capacity for cross-LAC operations, thereby increasing the danger of war. The year 2021 has seen an uptick of Chinese activity in other parts of the LAC, in the central sector between Ladakh and Nepal, as well as in the east in the area near Tawang.

Other issues, too, will impact the situation in the future. Among these are the relationships of China with the United States and the European Union. A new administration in Washington has brought little change since it, too, sees the US in "intense competition" with China. There appear to be shifts in EU attitudes as well, which are manifesting themselves in the commitment of countries like France, Germany and the UK to a higher profile in the Indo-Pacific region. These will inevitably play into the postures adopted by New Delhi and Beijing in the coming years.

1

BREAKDOWN

On 6 June 2020, a helicopter with Lt Gen. Harinder Singh, Commander of the Indian Army's XIV Corps, landed on a specially prepared helipad built on a disused airfield near the village of Chushul, that overlooks Pangong Tso, a brackish 134-km lake shared between China and India. From there the general drove along a road which is known as the Spanggur Gap to a small Chinese base at Moldo, on the shores of another nearby lake, the Spanggur Tso. Here, waiting, was a Chinese team led by Major General Liu Lin, Commander of the South Xinjiang Military District of the Chinese People's Liberation Army. The corps-commander level meeting was convened only after lower level military meetings on 18, 20, 22 and 23 May failed to reach any consensus, as neither did diplomatic consultations.

The two conferred for six hours, with the Indian team patiently conveying to their Chinese counterparts that they would have to pull back from the areas of eastern Ladakh into which they had moved since April 2020. These were contested areas claimed by both sides, which by agreement were patrolled by them following protocols that had been arrived at in the last thirty years. But now, Chinese forces had created blockades on the north bank of Pangong Tso, in the Kugrang river valley, the southern half of the Depsang Plains, and the Charding-Ninglung Nala area, south of Demchok, to prevent Indian patrols from reaching areas which they used to earlier.

The Chinese side complained that India was building a road from the junction of the Shyok and Galwan rivers several kilometres up the Galwan river, into Chinese territory. The Indians, in turn, told the Chinese that the Line of Actual Control (LAC) was, at least, 8 km away from this confluence and the Chinese already had road proximate to that point. The Chinese insisted that their territory was up to the junction of the Shyok and Galwan rivers, and that they were exercising their claim.

Not surprisingly, the Chinese side refused to acknowledge any fault, and offered mirror comments saying that it was the Indians who had crossed the Line of Actual Control and carrying out provocative actions and were improving their infrastructure in the region in violation of agreements.

The two military officials did not issue any joint statement. But later it transpired that they had agreed on a sequence of "disengagement" of forces in certain areas, followed by "de-escalation." This meant that in the first stage troops in contact with each other would be pulled back and, subsequently, the two sides would remove the additional forces that had been brought in.

It was only the next day that India's Ministry of External Affairs declared itself to be satisfied and said that the talks "took place in a cordial and positive atmosphere." The statement said that the two sides would continue their military and diplomatic engagement to resolve the situation and "restore peace and tranquility in the border areas." There was also the usual bit in the statement about the seventieth anniversary of Sino–Indian relations and the apex agreement between Prime Minister Narendra Modi and his counterpart President Xi Jinping to maintain peace and tranquility.[1]

In February–March 2020, the Chinese had been conducting their routine annual exercises in western Tibet some 200 km away from the LAC. All countries make some precautionary deployments when a neighbour conducts a military exercise. The annual Indian Army–Indo-Tibetan Border Police (ITBP) exercise takes place in the Depsang region in March with troops from other areas being brought in as well. But when COVID-19 infections surfaced among the soldiers in mid-March in line with the draconian lock-down Prime Minister Modi had instituted across the country beginning the third week of March, the exercise was postponed.[2]

When the Chinese began to move some of these combat forces westwards towards the LAC, the Indian Army did not pay heed, even though they had received intelligence reports regarding their movement.[3] On 5 May concentrations of Chinese forces had appeared near the Galwan valley and Gogra-Hot Springs area in the Kugrang river valley, but even now, the Indian Army had not appreciated the seriousness of the threat. Chinese border guards had begun blocking India efforts to patrol to Finger 8 in the north bank of Pangong Tso and the Kugrang river valley beyond Gogra Post. On 9 May, there had been a major scuffle near Finger 5 in the north bank of the Pangong Tso when sticks and stones were used and scores on both sides had been injured. These "fingers" were ridges that came down from the heights to the north bank of the Pangong Tso. There were eight distinct ones, and where the Indians saw their border lying at Finger 8, the Chinese claimed that it was at Finger 4 and prevented Indian patrols from going to the area beyond it. In two other areas, Depsang in the north and the Charding-Ninglung Nala near Demchok, the PLA established effective blockades as well.

Separately and thousands of kilometres away, on 9 May there had been a clash between Indian and Chinese troops near Naku La in northern Sikkim, where a dozen Indian and Chinese soldiers had been injured.[4] But this was not related to the developments in Ladakh.

Earlier in January Army Chief M.M. Naravane had told reporters that after the Wuhan informal summit, Indian and Chinese forces were following "strategic guidelines" and resolving local issues locally and not allowing them to escalate. On 14 May he told reporters that "temporary and short duration faceoffs" were routine in an area where both sides had overlapping claims of the LAC.[5]

Later that day, responding to reports of face-offs in the Pangong Tso region, the Ministry of External Affairs official spokesman Anurag Srivastava made an anodyne statement at his official briefing that India and China "attach utmost importance to maintenance of peace and tranquility in all areas of the India–China border regions." Adding that in their recent informal summits Prime Minister Modi and President Xi Jinping had also directed their militaries to "earnestly implement various confidence building measures… as a result, India–China border has largely been peaceful."[6]

So, the problem was not the lack of intelligence, but its assessment. On 17 May the PLA forces occupied the ridge lines of Finger 4 and moved to its southernmost tip to block any Indian moves eastwards. It was at this point the Indian side realized that they had a problem in hand. Though the Indian side accused the Chinese of "breach of trust" in doing so, in reality, they had been caught napping. Meanwhile the Indian Army, though taken by surprise initially, had begun to rush another two divisions, some 50,000 men, into Ladakh along with their heavy equipment and weapons to counter the Chinese deployment.

The more troubling ingresses were in the Galwan river valley and near Gogra Post, north west of Pangong Tso. Over the years, India and China had faced off at several points along the Line of Actual Control in Ladakh where they had overlapping claims—in Pangong Tso in 2008, 2017 and October 2019, the Depsang Plains in 2013, in Chumar in 2014 during Xi Jinping's visit to India. In fact, there had never really been problems in the Galwan or the Kugrang area and there had been no indications in the decades past that the Chinese had any overlapping claims with the Indians in Galwan.

The Galwan valley was a sensitive area for India since the LAC was proximate to the newly built 255-km Darbuk–Shyok–Daulat Beg Oldi (DS-DBO) road that ran along the Shyok river and which India had carved out with the greatest of difficulty to establish its link with its northernmost post at DBO, a little short of the Karakoram Pass which marks the border between India's Ladakh and China's Xinjiang province. But this road had been decades in the making and surely the Chinese were aware of the Indian efforts to construct it. The DS-DBO road had been formally opened only in April 2020, and it enabled India to reinforce its northernmost areas adjacent to Daulat Beg Oldi, but also aided the effective policing of the Line of Actual Control in Galwan, Jeong Nala, Raki Nala and the Depsang Plains.[7] And now, the Indian side had begun constructing a lateral road leading off from this DS-DBO road into the Galwan valley. Further up the valley was a place where the Indians and Chinese had clashed in 1962 as well.

The first reports of the developments appeared in the Chinese media on 18 May. Guo Yuandan of the *Global Times* said that the Chinese forces "had strengthened control over the Galwan river valley area." Citing military sources he said that earlier the Indian side had "crossed the line into Chinese territory in the Galwan river valley area...erected barriers and blocked normal patrols of the Chinese border troops, deliberately provoked incidents and tried to unilaterally change the status quo."[8] This was in fact a mirror image of what the Chinese had done.

By the end of May, according to a report, main battle tanks and towed artillery had been deployed in the north and east of Gogra and Hot Springs. In the Galwan river valley, though, most of the vehicles appeared to be part of a construction team, presumably set to extend their road all the way to the junction of the Shyok and Galwan rivers.[9]

At this time, towards the end of May, there was little clarity in India as to what was happening. In an interview with *The Times of India*, former foreign secretary and China hand Shyam Saran noted that such incidents were not unusual "in zones where there is a difference in perception regarding the alignment of LAC. These usually get resolved in accordance with well laid down SOPs observed by both sides." He did note, however, that the frequency of such incidents had been increasing because of "[the] significant improvement in the border infrastructure on both sides."[10]

However, retired Lieutenant General H. S. Panag, a well known commentator who had once commanded India's Northern Army, referred to the reports surfacing about Chinese intrusions and said, "we have once again been surprised both at the strategic and tactical levels." This was echoed months later by another senior military officer, Major General Yash Mor. A somewhat ingenuous explanation was given by General M. M. Naravane in January 2021 when he said that the Indian Army was aware of the Chinese mobilization in eastern Ladakh, "but we could not anticipate their intentions. This was [their] first mover advantage."[11]

It was only on 2 June that India provided the first official confirmation of the developments, when India's Defence Minister Rajnath Singh told a TV channel that it was true that a "sizeable number" of Chinese troops had moved into eastern Ladakh, to disputed areas that India also claims, and thereafter, India had taken all necessary steps to deal with the situation. He said a meeting between the two senior commanders would take place on 6 June.[12]

Writing in the pro-China *Hong Kong News*, on 4 June, Mao Yuelin said that Chinese moves, which included the 4-km push across the LAC in the Galwan area, were "returning to the line of occupation in 1962 and establishing it as the 'line of Actual Control' (LAC)" and signaling that there "is no gray area that can be eroded by India." In his view, the reason for the Chinese action was the changes in the *status quo* that India had wrought by building infrastructure like the DS-DBO road.[13]

Later in September 2020, Rajnath Singh provided an authoritative version of what happened when he told Parliament that the Indian side had, since April 2020, noticed a Chinese buildup in areas adjacent to eastern Ladakh. By early May "the Chinese side had taken action to hinder the normal, traditional patrolling pattern of our troops in the Galwan Valley area." An effort was made to address the issue through local commanders, but by mid-May, the Chinese began "several attempts to transgress the LAC in other areas like Kongka La, Gogra and the north bank of Pangong Tso." It was to address these issues that the meeting of the senior commanders had been convened in Moldo on 6 June.[14]

He did not mention the Chinese actions in blocking Indian patrols in Depsang, the rest of the Kugrang river valley beyond Gogra Post, or the Charding Nala area of Demchok. In fact, in total, by the end of May China was controlling 1,000 sq. km more of Ladakh than it had been at the beginning of April. Citing a senior government official, Vijaita Singh reported in *The Hindu* that 900 sq. km of this was the outcome of the blockade in the Depsang area, which we will discuss below. Another 20 sq. km was in the Galwan valley, 12 sq. km in Hot Springs near Kongka La, 65 sq. km on the north bank of Pangong Tso and 20 sq. km in Chushul on the south bank.[15] Even this may not have been the whole story. This does not take into account the entire Kugrang river valley and the Charding Nala area, which could have added another 1,000 sq. km to the total.

The Galwan incident

The 65-km Galwan river flows from the eastern side of the Karakoram range westwards to join the Shyok river. In 1956 Chinese maps showed the river to be part of Indian territory. But in 1960 the Chinese claimed most of it, leaving a small length some 7–8 km in extent on the Indian side. In the 1962 war, the Chinese had wiped out an Indian post near Samzungling, adjacent to where the river originates, but even at that point, their claim remained a little short of the Shyok-Galwan confluence. (See Map 1)

When India resumed patrolling the border in the late 1970s, it defined its LAC by establishing Patrolling Points (PP) along the entire LAC beginning with PP 1 near the Karakoram Pass. PP 14 was at the point where the Galwan river, which comes from a south-easterly direction, turns sharply westwards and flows into the Shyok, 7 km away. Through the next three decades, Indian patrols regularly visited PP 14, till in May of 2020, they found Chinese border guards blocking them from reaching that point. Further, through official statements, China now expanded its claim to all the Galwan valley.

The PLA had not been happy when, in 2019, the Indians finally completed their Darbuk–Shyok–Daulat Beg Oldi road enhancing their logistics to their northernmost posts. But what riled them more was that the Indians soon began to build a road eastwards to service their claim along the Galwan valley. By the time of the clash of 15 June, they had bridged the Shyok and reached 3 km upriver and were on the verge of completing another 60 m Bailey bridge that would enable them to reach PP 14 easily by road.[16] The Chinese had their own road on their side of the LAC along the river valley from Samzungling, which had been constructed years earlier. Their worry was the possible Indian use of linking the roads in a war to mount a threat to Aksai Chin from a new direction.

On 6 June 2020, unbeknownst to the media, at least, at that time, Generals Singh and Liu had agreed to begin a process of disengagement and de-escalation and meetings were planned between military officers at junior levels to coordinate the exercise over the next two weeks. On 12 June, speaking in the north Indian city of Dehra Dun, Indian Army Chief General M. M. Naravane had said that everything was under control at the borders and, as a result of talks between the two militaries, "a lot of disengagement had taken place." He said both sides were dis-engaging in a phased manner: "We have started from the north, from the area of the Galwan river valley where a lot of disengagement has taken place."[17]

In the 6 June talks the Chinese seem to have accepted that this was clearly on the Indian side of the LAC. During the division-commander level meeting of 12 June both sides had agreed to pull back their troops by about a kilometre each to prevent the kind of hand to hand brawls that had been taking place in Pangong Tso. The Chinese side had removed an observation tower and two tents they had pitched at a point near PP 14, which is a couple of hundred metres ahead of the LAC. While dismantling their positions, the Indian officer in-charge of the area, Colonel B. Santhosh Babu, who headed the 16 Bihar regiment, met and interacted with his Chinese counterpart, Senior Colonel Qi Fabao, whose forces were camped further upriver.

But then came reports that the PLA had once again pitched tents at the spot and rebuilt their observation post. Colonel Babu was given an earful by his higher commander and he rushed to investigate. The colonel and his men reached the area some thirty minutes before sunset on 15 June and asked the Chinese why they had returned. At some point the verbal altercation became violent and the Indians not only demolished the rebuilt observation tower but razed the tents pitched by the Chinese.[18]

By this time it was dark and freezing and suddenly fresh Chinese reinforcements arrived along both banks of the Galwan and took up positions on an adjacent high point and set upon the Indians with stones, clubs and sticks and a furious hand-to-hand brawl ensued involving some 300 men. At some point the colonel was hit by a stone and fell into the river and casualties piled up on both sides. There was a lull for an hour when the soldiers recovered Babu's body.

By this time Indian reinforcements in the form of two commando platoons had also arrived while the Chinese, too, had reinforced their men. Now commenced a third phase of the brawl, that continued past midnight with many on both sides hit by stones, others falling into the river. Only after five hours of this primal battle did things calm down. Medics arrived, bodies and the injured were exchanged. When the dust settled the next morning, twenty Indian soldiers lay dead, scores were missing and more than eighty injured. Many had died because of exposure at the high altitude and the lack of immediate medical attention.[19]

Subsequently, just after the pull-back at Pangong Tso had been announced and implemented in February 2021, the Chinese released a video which purported to show their version of the incident. In this video, shot along the banks of the Galwan river, Senior Colonel Qi is first seen explaining the situation to an Indian officer, who could be

Colonel Babu. Thereafter, the video shows Indian soldiers armed with batons wading across the river and Senior Colonel Qi spreading his arms out to physically block them. At this point an Indian officer wades up and confronts him and a brawl breaks out between the clearly over-whelmed Chinese force and more than 150 Indian soldiers. Senior Colonel Qi organizes the fight back, but is seen to be hit on the head. By the time the Chinese reinforcements arrive, it is already dark and the fighting continues. According to the video, four Chinese PLA per-sonnel were killed and Senior Colonel Qi was severely wounded.[20] Simultaneously, a lengthy article appeared in the Chinese military newspaper detailing the heroism of Senior Colonel Qi and his men.[21]

In October 2021, the Chinese side began to release a series of pic-tures and a video on Weibo which suggested that the clash had been far worse than previously thought. The pictures showed scores of Indian soldiers in Chinese custody, as well as their personal arms that the Chinese had seized. This confirms the fact that the Indian soldiers had, indeed, been armed, but for some inexplicable reason not used their weapons even in the face of the dire threat they confronted.[22]

What is intriguing is the location of the video. While Indian reports said that the fighting was near the point where the river makes a 90° turn to the west and flows towards the Shyok, an area clearly on the Indian side of the LAC, some Chinese accounts suggest that it was about a kilometre-and-a-half upriver but, even here, the LAC ought to be on the Indian side as per the latitude and longitude provided by the Chinese side to their Indian counterparts in the official talks of 1960.[23]

Whatever be the case, both sides fell back around midnight, and senior officers of the Indian Army and PLA held an emergency meeting early next morning at the point of the clash and both sides collected their dead and injured. Reconciling the circumstances and the different versions, it would appear that this was a local situation that got out of hand. Many of the details remain blurred given the Chinese reticence about these things, but also the deliberate decision on the Indian side to obfuscate matters. The Chinese side has put out the video, but so far there has been radio silence from the Indian side.

By military standards, or even by the previous measure of casualties in clashes between India and China, twenty or twenty-five is a small number. Fighting insurgencies and maintaining a hot Line of Control with Pakistan has inured Indians to the occasional casualties on its border with Pakistan. But its shock value came from the fact that the nearly 4,000-km disputed border with China, though manned by their respective militaries, had not seen a single shot fired in anger since 1975. In the past decade there had been scuffles and a few injuries, but that was all, and now twenty-four soldiers had been killed, and maybe over 150 injured and perhaps 100 or so taken captive.[24]

Just why the Chinese pulled back from their forward position and then returned, triggering the Indian reaction, is not likely to be known. As of now, Beijing has developed its own narrative of being wronged by the Indian side. But, as M. Taylor Fravel has noted, "China did not intend the Galwan clash to occur, they wanted to disengage and Chinese diplomats wanted to put the genie back in the bottle." But clearly something went awry somewhere. As it is, the Chinese surprise push all along eastern Ladakh triggered a very strong Indian reaction and created the conditions under which something like this could happen.[25]

Reaction

The immediate government of India response was to fudge. The public reaction, especially to the death of the soldiers at Galwan, was of shock, surprise and anger and expectations were that the hardline nationalist Modi government would give a befitting reply. The incident had taken place on Monday night and ended in the early hours of the next day. Through Tuesday, even though the Indian government knew that 20 soldiers had died and 100 or so were captive, they said that only 3 personnel had been killed. For good measure it was also put out that 5 Chinese soldiers had also died. It was only on late Tuesday evening through a news agency, that another 17 dead were acknowledged, though it was claimed that these 17 had been critically wounded and died only later.[26] The putative Chinese dead was now hiked to 43, again through friendly news agencies. There was no mention of those taken captive.

The bulk of the captives were released within the next two days. On Wednesday 17 June, *The New York Times* broke the story, citing two Indian military officials, who spoke to them anonymously, but presumably with authority, to reveal that "a number of Indian soldiers" had been captured in the fracas that began "after Indian troops on Monday set fire to tents erected by Chinese soldiers."[27]

But this was not officially acknowledged. All that the government did was to wait another 24 hours for the negotiated release of the captives—who reportedly included a lieutenant colonel and three majors—to claim on Thursday evening (18 June) that "no Indian troops are missing in action." The Chinese had wanted to release them at the Moldo border meeting point, but after hard bargaining agreed to release them in Galwan itself.

The first Chinese reaction came through on Tuesday when a spokesman of the PLA's Western Theater Command, Colonel Zhang Shuili, accused the Indian side of "deliberately launching a provocative attack" and violating the agreement arrived at during the senior commanders meeting on 6 June. He went on to add that "the sovereignty of the Galwan Valley has always belonged to China." Accusing the Indian Army of violating existing agreements, he called on the Indian side to restrain the troops and "stop all infringements and provocative actions."[28]

On 17 June, Hu Xijin, editor of the *Global Times*, had mocked the Indians, saying in a Twitter post that the seventeen injured had "reportedly died due to lack of in-time rescue" which reflected the lack of capacity of the Indian Army to provide emergency treatment. "This is not an army with real modern combat capabilities at plateau. Indian public opinion needs to stay sober."[29]

Prime Minister Modi's first response came through impromptu remarks on Wednesday 17 June, when he declared that India would "firmly protect every inch of the country's land and its self-respect." Expressing his condolences to the families of those who had died, he added that "on provocation, India will give a befitting reply." Note, this was the day that *The New York Times* story on the capture of ten Indian soldiers and officers had appeared and the Indian side had refused to acknowledge it.

This was also the day when the External Affairs Minister S. Jaishankar spoke to his Chinese counterpart Wang Yi and protested "in the strongest terms" the Galwan development. He said that even as efforts to resolve the issue were going on "the Chinese side sought to erect a structure in Galwan valley on our side of the LAC" and this had eventually resulted in the clash. He said that the Chinese side should "strictly

25

respect and observe the Line of Actual Control and should not take any unilateral action to alter it."[30]

However, soon the tenor of the Indian government's remarks changed. They began to flatly deny that any incursion had taken place. This was reflected in the government's convoluted position after an all-Party meeting on 19 June when, speaking in Hindi, Prime Minister Modi said, "no one had intruded across our border, nor has any of our post been captured by another party."[31] The official Prime Minister's Office video recording of his remarks has since excised these lines.

After a storm of protest from people wondering what then was happening in Ladakh, the next day the Prime Minister's Office made a somewhat bizarre clarification that the PM was speaking of the "here and now," not what had transpired earlier. Its statement claimed glibly that Indian soldiers had "foiled the attempt of the Chinese side to erect structures and also cleared the attempted transgression at this point of the LAC on that day." Ergo, there *is* no ingress into Indian territory. There was nothing said about whether there *had been* any, or that there continued to be some in other areas.[32]

There was no acknowledgement that the Chinese had, indeed, established positions across the Indian LAC and had removed their tents only after the 6 June agreement, and that the brawl, that took the life of Colonel Babu and nineteen other soldiers on 15 June, had occurred when they refused to remove one such structure within an area nearly a kilometre inside Indian territory. There was not a word about the injured and those held captive. And no word about Chinese actions in other areas where they had transgressed in what for long had been an accepted part of the Line of Actual Control.

Having positioned himself as a nationalist and, indeed, a belligerent defender of India, the prime minister suddenly adopted a restrained tone. Which was all for the good, but baffled his ultra-nationalistic fan base. But there must have been sound reasons for his stance. Perhaps this was part of the deal that had led to the release of 100 or so soldiers who had been in Chinese custody since the incident on 15 June. So far neither the Chinese, nor the Indian side has acknowledged what is clearly an embarrassing fact. Or perhaps it was that the prime minister who boasts of being tough in every situation had to acknowledge discretion had to be the better part of valour in the face of a difficult adversary, who could inflict a humiliation on him, as it had done with Jawaharlal Nehru.

Modi's "no intrusion" claim made New Delhi perform all manner of contortions to at once blame China for intrusions, and at the same time praise the Indian troops for preventing them from doing so, and simultaneously negotiate with China to pull back from the areas they had occupied or where they had established blockades. This soon became painfully apparent. In early August, the Ministry of Defence put up a note on its website on what it said was "Chinese aggression on LAC." The note said that "Chinese aggression" had been increasing "and more particularly in Galwan Valley since 5th May 2020." It then went on to add that the Chinese side had "transgressed" (a usage peculiar to the LAC, meaning they had come into the Indian claimed areas) in Kugrang river, Gogra and North Bank of Pangong Tso on 17–18 May. It referred to the 6 June meeting and the 15 June breakdown, and again spoke of the situation in eastern Ladakh as "arising from unilateral aggression by China." However, within a day, the Ministry of Defence had taken down the note from the website.

On 19 June, the Chinese Foreign Ministry spokesperson Zhao Lijian, of the Wolf Warrior fame, put out the Chinese official version of the incident, which was a mirror of the Indian position. He said that the Chinese had been patrolling this region for a long time, but Indian troops had "continuously built roads bridges and other facilities at the LAC in the Galwan Valley." China had protested but to little avail and, on 6 May, Indian troops had crossed the LAC and fortified an area preventing the PLA patrolling. On 6 June, India had agreed to withdraw personnel and demolish the fortifications and promised they "would not cross the estuary of the Galwan river to patrol and build facilities." On 15 June when things were appearing to be cooling down, Indian forces suddenly crossed the LAC again and "violently attacked" the Chinese forces "triggering fierce physical conflicts and causing casualties."[33]

It is not surprising that Chinese scholars used Modi's statement to claim that it was India which had crossed the LAC and provoked the incident. Jin Yinan, a leading military commentator and professor at the National Defence University of the PLA, quoted Modi to argue the case and observed that the action was probably the action of a small number of soldiers "who wanted to be promoted, wanted to get attention… went beyond the boundaries of right and wrong." He also added that the PLA had "taught India a lesson in the Galwan river valley."[34]

On 25 June, speaking to the Indian news agency PTI, the Chinese ambassador in New Delhi, Sun Weidong, squarely blamed India for the developments. He insisted that the entire Galwan valley belonged to China and that India had surreptitiously entered it on the night of 6 May and sought to develop a permanent presence there. Following the 6 June talks, the Indians had promised that they would not "cross the estuary of the Galwan river" and the two sides had actually "agreed to build observation posts on either side of the Galwan river mouth." But the Indians had reneged and demanded China dismantle its post and this triggered the conflict.[35] If you work with the assumption that by the record, the Chinese should have been some 7–8 km away from the mouth of the Galwan, it becomes difficult to understand just what position the ambassador was putting forth.

The most striking thing about these statements was the claim that the LAC was at the estuary of the Galwan, as it enters the Shyok. This is, as we have noted, at least 7–8 km away from the point where the Chinese had themselves said that their claim line lay in official talks in 1960, when they had provided the Indian side with the coordinates of the point at which their border ran across the Galwan.[36]

New Delhi's first response, on 29 June, was to ban the popular app Tik Tok in India on national security grounds; subsequently, more than 300 apps were banned. There were public calls to boycott Chinese goods. New Delhi also began the process of cancelling road and railway contracts of Chinese companies and restricting Chinese foreign direct investment to the country. But looking back these steps did not amount to much.

Pangong Tso

Though the deaths of Indian and PLA personnel following the clash in the Galwan became the focus of the 2020 events, they had actually come after a month and a half of some serious scuffles in the Pangong Tso lake area. The 134-km, brackish L-shaped lake, is some 5 km at its widest point, and lies at an altitude of nearly 14,000 ft (4,250 m) and is known for the incredible shades of blue visible in its waters. The LAC between

India and China runs through it in such a way that 45 km of the lake fall on the Indian side, and 90 km on the Chinese side. The problem is along the north bank, where there are eight major finger-like ridges coming down into the lake, numbered Finger 1, 2 and so on. (See Map 2)

According to India, the well established boundary between India and Tibet was at its narrowest point which was also roughly its midpoint. Some 2.5 km north-west of it was the ruined Fort Khurnak. British and other foreign travellers of the nineteenth century have cited different points at which they say the Ladakh–Tibet boundary lay. This is an area which does support some sparse population in both Ladakh and Tibet.

The Chinese started showing up at Fort Khurnak in 1958, India protested, but the Chinese insisted it was on their side of the border, and by 1959 had established themselves there. 1962 saw intense fighting on both its banks, as well as around its neighbouring Spanggur Tso lake. After the war, the Chinese established what they said was a civilian post at Khurnak. They did not withdraw from the area they had captured, which was to a point 15 km west of Finger 8 called Sirijap.

Till the Kargil War of 1999, Indian troops patrolled till Sirijap regularly. When forces had to be thinned out and India was distracted with the operations in Kargil, the Chinese extended their road through Sirijap to Finger 8. Thereafter Indian patrols were blocked at Finger 8 and, for their part, the Indian side set up a permanent post at Finger 4, and blocked the Chinese patrols to Finger 2.

For the last 20 years the Indians were patrolling to Finger 8 and the Chinese to Finger 4, and sometimes Finger 2. This led to some scuffles such as the one in 2008. Then, during the Doklam standoff, there was a serious clash in 2017 when scores of personnel were injured as Indian and Chinese personnel slugged it out. Again, in September 2019, there was an incident, but it was quickly brought under control.

In May 2020, as part of the Chinese push on the LAC, the Chinese forces began to prevent Indian access to Finger 8 by establishing a blockade at Finger 4. There were episodes when a senior Indian commander's helicopter was buzzed while flying over the lake. And then on the night of 5/6 May there was a free-for-all at Finger 5 between some 250 Indian and Chinese troops where sticks and stones were freely used. There were injuries on both sides, with an estimated 70 Indian personnel being hospitalized. From the Indian point of view, the

Chinese had systematically nibbled at the Pangong Tso north bank and come in some 23 km into what India considered its territory.

Gogra–Hot Springs, the Kugrang river valley and the Charding Nala

There has been considerable focus by the media in India on the incidents in Galwan and Pangong Tso. This is not surprising because both sides suffered casualties in these incidents. But from the Indian point of view, the developments in Charding Nala, Gogra–Hot Springs and Depsang are, perhaps, more serious in that Indian border guards are being prevented from patrolling important chunks of territory through blockades established by the PLA at strategic points. In some places, like the Charding Nala, which is adjacent to Demchok, the PLA takes advantage of its superior road network to pre-empt the movement of Indian patrols on an almost daily basis.

In the case of the Gogra–Hot springs area, there were serious ingresses in the area of the Kugrang river valley (PP 15) and the Gogra Post (PP 17 and 17A). This is an important area, close to the Kongka La pass where there was a serious incident in 1959. In the Chinese reckoning, Kongka La marks the border, while the Indians say it is a few kilometres more to the east at Lanak La. The Line of Actual Control as observed by India follows the description provided by the Chinese when they outlined their version of the boundary in 1960. This is the watershed between the Kugrang and Changlung rivers.

Clearly, the Chinese are seeking to push the LAC to the Kugrang river itself. The Kugrang valley provides one route of access to the Galwan valley. Tactically, the Chinese are at an advantage in this area, but a road from Phobrang across Marsimik La to the Hot Springs area completed in 2013 may have triggered sensitivities, especially since north-east of Gogra, the Chinese have found a virtual mountain of zinc at Huoshaoyun which falls within the larger Indian claim to Aksai Chin. (SeeMap 3)

Depsang

We will discuss the Depsang incursion of 2013 in some detail later in this book. Intriguingly, in 2020, though the overwhelming attention was paid to the developments in Pangong Tso and Galwan, the situation in Depsang had much greater strategic significance. Reports in June had suggested that the Chinese had moved forces in this area as well, and that they had resumed a blockade of India patrolling in a crucial area, the way they had done in 2013. The blockade of a point suggestively called Bottleneck or Y-Junction prevented Indian border forces from patrolling a significant part of their claim line. (See Map 4)

In his statement in Parliament on 15 September, Defence Minister Singh had made no mention of Depsang. Yet, there was a problem there, as evidenced by the fact that in August, India and China held major-general level talks at the meeting point on the Chinese side of the LAC, near Daulat Beg Oldi (DBO). The meeting came a week after the fifth round of corps-commander (lieutenant-general)-level meetings that had been taking place at Moldo, near Spanggur Tso.[37]

In an interview with a news channel in mid-February 2021, Lt Gen. Y.K. Joshi, the new Northern Army Commander, reiterated the official view that no land had been ceded to the Chinese. Asked about the Depsang situation, he said, "this predates the present situation. This is a legacy issue." Pointing to the differing "Lines of Perception" here, he said that the saving grace is that "the troops are not in contact."[38]

There was a telling rejoinder to this months later when retired Lieutenant General Rakesh Sharma, a former commander of the XIV Corps looking after Ladakh, wrote in the journal of the pro-government Vivekananda International Foundation questioning the narrative that had been put out on the developments in the Depsang region. Principally, he took issue with the theory that this was a "legacy issue" and that Indian forces had not been able to visit PP 10–13 since 2013. He said that despite difficulties, including the PLA obstructionist tactics, a "minimum of eight to ten patrols per year from 2013–2019" would have visited the area for a period of five to six days at a time. He said that the detailed debriefing of the patrols would exist with the authorities.[39] Reports suggest that the last Indian patrol to visit the area may have been in January–February 2020.[40]

But General Joshi didn't deny that there remained a situation in Depsang, which if you look at Map 4 is pretty serious. By blocking the Indian patrols at the Y-Junction, the PLA's border troops have been denying access to Indian patrols going to patrolling points PP 10,

PP 11, PP 11A, PP 12, and PP 13. These patrolling points are in an arc of around 20 km from PP10 on the Raki Nala to PP 13 on the Jeong or Jiwan Nala. But the patrolling points are not the LAC, which lies anywhere up to 5–8 km further east.

By blocking Indian patrols, the Chinese have effectively denied access to an area some 900 sq. km in extent, by far larger than the incursions on other parts of the LAC. With regard to the Chinese deployment of some 17,000 troops and armoured vehicles opposite the Indian positions in the area, India was compelled to respond in kind. Through July, deployments were made from PP 1 near Karakoram Pass, down to the blocked patrolling points. The Indians sent in tanks and heavy artillery by road and by air to match the Chinese with a division-sized deployment of their own.

Daulat Beg Oldi (DBO) is the terminus point of the new DS-DBO road that goes along the Shyok river, past its conjunction with the Galwan. This is 10 km or so short of India's northernmost point, the Karakoram Pass and the LAC lies just 8–9 km to its east. In the flat terrain of the region, the road is unconscionably close to the LAC, as is the airfield at DBO, which was used to maintain the region before the road was completed. Given the terrain, good defensive positions are not easily available. In terms of vulnerability, this is far more sensitive for India than either Pangong Tso or Galwan.[41] Having long lived with a situation where the Indian capabilities were limited because they had to be maintained by air, the Chinese began to feel that the new road enabled India to build a capacity which could threaten them northwards beyond Karakoram Pass and eastwards to their highway (No. 219) linking Xinjiang with western Tibet. (See Map 1)

Elusive disengagement

By early July there were reports that both sides were disengaging in Galwan as well as Pangong Tso. Following a two-hour conversation on 5 July between the topmost officials dealing with Sino–Indian relations—the Indian National Security Adviser Ajit Doval and his Chinese counterpart State Councillor Wang Yi—both sides moved back 1.5 km each from the site of the 15 June clash in Galwan. There were claims that there would also be disengagement in the Kugrang river valley, but they turned out to be untrue. However, there was no movement back from Finger 4 in Pangong Tso at this point in time.

Indeed, on 28 July, the Chinese Ministry of Foreign Affairs spokesman declared that most of the disengagement was done "and the situation on the ground is de-escalating." This was immediately contradicted by the Indian side which said that while there had been some progress, "the disengagement process has not as yet been completed."

In his Independence Day speech on 15 August, Prime Minister Modi had spoken of giving a befitting reply to those challenging India's sovereignty "from LoC to LAC", an oblique reference to Pakistan and China. When asked to comment on this, Chinese spokesman Zhao Lijian took a laid back stance, saying that the Chinese side had taken note of the speech, and it "stands ready to work with India to enhance our political mutual trust, properly manage our differences, step up practical cooperation…."

But when it came to working on the nuts and bolts of a three-step plan that would see disengagement, de-escalation and a restoration of patrolling rights in the areas over which both had claims, the Chinese response remained elusive. As far as they were concerned, "disengagement" or mutual withdrawal would be from the positions they had freshly occupied, while the Indian side wanted them to go back to the positions they were in April 2020.

Seeing that the talks on disengagement were not going anywhere, the Indian side executed their counter-move. At the end of August 2020, India used the Special Frontier Force, made up largely of Tibetan exiles, in an operation to occupy some key heights—Gurung Hill, Magar Hill, Mukhpari, Rezang La and Rechin La—on the Kailash range on Line of Actual Control along the south banks of the Pangong Tso and overlooking the smaller lake, Spanggur Tso. (See Map 2)

Copying the Chinese style, the Indians said that their move had been one of pre-emption, to prevent the Chinese from occupying those heights. It was implied that they had occupied heights on the Chinese side of the LAC, but that was later denied. At one level this was a precautionary move, within the Indian LAC, to hold positions that were important to defending the Chusul area and its vulnerable lines of communications to Leh. But at the same time, those heights gave the Indians an overview of Chinese bases in the Spanggur area that are important for their military posture in the area.

The unusual display of aggression by the Indian forces took the Chinese aback. The Chinese attempted to do a Galwan on Indian positions on Mukhpari peak, the highest point in the area, and overwhelm its defenders by PLA personnel armed with sticks and lances. But the Indians were prepared and this time fired warning shots over their heads. Even more sustained firing took place at a point where Fingers 3 and 4 merge as the two sides began jockeying to occupy the ridges descending into the Pangong Tso. Both sides issued statements accusing the other side of firing. Whatever be the case, this was the first time since 1975 that gun shots were being heard at the LAC.

After the pre-emptive occupation of the heights, the Indian Army also deployed its infantry combat vehicles and tanks wherever they could and also fenced off the posts to prevent them from being overrun Galwan style. In turn, the PLA paraded its tanks and mechanized infantry squads and soldiers in their base area at Spanggur Tso. Essentially both sides were displaying force, rather than planning any serious military operation. Seven months later, speaking at a press conference in New Delhi, US Secretary of Defence Lloyd Austin said, in response to a question, "To my knowledge we've never considered that India and China were on the threshold of war."[42] This was evident in the first place from the Chinese deployment of just a two-division strong force to back up its operation to push the LAC westward and also from India's counter-deployment, which was approximately of the same size. If either side contemplated war, the levels of deployment would have been greater.

A 5-point joint statement following a meeting of India's External Affairs Minister S. Jaishankar and his Chinese counterpart Wang Yi on 11 September 2020 in Moscow at the sidelines of a ministerial meeting of the Shanghai Cooperation Organisation (SCO) was intriguing. After genuflecting to their respective supreme leaders' wisdom, the statement called for a continuation of a dialogue to "quickly disengage, maintain proper distance and ease tensions." The emphasis was on disengagement, not *status quo ante*. Indeed, a striking feature of the joint statement was that the words "Line of Actual Control" were simply not mentioned at all. All references were to "border areas." And equally intriguingly, given the circumstances, was the last clause, which said that the two sides need to "conclude new Confidence

Building Measures (CBMs)" to maintain peace and tranquility in the border areas. Considering that the two were currently picking up the pieces of the earlier CBMs stretching back to 1993, it defied imagination to understand what the new measures could be, short of declaring that they had come to an agreement on the boundary itself.[43] There was some speculation whether this implied some new formulation in border management, but as of now it remains occluded.

Frozen positions

As autumn came in 2020, both sides began to think of the winter which would be their main adversary soon. The winter in Ladakh is not ordinary. It comes with high winds, snow and bone-chilling cold with temperatures going down to minus 30° Celsius at heights where breathing is difficult at the best of times. Troops began to dig in, winter hutments and equipment were hastily set up. Both sides also knew that some positions they had established could well become untenable.

In the 1970s, when anti-freeze was not commonly available, vehicles were required to drain their water radiators for the night for fear it would become ice and crack them. Army truck personnel would light a small fire under the fuel tank to prevent it from freezing and the bonnet of the trucks were often padded. As for humans, besides all the nasty things it does to your metabolism, exposure can kill quickly. It's not surprising that 17 of 20 Indian personnel who died in Galwan did so because of hypothermia and that, too, in high summer. Besides things like frostbite, skin-bonding occurs when exposed skin can actually stick to a metallic surface and be ripped off.

Just how unforgiving the climate is in the region has been known. In 1962, an entire company of the India's Kumaon regiment fended off repeated Chinese attacks at Rezang La pass, near Pangong Tso, till they were overwhelmed. When the following year search parties went to recover their remains, they found many had been frozen in battle positions in their shallow trenches. The Indian Army Photo Service has never released those graphic photographs depicting the valour and fortitude of the soldiers.

With the two highways—Srinagar-Leh and Leh-Manali—shutting down in winter, the Indian Army began preparing for winter by its routine stocking of rations, fuel, clothing and tents to protect against the biting cold. Because of the increased deployment, the Indians had to redouble their logistical effort. They also had to make an urgent purchase of high-altitude winter clothing from the United States under the 2016 logistics exchange agreement (LEMOA). Purchases were also made from Europe.[44]

The Chinese side also did the same. A *Global Times* report spoke of new heated barracks for the troops, portable oxygenators and winter clothing with heated vests, lightweight boots and down jackets. There were other technology touches like the use of optronic devices to surveil the border, fibre optic cables for secure communications, and even a high-tech kitchen vehicle to provide hot food at very cold locations. The report tartly spoke of India's "relatively weak industrial foundation" making it hard to produce "cold-resistant military logistical supplies like windproof goggles, sleeping bags and tents."[45]

There were hopes that the two sides could actually manage a pull back to avoid the worst of the winter months. At the beginning of November 2020, there was a brief flurry when Nitin Gokhale, a well connected journalist, put out a news report that the Indian and Chinese commanders had agreed on restoring *status quo ante* as of May 2020 in the Pangong Tso area. All that remained was the sequencing of steps. Writing for his own portal, Gokhale said that this had been agreed to in the eighth round of talks between the Corps Commanders on 6 November. The PLA would remove all temporary structures and deployments it had made between Fingers 4 and 8 and go back to the latter position in Pangong. Once done, both sides would agree to treat the area as a "no patrolling zone." The second step would be to pull back heavy armour and artillery to their depth areas to reduce chances of conflict. The report claimed that Indian counteraction in the Pangong Tso area, by occupying the heights along the Kailash range, was what had pressured China to agree. It also said that the issue of Depsang would be taken up later.[46]

Two days later, the *Global Times* poured cold water over the report and said that such assertions "are inaccurate and not helpful." It accused the Indian media of deliberately projecting "India's tough stance through partially true and partially false information with the aim of stirring up domestic nationalism."[47]

Through the fog of rhetoric, it was still possible to see that perhaps a process was still on, though working at a snail's pace. After all, the basic decision on disengagement had been taken at the very first meeting on 6 June. The problem had been that, for a variety of reasons, almost all related to the poor handling of the situation locally, the Galwan process had gone awry resulting in the horrible incident. But subsequently, the two sides did disengage there. They also pulled back in the Gogra–Hot Springs area a bit.

The five-point "consensus" that the two foreign ministers had agreed to on 6 September in Moscow appeared to be the practical basis on which the talks were now being conducted to "quickly disengage, maintain proper distance and ease tensions." The sixth round of talks between the military officers had seen agreement that the two sides would not send more troops to the front "and avoid taking actions that may complicate the situation."

Gokhale's report and the Chinese denial came after the discussions of the eighth round of talks between the military officials had been held on 6 November. At the meeting of the Working Mechanism for Consultation and Coordination (WMCC) for India–China boundary affairs that took place via video on 18 December, the two sides agreed to hold another round of talks to take forward their slow-motion disengagement process.

This led to the next military commander-level meeting, the ninth round, which took place on 24 January, two-and-a-half-months after the previous one. Whether it was the experience of winter, or some other hard bargaining, in the end, this round delivered results though they were revealed two weeks later.

The news of the disengagement was released on 10 February in simultaneous statements by the Chinese foreign and defence ministries. Wang Wenbin, the foreign ministry spokesman, said that riding on the decision taken by the two foreign ministers at a meeting in September 2020 and the subsequent commander-level talks in Ladakh, "the frontline forces of the Chinese and Indian armed forces began to organize disengagement in the Pangong Lake area on 10 February" adding that "We hope the Indian side will work with China to meet each other halfway... and ensure the smooth implementation of the disengagement process."

There was no word from the Indian side that day, but on 11 February in a statement in the Upper House of Parliament, the Rajya Sabha, India's Defence Minister Rajnath Singh confirmed the disengagement. He said as per the agreement, the Chinese would keep their presence east of Finger 8 and India would do so near Finger 3. In the area in between there would be a "temporary moratorium on military activities," or a buffer zone. He said a similar process would take place along the south bank, but did not detail the area of withdrawal. The minister said "outstanding issues" would be taken up in further discussions.

Following the eleventh round of talks between Indian and Chinese military officers at the Chushul-Moldo meeting point in April 2021, the Indian media reported that the Chinese were refusing to budge from the Kugrang river valley area. According to a report, the Chinese said that the Indians "should be happy" with what has already been achieved. According to the report, the Chinese were still there at PP 15 and PP 17A with about a platoon-level force, along with their vehicles.[48]

Assessing the situation, Lt Gen. H.S. Panag, former Northern Army Commander, noted after the eleventh round discussions, that while disengagement had been done in Pangong Tso, there was no change in Gogra–Hot Springs and the Kugrang river valley, Depsang Plains and the Charding Ninglung area south of Demchok. In his view, the Chinese were unlikely to compromise on the Depsang and Demchok area since "these areas are east of its 1959 claim line." In the Kugrang area, China might agree to create a buffer zone "entirely in our territory."[49]

The twelfth round of talks in July 2021 had succeeded in getting agreement on disengagement at PP 17A near Gogra Post, but later it transpired that the process was only partial. Almost all commentators agree that the thirteenth round of military talks between XIV Corps commander Lt Gen. P. G. K. Menon and the South Xinjiang Military District chief of staff, Maj. Gen. Zhao Zhidan, in early October 2021 ended in a stalemate. The statements of both sides indicated a hardening of positions.

The PLA's Western Theater Command spokesperson Senior Colonel Long Shaohua accused the Indian side of "persisting in its unreasonable and unrealistic demands" and warned that "instead of misjudging the situation, the Indian side should cherish the hard won situation in the China-India border areas." His Indian counterpart blamed Beijing for not being "agreeable to its constructive suggestions" and failing to provide "forward looking proposals" to defuse the Sino–Indian military confrontation in eastern Ladakh "which would facilitate progress in bilateral relations."[50]

The Indian statement was remarkable for the manner in which it delicately skirted the issue of the Chinese withdrawal by talking of "constructive suggestions." Needless to say, it didn't really spell out just where these "forward looking proposals" were to be deployed. Even now Depsang and Charding Ninlung Nala had not been mentioned. The talks took place in the background of an uptick of the PLA's activities in the central sector and Arunachal Pradesh in the east.

The fourteenth round of India–China senior military officers' talks was on 12 January 2022. In line with previous rounds, the two sides had extensive discussions going late into the night. But there was no progress in India's efforts to get the PLA to vacate its ingresses in the Kugrang river valley, Depsang and the Charding Ninglung Nala (rivulet). However, and significantly, the two sides did issue a joint statement saying that they had "agreed to consolidate on the previous outcomes and take effective steps to maintain the security and stability on the ground...."[51]

Actually, right throughout this process, besides the corps commander-level talks at Chushul-Moldo, the two sides have been continuing a military dialogue at the level of major-generals at other points like Daulat Beg Oldi. According to one report, between the May 2020 faceoff and July 2021, there had been ten major-general level talks, fifty-five brigadier-level ones and around 1,500 calls in the two hotlines that function from Chinese local headquarters to Chushul and DBO.[52]

Looking for answers

The events of the summer of 2020 took China and India's relationship to breaking point. As former National Security Adviser, Shivshankar Menon, noted later that year, the Chinese successfully compelled India to cede ground in "a successful salami-slicing maneuver." Now both sides were calling for a negotiated solution to the crisis, but their perspectives varied: India wanted *status quo* as of April 2020, while China wanted India to disengage, de-escalate, create buffer zones and negotiate "new confidence building measures" based on the new positions.[53] The creation of the "no-patrolling zone" in Pangong and Galwan suggested that they had, to an extent, succeeded.

Former Foreign Secretary Shyam Saran's view was that in the past the Chinese had used carefully calibrated tactics to heat up the LAC, without letting things boil over. But the events of 2020 saw a change of operating procedure since it was aimed at carrying out a substantial alteration of the alignment of the LAC. But they did not expect the tough Indian response, and so the Chinese were forced to back off, because the other option for them would have been to escalate the situation, for which they were clearly not ready.

That the Chinese had not come to make war, even though they had brought substantial numbers of troops along with their artillery and armour, was obvious from the very fact that fists, stones and sticks were used—and displayed—in their push, suggesting that the aim was limited to changing the LAC in a relatively minor way in eastern Ladakh at some key points. Saran rhetorically posed the question as to whether the Chinese had bitten off more than they could chew. The disengagement agreement provided its own answer to that question.[54]

The main Chinese narrative, according to Mathieu Duchatel, who looked at the publications of more than two dozen Chinese writers, was to establish a narrative "to put the blame on India." According to him the "red thread running through Chinese analyses" is to argue that it was Indian behaviour which compelled China to "abandon its long standing practice of self-restraint in managing the disputed border."[55]

Yun Sun, a Chinese-American scholar at the Stimson Center, said that China was "pushing for territory [it had] occupied in the 1962 war." She said that the Chinese believed that a lot of the infrastructure construction on the Indian side was going on in areas that Beijing had withdrawn from after the 1962 war.[56]

There is some validity to this when you look at Map 1. It gives us an idea as to where the Chinese had reached in 1962 and where they pulled back to for a while. If you focus on the individual area of the map, you can see why they are active in the Depsang Plains where India contests their claim, in the Kugrang and Kongka La region where they had come in towards Tsogstsalu, and Demchok where they had captured areas both sides of the Indus, including Charding La. The one region where they are clearly going beyond is Pangong Tso where they have in the past decades already occupied territory west of Sirijap. And the one region where it shows up the Chinese is the Galwan river where the extent of the Chinese claim is short of the confluence of the Shyok and Galwan.

Writing in *The Washington Post*, the scholar M. Taylor Fravel pointed to the Indian efforts to strengthen its border defences as a major trigger for the eastern Ladakh crisis in 2020. In particular, he referred to the DS-DBO road "greatly facilitates the lateral movement of Indian forces along this part of the western sector."[57] Incidentally, the DS-DBO road is not the only link to Daulat Beg Oldi. India has also constructed an alternate alignment involving some 90 km, from Sasoma, through the Saser La pass to Gapshan and Daulat Beg Oldi. This will be far less vulnerable to interdiction than the DS-DBO road. Part of this road has already been constructed. What India needs to do is to fix some issues relating to its construction in the glaciated area around Saser La. (See Map 1)

The unhappiness over India's connectivity projects is only one part of the motivation for the Chinese actions. At the end of September 2020, in response to a query by *The Hindustan Times* correspondent in Beijing, Sutirtho Patranobis, the Chinese foreign ministry spokesman said that China abided by the Line of Actual Control as proposed by Premier Zhou Enlai to Prime Minister Jawaharlal Nehru on 7 November 1959. The Chinese foreign ministry statement in Mandarin declared that the "LAC is very clear, that is the LAC on November 7, 1959." Second, it said that "Since this year, the Indian Army has continued to arrive and illegally cross the border, unilaterally expanding the scope of actual control."[58]

This November 1959 line is a bit of a chimera and its reappearance in 2020 is striking. It has never been delineated on a map or described in any detail. The Indian spokesman lost no time in responding that "India has never accepted the so-called unilaterally defined 1959 Line of Actual Control (LAC). This position has been consistent and well known, including to the Chinese side." He pointed to the numerous agreements that the Chinese side had signed with the Indians accepting the need to clarify the LAC at points where the two sides differed, and said that "the insistence now of the Chinese side that there is only one LAC is contrary to the solemn commitments made by China in these agreements."[59]

On the same day, responding to a question, the Chinese spokesman Wang Wenbin added two more to the list of grievances that may have motivated the Chinese actions: that "China doesn't recognize the so-called 'Ladakh Union Territory' illegally set up by India and opposes infrastructure building aimed at military contention in disputed border areas."[60]

India's government had demoted and split the state of Jammu & Kashmir into two Union Territories of Jammu & Kashmir and Ladakh in August 2019. At the time, the Chinese spokeswoman had accused India of undermining "Chinese territorial sovereignty by unilaterally changing its domestic law." She had urged India to "exercise prudence in words and deeds concerning the boundary question… and avoid taking moves that further complicate the boundary question."[61] Though the Indian side professed to be shocked by this view, it was not all that surprising considering that the *de facto* number two in the Indian government, Union Home Minister Amit Shah, had declared that parts of the new Union Territories of Jammu & Kashmir and Ladakh were occupied by Pakistan and China respectively, and "we are ready to give our lives [to regain them]…"

This issue clearly rankled. In October 2020, when asked about India's inaugurating a series of new bridges to provide access to the border with China, the spokesman Zhao Lijian responded, first, that China does not recognize the so called "Ladakh Union Territory" or for that matter "Arunachal Pradesh," and "opposed infrastructure building aimed at military contention in disputed border areas." He went on to point out that India had stepped up this activity for some time now and that "This is the root cause of tensions."[62]

Imagery analyst Chris Biggers told Sushant Singh that what was striking about the developments in 2020, was "the visible asymmetry between the respective sides' forces and the relative speed of their deployment." According to him the latter phenomenon appeared to be an outcome of advanced planning on the part of the Chinese going back to around August 2019.[63]

The area of DBO and the Depsang Plains is important to both China and India. On the one hand, it offers India an area in which it can, at least theoretically, launch offensive operations that can interdict China's 219 Highway and move either north to Xinjiang, or south to western Tibet. On the other hand, a Chinese push in the area can open up the Shyok and Nubra valleys and threaten Leh and Indian deployments in the Siachen glacier.

The Chinese push in Galwan seemed to be aimed at a desire to block the Indian construction of a lateral road along the river to service its post. In the first meeting of the top commanders in June 2020, the Chinese had complained about this Indian activity. And, as events indicated, they sought to push their own road to the point of confluence between the Galwan river and the Shyok river even though at least the last 7 or 8 km would have been clearly on the Indian side of the LAC.

This is evident from a close examination of a map disseminated by M. Taylor Fravel in a Twitter thread based on a Chinese map showing the dispositions during the 1962 war. What it reveals is that the Chinese did not claim their border line to be at the confluence of the Galwan and Shyok rivers, but near the bend of the Galwan, some 7–8 km east of the so-called estuary.[64]

The reason why this claim is now being extended to that point is simple. Across from what the Chinese have been calling the "the estuary" or the confluence of the Galwan with the Shyok river, runs the DS-DBO road. If China gets a position at that point, it not only surveils the road every hour of the day or night, but is able to interdict it with nothing more than a machine gun.

Likewise, it shows that the Chinese claim line runs parallel to the Kugrang river, along with its watershed with its tributary, the Changlung. Chinese actions here in blocking Indian patrolling up the valley are as inexplicable as they have been in Galwan. The only motivation could be a general desire to push the LAC westwards, as a means of creating a buffer to protect their 219 Highway.

The Indian reaction to the developments in Galwan and elsewhere in eastern Ladakh clearly took Beijing aback. They could not understand why such a limited clash in a disputed region was being taken so seriously in India. A lot of it had to do with the over-the-top Chinese action on the LAC but some was the result of the reportage of the media, both conventional and social. Writing in 2017, in the wake of the Depsang and Chumar incidents on the LAC, the scholar Zhang Li noted that China had "often emphasized the cognitive difference between the actual control line and the complexity of the Sino–Indian border issue" and the importance of handling inevitable problems along the LAC.[65] In other words, there was a need to differentiate between the boundary issue and the inevitable problems arising out of the differences over the LAC. But that was something scholars could do, not the ordinary folk who tended to react emotionally.

There was, of course, the larger geopolitical picture as well. The Indian discomfiture over the 2020 incidents could not but have sent its own message to India's neighbours like Bhutan, Nepal and Sri Lanka. Further compelling India to pour additional resources from its already strained defence budget to upgrading its LAC deployment is the surest way of crimping plans by New Delhi to play a larger maritime role in association with the US and Japan in the Indo–Pacific. As a result, India may be pushed further into the US embrace, but that would be assuming that Washington wanted India to play a greater military role in the western Pacific. As events turned out, in 2021 the US, UK and Australia decided that it was better to create a tighter new Australia–UK–US (AUKUS) alliance, which had a clear military intent.

2

THE SINO–INDIAN BORDER DISPUTE

Asian neighbours, India and China have had a fraught relationship in relation to their borders ever since the birth of the People's Republic of China (PRC) and the Republic of India, in October 1949 and January 1950 respectively. The principal reason is that both assert the territorial limits of the empires they succeeded—the Chinese the Qing, and the Indians the British. The problem arose when the PRC established Chinese authority over Tibet in terms quite different from those of the Qing. The British had assiduously sought to maintain Tibet as a buffer between the two empires, in some ways virtually gifting the Chinese "suzerainty" over Tibet, which only served to buttress Chinese claims over Tibet.

The Sino–Indian border faces off the new Union Territories of Ladakh and Jammu & Kashmir (western sector), Himachal Pradesh and Uttarakhand (central sector), Sikkim and Arunachal Pradesh (eastern sector) with China's Xinjiang and Tibet Autonomous Region. The Indians put the length of the border variously at 4,057 and 3,488 km, while the Chinese say it is a little over 2,000 km long. This discrepancy arises because the Chinese do not include the border with Pakistan and then, their straight line border in the foothills of Arunachal Pradesh helps make for that figure. (See Map 5)[1]

The eastern border is formed by the McMahon Line, which was delineated on a map and was attached to an exchange of notes in March

1914 between India and Tibet in Simla. In April, the Chinese representative initialled both the map and a convention signed by the British and Tibetan representatives, but later refused to sign it. His government later repudiated his actions. The Chinese government objections were not to the depiction in the map of the Tibet–India border, but to that between Tibet and China. So, China was not a signatory to the convention signed in Simla some three months later in July 1914 that defined the Tibet–India boundary in the north-east. It was only in the mid-1930s that Chinese maps first began to show the areas south of the McMahon Line as the border.

The western border, as we will see, was more complicated.

This border, as we noted, almost in its entirety comprises of a desolate mountainous region which is snowbound through much of the year. As a result it is largely uninhabited. Boundaries were really defined by the mountain passes through which trade took place, and both sides knew where the border lay. When the snows melted, shepherds moved to the pastures, which could be on this or that side, but again the boundary itself would be pretty familiar to the locals, though not to the Chinese, whose suzerainty was exercised by officials living in Lhasa or Kasghar.

In their argument in the 1950s, both sides asserted that there was a traditional and customary boundary, the only problem was that it was very different for the two sides.

From the historical point of view, Stephen A. Hoffman has pointed out that India probably had a relatively stronger case than China. But by insisting that "linear borders had been conclusively 'delimited' by history and 'discovered' through a documentary investigation, the Indian case became vulnerable."[2] Further, in the modern era, it was not simply possible to assert "traditional and customary" boundaries; what the two new nations needed to do was to sit down and delineate and demarcate their boundary after negotiations that were bound to involve give and take. But, as we will see, that did not happen.

India did little to oppose the Chinese invasion of Tibet, which the new People's Republic saw as a "liberation" of the region which had known *de facto* independence since 1911. In any case, there was little New Delhi could have done, considering the domestic commitments of its army. Somewhere in the as yet classified files, say some of my diplomat friends, there is a written document signed by the first Indian commander-in-chief General K.M. Cariappa formally informing Prime Minister Nehru that India lacked the military wherewithal to intervene in Tibet.

As it is, in line with his worldview, Nehru reduced India's annual defence expenditure and in 1951, even as the Chinese were establishing themselves in Tibet, the Indian Army was shedding 50,000 personnel. The Chinese were diplomatic, their communication links were a nightmare and they were aware that the supplies to feed their army in Tibet would have to come through the port of Calcutta (now Kolkata) in India.

The Chinese played the Indians well on the border. Besides their immediate need for consolidating Chinese authority in Tibet, India was important to the nascent People's Republic of China in many other ways at that time. It self-consciously refused to align with the western powers, it played a significant role as a neutral in the Korean war that pitted the People's Republic of China against the United States. Further, it adopted a principled role in demanding that China's UN seat, with a veto-wielding power, be assigned to the PRC rather than continue with Taiwan. Indeed, there is a contemporary equivalent of an urban myth that in the 1950s the US offered China's seat in the UN Security Council, which was then held by Taiwan, to India and Prime Minister Nehru turned down the offer.

Nehru was not entirely guileless on the issue and even as the Chinese were establishing their authority in Tibet, India was also doing so south of the Himalayas. In early 1951, a platoon led by Major Renmao 'Bob' Khating, asserted Indian authority at the monastery at Tawang by expelling its Tibetan administrators, with no protest from Beijing. India signed fresh agreements with the Himalayan states of Nepal, Sikkim and Bhutan to update the relationships they had had with the British Empire.

In 1950 when Nehru announced on the floor of Parliament that "Our maps show that the McMahon Line is our boundary and that is our boundary—map or no map," the Chinese did not react. Unbeknownst to the Indians, they were busy planning to build a highway linking Xinjiang with Tibet through territory which India claimed. In fact, when the Chinese told the friendly Indian ambassador K.M. Panikkar in 1951 that there was no territorial dispute between the two countries, the Indian side took these Chinese professions at their face value, and Nehru issued a directive in mid-1953 saying that the border issue did not need to be raised in talks with the Chinese.

Some years ago, at a reception in New Delhi in a European embassy, the new ambassador of China to India and I engaged in a long conversation on the border. He was refreshingly frank and acknowledged that in 1950 neither India nor China effectively administered the Aksai Chin, the so-called "desert of white stones" which is claimed by India, but occupied by China. "But China needed the area, India didn't and so we established control." He was referring to the fact that India had no real need for that inhospitable piece of real estate, where Nehru famously said "not a blade of grass grows," while the Chinese understood that a road through that region would offer them an all-weather route to Tibet. Looking at the record, he was right since there was no habitation or even pastures there: Aksai Chin was a kind of no-man's land.

That seems to be as fair a way of looking at the issue as any. But it was also a slight overstatement of the issue. As John Garver has pointed out, the PLA built three roads into Tibet and the one from the north, through Qinghai, was completed first in 1950, the second through Sichuan came through in 1954 and the Aksai Chin road was opened only in 1957. In addition to these, three new routes through Sichuan were also constructed between 1956 and 1957.[3] It was not as if the Chinese military occupation of Tibet required the Aksai Chin road, although once things went out of control following the rebellion of 1959, it became crucial for the control of western Tibet.

The Tibet Treaty of 1954

India made an enormous blunder when in 1954 through an agreement it surrendered all its rights in Tibet, and got nothing in return. It is not that there was no rationale to settle the issue. From the beginning it had been clear that there was little India could do in Tibet and conceding colonial rights that India had inherited from Britain there seemed logical. Nehru's strategy was to accommodate the Chinese so as to encourage them to retain Tibet's autonomy. Even the 1954 treaty was part of that design. Further, by early 1954, it appeared that Pakistan was set to become part of the western alliance system. India needed to ensure that it did not get into a two-front situation. Stabilizing the situation with China looked like a good proposition.

In turn, the Chinese, who were not quite settled in Tibet and were coming to grips with its vastness and poor infrastructure, also felt that they needed to make a deal. In any case, they could not have been unaware of India's lack of military capacity vis-à-vis Tibet, and neither could they ignore their own dependence on Kolkata port to consolidate their authority there.

The April 1954 "India–China Agreement on Trade and Intercourse between India and the 'Tibet region of China'" was a splendid diplomatic victory for China. India conceded all its diplomatic, commercial and military privileges in Tibet and got nothing in return. Worse, for the first time, India conceded in a formal document that Tibet was an integral part of China. Considering that India's eastern border, the one that separates Tibet and Arunachal Pradesh, is defined by the McMahon Line, which was based on an agreement between India and Tibet, it was an egregious blunder not to obtain some kind of a clarification on the issue.

Negotiations on a Sino–Indian Treaty on Tibet had begun in December 1953 with Nehru directing his officials that the issue of the boundary was not to be raised and in case the Chinese raised it, "we should express our surprise and point out that this is a settled issue."[4]

Nehru actually believed that with the agreement, the issue of the border had been laid to rest. The reference to six passes in the central sector in the agreement was taken as an assumption that the Chinese had accepted the customary and traditional boundary across its entire length.

Just how India was played became apparent in reading the opening remarks of the interlocutors of the two sides. In his opening remarks welcoming the Indian delegation in Beijing, Premier Zhou noted that both sides agreed on common principles and on their basis "all outstanding questions between us *which are ripe for settlement* can be resolved smoothly" (emphasis added). In his response, Ambassador N. Raghavan, who led the delegation, spoke of how "*all outstanding issues*" could be resolved under Premier Zhou's guidance.

In the talks the Chinese spelt out the five principles. These were: mutual respect for each other's territorial integrity and sovereignty;

mutual non-aggression; mutual non-interference in each other's internal affairs; equality and mutual benefits; and peaceful co-existence. By adhering to them, the two sides could resolve "all pending questions *that were ripe for settlement"* (emphasis added).[5] At this time, it is important to note, the Aksai Chin issue had not yet arisen as India had not discovered the road that the Chinese had begun constructing there. Indeed, the Chinese very cleverly deflected an Indian effort to take up the issue of trade between Tibet and Ladakh.[6]

Even a sympathetic observer like Dorothy Woodman was to write in 1969 that it was "extraordinary" that the Indian side did not raise the frontier issue. The negotiations over the treaty was a missed opportunity. "A settlement might have been reached on Aksai Chin and McMahon Line in 1954," but the Indians had themselves tied their own hands "by agreeing to a Chinese proposal that frontiers should not be discussed."[7]

Thus, came the brief era of "Hindi-Chini bhai bhai" (India and China are brothers). Zhou Enlai visited India for the first time in 1954, 1956 and then in 1960. Crowds waving Indian and Chinese flags lined the roads in Mumbai, Kolkata and Delhi. I was witness to this in Mumbai as a small child as Zhou emerged from the airport standing in an open car and waving to the school children lined up to greet him. The boundary issue was not touched upon in his talks with Nehru.

Yet, there must have been a nagging worry somewhere at the back of Nehru's mind. He had made a ringing declaration in Parliament in November 1950 that "the frontier from Bhutan eastwards had been clearly defined by the McMahon Line, which was fixed by the Simla Convention of 1914." The Chinese had made no comment on this at the time. And the Chinese seemed to have largely accepted the central sector, but what about the western?

Nehru could not have been unaware that most official maps in India did not show any boundary between India, Xinjiang and Tibet, till Nepal. When India was consolidating itself as a nation, the Ministry of States headed by Home Minister Sardar Patel issued two White Papers in 1948 and 1950 on Indian states. Both had an official map of India, one depicting the boundary as of Independence Day, that is, 15 August 1947. The other showed the boundaries as of the time India became a republic, on 26 January 1950. The northern and eastern boundaries of Kashmir, as well as that of the central sector till Nepal, were shown with a legend noting "boundary undefined." The 1950 map did have a colour wash covering the region, where the 1948 map did not. The McMahon Line in the east was depicted with a dotted line with the legend "boundary undemarcated."

In July 1954, Nehru ordered the withdrawal of all the old maps and their replacement by one which showed a firm boundary around Aksai Chin, as we see it now.[8] In his return visit to Beijing in October 1954, the issue of the border was briefly raised, with Nehru himself feigning that it was unimportant since it was settled. But he did raise the issue of maps in China showing parts of India within their border. Zhou neatly side-stepped this by saying those were old KMT maps. As of this point, there was no official People's Republic of China claim on Aksai Chin, but we now know they were racing to complete a road through it to connect Xinjiang with Tibet.

Looking at Nehru's record, A.S. Bhasin has noted, "Nehru did not realise that international borders are not settled unilaterally but in consultation with the other stakeholder." Instead, he virtually took the position that the Chinese accept the borders as delineated in the Indian maps. "Since Nehru had unilaterally declared Indian borders and made them non-negotiable and had even altered them, he expected the others to fall in line and accept the alignment drawn on Indian maps."[9]

Assessing Nehru's handling of the situation in the mid-1950s, former Foreign Secretary Nirupama Rao has charged him with both acts of commission and omission. The principal omission was not to have raised the issue of the border during the negotiations over the 1954 Tibet Agreement. And his major act of commission was to order his officials to show the Indian border as defined and settled through a fiat, rather than a bilateral agreement.[10]

* * *

But if India continued to whistle in the dark on the border, the Chinese were playing a subtler game. From 1955 onwards reports kept coming in about a road the Chinese had built through Aksai Chin to connect Xinjiang with Tibet. Many of the early reports were simply ignored by New Delhi. Finally, in September 1957, the *People's Daily* printed a small map showing the road and also announced the road, but Indian officials were unable to determine whether it went through Indian territory.

In June 1958, India sent out two patrols to verify the situation on the ground. Both parties found the road, though one group was arrested by the Chinese and "deported" through the Karakoram Pass; the other returned confirming the road there within what India considered its territory. When yet another article appeared in a Chinese publication showing its alignment, India made an official protest. The Chinese again made an ambiguous response claiming that the area had yet to be surveyed and that it would consult with the countries concerned before making any changes.

In December 1958, Nehru wrote a friendly letter to Zhou on the border issue. He referred to the 1954 treaty negotiations and noted that "no border questions were raised at the time and we were under the impression that there were no border disputes between our respective countries." He referred to his Beijing visit of October 1954 and of raising the issue of some Chinese maps, to which Zhou had then said that they were "pre-liberation" ones which had not yet been revised. He recalled that during Zhou's India tour of 1956, the matter had resurfaced yet again, and Zhou had again replied that these were old maps. He also referred to his conversation where Zhou had assured him that the Chinese would recognize the McMahon Line as the border in the east after consulting the Tibetan authorities.[11]

In his response, on 23 January 1959, Premier Zhou Enlai for the first time informed Prime Minister Jawaharlal Nehru that actually, "the Sino–Indian boundary has never been formally delimited," either by a treaty or any kind of agreement.[12] As a consequence, Zhou wrote, "there are certain differences" over the border. They had not been raised earlier "because conditions were not ripe for settlement." Chinese maps may not all be accurate on every point, he said, but changes could only be made after surveys and consultations with other countries. He did note, though, that the Chinese government was willing to take "a realistic attitude towards the McMahon Line." He proposed that the two sides maintain the status quo, "each side keep for the time being to the border areas at present under its jurisdiction and not go beyond them."

The penny did not quite drop for the Indians even now. Nehru's response of 22 March 1959 was to try and convince the Chinese that they need not worry too much about these details, the Indian side had already done the homework and found that the border was actually a settled matter. After expressing some surprise at the Chinese note, the Indians provided a detailed account of the Indian case in Sikkim, the Ladakh region and the McMahon Line. In all three Nehru said, "there is sufficient authority based on geography, tradition as well as treaties for the boundary as shown in our published maps."[13]

As the two prime ministers traded letters, another key development had occurred. On 10 March the Tibetan revolt broke out, there was fighting in Lhasa and the Dalai Lama fled to India and was given asylum on 31 March 1959.

Tibet was a key element in China's calculations with regard to India. An independent Tibet would vastly complicate China's security. The Indian role here was quite crucial: since India bordered Tibet the links between India and Tibet were extensive, not just physical since the closest port to Lhasa through which it got its supplies was Kolkata, but also cultural.

But where India felt that all it was doing was accepting the British-conferred notion that China was the suzerain of Tibet, the Chinese simply saw it as an acknowledgement of its sovereignty, a major achievement. In any case even this fictional suzerainty was cast aside after the Chinese crushed the revolt and the Dalai Lama had fled.

Tibet has, of course, been the long shadow that has affected Sino–Indian relations. The revolt was a culmination of Tibetan resistance that had begun to build up since the mid-1950s as the Chinese sought to impose their control over the country, beginning with the Kham and Amdo areas. The March 1959 uprising added to Chinese sensitivities, layered as they were over concerns of the CIA support to the Tibetans.

The CIA had from the early 1950s established contact with Gyalo Thondup, the Dalai Lama's elder brother, and other leading Tibetan notables living in the Kalimpong area of north Bengal. In 1957, it began to use the Kurmitola airfield in East Pakistan, overflying India clandestinely and dropping Tibetans back to their homeland. From 1958 onwards, as Tibetan resistance increased, the support was stepped up to what was now called the National Volunteer Defence Army. Over the next three years, the US carried out 30 or so air drops to provide arms, ammunition and some money to the Tibetan groups who, in reality, never did pose a significant threat to the PLA.[14]

Just how much did the Indians know of what was happening at the time? The issue had been discussed with Bhola Nath Mullik, the Indian intelligence chief, during the latter's visit to Hawaii. But Bruce Riedel, a CIA veteran who looked at the issue in 2015, says it is not clear how much detail he was given: "likely the Pakistan role was not emphasized." But Mullik had sources in the Tibetan refugee community in India and he would have pieced together the story. Given his proximity to Nehru, it is more than likely says Riedel that he kept the prime minister informed as well.[15]

The Chinese sought to walk a tightrope on the developments in Tibet. A lengthy editorial in the *People's Daily* criticized Nehru's statements in Parliament in April–May 1959, even while upholding the notion of Sino–Indian friendship. The editorial dwelt at length on the nature of Tibetan society, the reaction of the world to the revolt, and claimed that the Dalai Lama had actually been abducted from Lhasa. It did acknowledge that "the Indian government had no desire to annex Tibet or send its armed forces to interfere in Tibetan affairs." India had recognized Chinese sovereignty over Tibet and handed over its posts and telegraph installations back to the Chinese. But while India had no desire to occupy Tibet or make it formally independent, the editorial said, "it really strives to prevent China from exercising full sovereignty over its own territory of Tibet." This was, in its own way, an accurate way of putting across the Indian view that the Chinese should honour their 1951 commitments on autonomy for Tibet.[16]

The Tibetan revolt and related developments delayed Zhou's reply, which came eventually on 8 September 1959. For the first time, China openly spoke of the claims to Indian territories. Zhou now said blandly, that the maps that he had earlier said were outdated, were more or less correct. And he went on to list the Chinese case on the boundaries in Ladakh, Tibet and in the east. He said that at the root of the issue was Tibet and the British aim of separating that region from China. Because India was the base from which the British operated, that was why there were "long term disputes and non-settlement of the Sino–Indian boundary question." He accused India of pursuing the British-initiated policy "not even scrupling the use of force to support its demand [to grant formal recognition to the British-initiated claims]."[17]

By this time several clashes had taken place between Indian and Chinese troops and patrol parties in the north-east. One reason for this was the Indian interpretation of the McMahon Line in places like Migyitun, Longju and Khinzemane, in modern-day Arunachal Pradesh. While these were based on established practices in interpreting boundaries along watersheds, they were, in the ultimate analysis, done unilaterally by New Delhi. And of course in relation to a country that had consistently refused to recognize the McMahon Line as the boundary.

That India was still talking past the Chinese became apparent in Nehru's reply of 26 September 1959 which again delved deep into history and India's historical claims. Indeed, the Government of India's White Paper Volume II included an appendix providing the historical background of India's Himalayan frontier. This would have made little impression in Beijing in any case: their goal was the consolidation of their control over Tibet and carving out strategic frontiers that they deemed vital for the defence of China.

But the ambush of an Indian police party at Kongka La on 21 October 1959 changed the texture of the debate. The event happened not too far from the site of the 15 June 2020 incident on the Galwan river and it had a similar chilling effect on Sino–Indian relations.

The patrol party was ambushed on its way to the border, which in the Indian reckoning was a little further east at Lanak La pass on the Changchenmo river. Ten personnel were killed and ten taken prisoner, including the head of the party, Karam Singh. One Chinese soldier died in the incident and the Indians were only released in mid-November after intense diplomatic exchanges. The Chinese aim, it became obvious, was now to physically prevent India from patrolling up to its border claim.

In his next letter of 7 November 1959, Zhou sought to bring down temperatures raised by the incident and consolidate the Chinese gains. He said that since disputes that had arisen needed to be settled peacefully, it was important to maintain the *status quo*. To create the right atmosphere for this, he proposed that both sides withdraw 20 km from "the so called McMahon Line" in the east and "from the line up to which each side exercises actual control in the west." The details of the line to which this "actual control" was exercised were not spelt out, and no map accompanied the letter. It was only through the next letter, on 17 December 1959, Zhou clarified that in the western sector, the "Chinese map published in 1956, correctly shows the traditional boundary between the two countries in this sector."[18] Whether this was the same line over which the Chinese were at that time exercising actual control was not clear.

This "November 7 1959 Line" has become the key point of reference for the Chinese. Subsequently, and most recently in September 2020, the Chinese have insisted that their claim on the border coincides with the 7 November 1959 declaration of Zhou.[19] They have constantly and consistently insisted that in their view, the boundary is defined by this date. The problem is that there is enough evidence to show that their move westward, especially in the Chip Chap river valley, came after November 1959. Then, there was a war where, in Ladakh, they eliminated a number of Indian posts in the Chip Chap, Depsang Plains, Pangong Tso and Demchok areas and did not withdraw, as they did in the east. Yet, they continue to insist to this day that they occupy 7 November 1959 positions. (See Map 1)

On 26 December 1959, the Chinese Ministry of Foreign Affairs sent a 5,000-word note to New Delhi detailing the Chinese case on the boundary in the format of a question and answer treatise. Question no. 1 was "Has the Sino–Indian boundary been formally delimited?" And the obvious answer was that it hadn't. The evidence put forward cited the legal invalidity of the 1914 convention and noted that "the Sino–Indian boundary was never discussed at the 1914 Conference."[20]

Question no. 2 was: "What is the Traditional Customary Sino–Indian Boundary Line?" So, while the Indian case was rejected in Question 1, in the response to Question 2, China simply asserted that there was a Chinese traditional customary line, and in the west it included 33,000 sq. km claimed by India for which China not only had documentary proof, but over which it actually maintained effective control, except for an area near Parigas (Demchok). Likewise, an elaborate argument was provided for the Chinese claim in the eastern sector.

Question no. 3 was: "What is the Proper Way to Settle the Sino–Indian Boundary Dispute?" The answer was that the two sides should, first, maintain *status quo* and then work towards resolving the dispute. By the way, the note also took issue with Indian claims that the 1954 Sino–Indian agreement implied that all issues, including those relating to the boundary, had been settled. It said that that agreement was merely about trade and intercourse, and "has nothing to do with the boundary question."

This note also had a "sketch map" of the Sino–Indian border. Though the map was not detailed, it did show the differing concept of the border. In the east, it showed that Indian claims went beyond the McMahon Line in places like Khinzemane, Longju, Migyitun and Tamaden. And in the central and western sectors it showed the Chinese boundary running from the Karakoram Pass, parallel but not touching the Shyok, thence to the Kongka La, across Pangong Tso and on to Demchok (Parigas) and then to the central sector.

At this time there was some back and forth between Nehru and Zhou Enlai over maps published in 1956 in China. Zhou confirmed that "the Chinese map published in 1956…correctly showed the traditional boundary between the two countries in this (Ladakh) sector." He added, with some chutzpah, that but for Parigas (Demchok) area, India has not occupied any Chinese territory east of this section of the traditional boundary."[21] In other words, in the west there was no dispute over the boundary from the Chinese point of view.

The US Library of Congress collection has a map, drawn before the Sino-Japanese war, but revised according to the new data and probably published in 1956 by the authoritative Cartographic Publishing House in Beijing. Incidentally, the scale of the map is 1: 6,000,000, roughly the same as maps offered in border talks between the officials of the two countries in 1960. If you zoom into the area of the present conflict, it is clear from the map that while most of the Aksai Chin area has been shown as part of China, the Galwan and the Chip Chap river valleys are distinctly on the Indian side. Also, if you look closely to the Pangong Tso Lake, the boundary is shown as cutting across at the point India had said it did, near Fort Khurnak, not at the present point more than a dozen kilometres away into the Indian border. If this map is the basis of the 7 November 1959 line that Zhou spoke off, then the Chinese have already encroached into thousands of square kilometres of what even they accepted was Indian territory in 1956.[22]

Where Nehru had once contemplated a possible deal involving Aksai Chin, his position now began to harden. India now categorically put forward its historical claim to the region describing its border claim in detail in a note to the Chinese in November 1959. Behind these developments, says Hoffman, "was a process by which Prime Minister Nehru abandoned his doubts about the historical case for the Aksai Chin."[23]

This set the stage for the arrival of Zhou Enlai in New Delhi in April 1960 for a week-long visit in which he and Nehru had seven meetings totalling 20 hours. His aim was to get Nehru to agree on a six-point declaration whose three key points were that both sides (1) accept there is a dispute; (2) affirm the existence of a Line of Actual Control (LAC) up to which each side exercised jurisdiction; and (3) work on a settlement that would take into account the "national sentiments" of the two sides towards the Himalaya and Karakoram mountains; in essence China was willing to accept the Himalayan watershed as the boundary, which meant leaving Arunachal Pradesh to India, if the Indians accepted the Karakoram watershed which would have had not just Aksai Chin, but also the Saltoro range, firmly on the Chinese side.

For a variety of reasons these points were not acceptable to India. Point 1, for example, would undercut India's assertion that there was no traditional frontier. Point 2 would imply an Indian acceptance that China had always been in possession of what it was claiming in Ladakh. Point 3 was a hint that a barter deal was possible, with China forgoing its claim in the east, if the Indian did so in the west.

Zhou's offer of a swap was not directly stated, but the Indian rejection was categorical. Nehru was dead set against any kind of a barter and was unable to accept the implicit bargain that China was offering, in its view, of one part of Indian territory for another. There is considerable controversy over whether a deal was indeed ever offered. Chinese writers have insisted that it was, while the Indian side are more tentative. In any case the Cabinet opposed any deal and Nehru held firm.[24]

Having examined the record on both the Indian and Chinese ends, Nirupama Rao has said that Nehru's was a "flawed assessment." He was convinced of the "correctness and sanctity of India's approach" and that there was no question of accommodating the Chinese position; "all that was necessary was to persuade the Chinese about the validity of the Indian case."[25]

The 1960 report of Chinese and Indian officials

There was one more act left in the drama of this negotiation. Zhou proposed a joint border commission that could work together to determine the border, while Nehru suggested that officials of the two sides meet to weigh the historical-legal evidence. Eventually, the two sides appointed a team of officials who met through the rest of 1960 and produced a voluminous report published in 1961. Each session of these talks would often go on over a month and here, according to Kalha, the Indian side produced 36 official Indian maps and 8 official Chinese maps in support of their claims, while the Chinese side presented 13 official Indian maps, and no official Chinese maps to back theirs.[26] As per the procedure, officials also clarified their claims to each other and, on occasion, provided the latitude and longitude of several key points that marked their border.

Both sides attached authorized maps showing their version of the alignment of the entire Sino–Indian border. The scale of the Indian map was 1: 7 million, while that of the Chinese was 1: 5 million. Such maps could hardly provide a detailed picture of their claims. But even so they are revealing. The map presented by the Chinese team showed most of the Chip Chap river valley as part of Indian territory; likewise, the Chinese claim line very distinctly avoided claiming the entire Galwan river valley, leaving a small section, where it meets the Shyok river, to the Indians. In the Pangong Tso region, too, the Chinese showed an area 20 km west of the Khurnak Fort as part of their territory despite the fact that in this area, in Sirijap, India had long maintained its posts.[27]

At the request of Indian officials, the Chinese did detail their LAC. They provided map coordinates of their western boundary, beginning from the Karakoram Pass, the boundary ran eastward to a point east of 78° 05'E, then it turned southwest to a point 78° 1' E and 35° 21'N where it crossed the Chip Chap river. After this, it turned southeast along the mountain ridge and passed through two peaks 6845 metres (78°12'E and 34° 57'N) and Peak 6598 metres (78° 13'E 34° 54'N. Thereafter it crossed the Galwan River at 78°13'E 34° 46'N. It then passed through peak 6,556 (approximately 78° 26' E, 34° 32' N), and ran along the watershed between the Kugrang River and its tributary the Changlung River to approximately 78° 53' E, 34° 22' N where it crossed the Changlung River and reached the Kongka Pass. It reached the Pangong Lake at 78° 49'E, 33° 44'N and crossed the southern bank of the Lake at 78° 43'E, 33° 40' N.[28]

As India's chief negotiator Jagat Mehta, later foreign secretary, put it, "In all honesty our evidence was uneven, but objectively and comparatively strong." In any case, he noted, "we could have no illusions of bringing about any difference in the ground realities, much less bringing about a Chinese withdrawal."[29]

The map the Chinese had produced in 1960 based their border on the Karakoram range in the west, the Himalaya in the middle sector and the Himalayan foothills in the east. According to Hoffman, "the Ladakh portion of it had probably been drawn by arbitrarily linking together geographical points that had only come under their control in the 1950s and 1960s. In these circumstances, a new boundary line had to be negotiated, in the meantime the status of the boundary was that it was a line along which both exercised actual control."[30]

By now it was clear that the position of the two sides on their border was radically different. India believed that the Sino–Indian border was based on custom and tradition that went back centuries and was based on natural features like watersheds and did not require formal definition. The Chinese believed that their boundary also followed a traditional customary line, but that it had never been formally delimited. According to Hoffmann, India "was determined to have *historic* borders" whilst the Chinese wanted to "delimit new *strategic* borders using both diplomatic and military methods" (original italics).[31] At the end of the day, the two sides needed to sit together, negotiate, delineate and demarcate their boundary. But the Indian position that the borders were already fixed and needed no negotiation set up the situation for a breakdown.

Garver has pointed out that in the 1950s, "Control of Aksai Chin was … essential to Chinese control of *western* Tibet and very important to its control over *all* of Tibet" (emphasis added).[32] With the Chinese viewing the situation from the point of view of what they felt was their national security, there was no room for compromise, leave alone time to be distracted by historico-legal claims.

In the scholarly literature the Sino–Indian border dispute has gone through various stages. In the first phase, India was seen as a victim of Chinese betrayal and expansionism. This view remains stuck even today in the mind of the public in India. Then, in 1970, came Neville Maxwell's *India's China War* which blamed Nehru and Indian policy for the 1962 war. Some correction was provided by Steven A. Hoffman's *India and the China Crisis* in providing nuances of the Indian position.

In an essay reviewing the issue, Srinath Raghavan has gone deeper into the way India saw the crises unfold and the motives and actions of the Indian players. He self-consciously avoided weighing the merits of the Indian and Chinese cases.[33] Yet, he does bring out that seemingly arbitrary actions of Nehru, such as unilaterally redrawing the maps of India in 1954, had a purpose other than to unilaterally settle the dispute on India's terms. This is a view which Bhasin has also underscored.

On the other hand, Chinese views have been fairly consistent. An article in *Quishi*, the Communist Party of China's theoretical journal, Kang Minjun, professor of history in Hebei, claimed that through the 1950s and even during the 1962 war, China tried to resolve the dispute through peaceful means. This was evidenced by its withdrawal, after the war, from Arunachal Pradesh. Whereas the Indian side had consistently refused negotiations and sought a settlement based on its unilateral border claims.[34]

Forward policy

In 1961, India came to the reluctant conclusion that the Chinese could not be negotiated away from Aksai Chin. So, somewhat late in the day, they devised their own strategy to push into the region. Though they had claimed the area, India had no administrative presence there. So far, they had been sending police patrols into the Chinese-claimed, but unoccupied, areas. Now the plan was to place posts of Indian Army personnel as far into the Aksai Chin region as possible in terms of logistics. Though executed by Intelligence Bureau and military personnel, the move was not a military one, but one which used military personnel to show the flag as it were. India established posts at Hot Springs, Daulat Beg Oldi, in the Chip Chap river valley and planned to do so in other places in the belief that the Chinese would not contest the process.

Nehru convened a key meeting that took place on 2 November 1961 with Defence Minister Krishna Menon, Army Chief General P.N. Thapar, Intelligence Bureau Chief B. N. Mullik, the foreign and defence secretaries and other officers attending. A directive was issued that in Ladakh the forces needed to patrol "as far forward as possible" from existing borders towards the international border—India's claim line. This would be with a view of establishing posts in a manner that would prevent the Chinese from advancing further. In the central and eastern sectors, too, posts were to be established. However, unless self-defence was an issue, a direct clash was to be avoided. An important caveat was that the posts should be established in such a way that they could be backed up by heavier concentrations of the army to provide logistics and security.[35]

But when the orders were transmitted next month, this key last point was omitted. In this way, the crucial link up of this "forward policy" with a larger buildup of defensive capacity in Ladakh was ignored. Actually, at this time, this was not really feasible. The road link between Ladakh and the rest of India had yet to be completed. The entire effort had to depend on air maintenance. But the generals went ahead anyway and ill-equipped troops with inadequate logistical support were pushed in to establish posts at altitudes of 14,000–16,000 ft (4250–4850 m).

The moves were not backed by the needed enhancement of the capabilities of the army, either in terms of personnel or equipment. The army simply ignored the larger imperatives of planning defences against a potential Chinese reaction, and was forced to deploy its forces in an untenable scheme of dubious utility.[36]

The forward policy predictably raised temperatures between India and China in the spring of 1962. The Chinese had been expanding westward since 1959 from their 1956 claim line. But since there were no Indians around, they were doing it at a leisurely pace. But in the spring of 1962, when the Indian Army began to establish new posts in the Chip Chap river valley, the Galwan and Changchenmo river valleys, Pangong Tso, and Demchok, the Chinese countered the deployments and very rapidly built up their forces in eastern Ladakh.

Even as diplomats exchanged notes of protest, the Indian and Chinese posts jostled for dominance, and there were occasional exchanges of fire but the balance of power was with the Chinese. As of September 1962, the Chinese had established 47 new posts as against the 36 the Indians had, the bulk of them in the Chip Chap region.[37] The Indians were at a disadvantage in terms of numbers and since they were either supplied by helicopters and airdrops, or yak and mule trains. They had to operate out of valleys, whereas the Chinese were connected by road to their highway and were able to occupy the heights around them. In the Chip Chap, Galwan and Changchenmo river valley areas the isolated Indian forward posts were effectively surrounded by the Chinese.[38]

In the eastern sector, the Indian forward policy called for occupying areas which the Indians interpreted to be on their side of the McMahon Line. We say "interpreted" because these were often at variance from the literal positioning of the line. The Indian side assumed that McMahon intended the high crest of the Himalayan watershed to be the border and so drew their own line, which was sometimes to the north of the actual line drawn.

War

Countering these moves was a more systematic and coherent Chinese policy which finally triggered the war. As Indian forces sought to cross the Namka Chu river to occupy Thag La ridge, north of Tawang in modern-day Arunachal Pradesh, the Chinese, who had been readying for war for some time, launched an attack on 20 October and destroyed the Indian brigade involved in the operation. (See Map 6) Over the next month, they decisively defeated the Indian forces and reached the foothills of Assam.

There was no action in the central sector. In the west, the war began on that same day, on 20 October, when it was still dark at 5 am, and soon all forward posts in the Chip Chap river valley area and the two in the Galwan valley were overrun. The next day, on 21 October, two more Indian posts in the Sirijap area in Pangong Tso were attacked and captured by the PLA. From 22 to 24 October, three Indian posts, one in Kongka La and two in the Hot Springs area, also fell. On 27 October Indian posts in Changla, Jara La and Demchok fell, and territory up to Dumchele occupied. The next phase, beginning 18 November, was a series of attacks on the Chushul area. Rezangla fell on the 18 November after bitter fighting with the Indians fighting to the proverbial last man and last round. Fighting carried on in the Chushul area till ceasefire.[39] (See Maps 1 and 2)

By and large the PLA was ordered to fight within the lines of the boundary claimed by China, which is their 1960 claim line.[40] But, in many places such as the Depsang area, the Chinese went beyond their claim line of 1960, since the Indians had withdrawn in the belief that they needed to consolidate themselves to defend Leh. Even in Pangong Tso where the Indian side had a slight edge, it remained passive when the main Chinese attack came on 18 November.

The Chinese announced they would cease fire as of 00:00 hours on 22 November 1962 and, as of 1 December, begin withdrawing to what they said were "positions 20 km behind the Line of Actual Control (LAC) which existed between China and India on November 7, 1959." India had little option but to accept: by this time, barring possibly Chushul, there was no contact between Indian and Chinese forces any way, either in the east, or the west.

In the east, the Chinese withdrew to the north of the McMahon Line, in the central sector there was no action. But in the west, there was an element of confusion since the Indians did not really have a clear idea, except in Chushul, as to the extent to which the Chinese forces had come in. As Shyam Saran has put it: "It was in the 1962 operations that Chinese forces created an alignment further west, which is, broadly, the current LAC."[41]

* * *

Why did India and China go to war in 1962? There have been several accounts of the war from both the Indian and Chinese sides. US scholar John W. Garver has rightly called on both sides to share responsibility for that war. In essence, he sees Indian policies, especially the Forward Policy begun in November 1961, for adopting an approach that was viewed by Chinese leaders "as constituting incremental Indian seizure of Chinese controlled territory." But, in turn, he notes, Chinese perceptions of Indian policies towards Tibet, a strong motivator for Beijing's decision, were "fundamentally erroneous."

Garver notes that Chinese studies of the 1962 war published in the 1990s were based on the belief, triggered by Mao Zedong himself in 1959, that India somehow wanted to attenuate Chinese control over Tibet, or actually overthrow it. This, of course, was an enormous and dangerous over-interpretation of the Indian desire to see an autonomous Tibet. Nehru was seeking to "induce Beijing to respect Indian cultural and security interests in Tibet within the framework of Chinese sovereignty of that region." Of course, the US operation to aid Tibetans added its own frisson, since the aircraft that parachuted the military supplies and agents came across the Indian border.

Indian leaders erred fundamentally in assuming that the Chinese would not respond militarily to the Indian Army establishing penny-packet posts in areas they controlled. But as for the war itself, it was a carefully planned Chinese venture. At the end of it all, notes Garver, Mao and his associates saw military power as "playing a central role in politics domestic and international," while their Indian counterparts actually believed that "war among the major powers was an obsolete phenomenon."[42]

In a recent book, Zorawar Daulet Singh suggests an element of geo-political misjudgment shaped both the Indian and Chinese behaviour in the late 1950s and early 1960s. Things were going well for India from the international point of view as the US adjusted its policy and began to emerge as a major aid giver to India; on the other hand, the beginnings of the Sino-Soviet rift were visible. A new Soviet approach saw them willing to provide high-performance Mig-21 fighters to India along with significant economic assistance. Nehru, says Singh, believed that the attitude of the two Great Powers would moderate Chinese behaviour towards India.[43]

The Line of Actual Control

The notion of the Line of Actual Control is peculiar to defining the border between India and China and it is worth examining its origins, nature and purpose. In early 2014 National Security Adviser (NSA) Shivshankar Menon explained the LAC as simply being "a number of points where we exercise actual control." Later in his book, he noted, that the term 'Line of Actual Control' has, in the main, been used by China to shape the border discourse in its own favour.[44] In essence it was to give some kind of legitimacy to the Chinese case in physically seizing the Aksai Chin.

So when, after routing the Indians, the Chinese said they would withdraw 20 km behind the LAC of 7 November 1959, what did they mean? For one, they clarified that the withdrawal referred only to military personnel; they would maintain administrative control in the 20-km zone on their side. In the east it was simple—north of the

McMahon Line. There had been no action in the central sector. But in the west this posed a problem. Indian posts had been wiped out in the Chip Chap, Depsang, Galwan, Changchenmo and Pangong areas, and withdrawn in others like DBO and Hot Springs. Only the Chinese knew in many areas as to where they had come to, and to which point they would go back.

Remarkably, through the war, the two prime ministers kept up their correspondence. For the Chinese, the effort was political positioning to show that theirs had been a defensive endeavour against Indian provocations. Because they were winning, they could also afford to show that they were magnanimous. So, four days after overwhelming Indian forces in Namka Chu, on 24 October, Zhou had reiterated his old proposal that the two sides withdraw 20 km behind the Line of Actual Control (LAC), and that the two prime ministers resume their talks.[45] Nehru's response of 27 October was to express some exasperation about proposals "which talk about 'lines of actual control' etc." which had baffled not just him but other governments as well. He said the simple way out was to revert to positions the two sides held on 8 September—the date before Chinese forces moved forward on Thag La ridge in the east. Attached to the letter was an annexure which was even more blunt. It said that the Chinese offer of withdrawal was meaningless. "What is this 'line of actual control' (LAC)?" it asked. Adding "Is this the line they have created by aggression since the beginning of September [1962]?"[46]

Zhou reiterated the points in his reply of 4 November 1962. But just how complicated things were is apparent from his own description of the line he had proposed on 7 November 1959, and the one he was proposing now as the one from which China would withdraw 20 km. To be specific, he said this LAC coincided with the "so-called" McMahon Line in the east, which was easy enough to grasp, but in the west and middle sector, "it coincides in the main with the traditional customary line which has consistently been pointed out by China."[47] Just where this line ran, of course, was another matter since the only official map India had of the Chinese-claimed border was the one provided in the *Officials's Report* in 1960 on a 1: 5 million scale map.

Nehru's response on 14 November, which incidentally was his birthday, and on the eve of an even bigger disaster for Indian arms in the east, the collapse of the Indian defences in Bomdi La, picked on this theme of the LAC. He said in the west, far from a coherent line, "what you call the 1959 'line of actual control' was no line but a series of positions of the Chinese forces on Indian territory" that had been established forcibly since 1957.[48]

The way India saw it the LAC in the west ran from their Spanggur post, to Khurnak Fort on the Pangong Tso, from there to Kongka La and then straight northwards to the Aksai Chin Road.

Zhou's response of 28 November was that not only would the Chinese forces go back from the positions they held on 8 September or 20 October 1962 but to those of 7 November 1959: "The line of actual control as taken on the basis of the extent of administration by each side at the time; it existed objectively and cannot be defined or interpreted according to the free will of either side."[49] Nehru's tart response of 1 December was that that is exactly what the Chinese had done— defined and interpreted the LAC according to their own will.[50]

In a note sent on 30 November, the Ministry of External Affairs had said that the Chinese side had circulated a map which had shown "large areas of Ladakh including Qizil Jilga, Shinglung, Dehra, Samzungling and areas to the west of those localities as within the Chinese line of actual control," while, in fact, some of these areas were occupied in late 1959 and in 1960 and others even later till September 1962.

Thereafter in the war, the Chinese had occupied another 2,000 sq. miles (5,000 sq. km). On the basis of this, India wanted "an objective and factual clarification" of the Chinese line of actual control, based on the position on the ground as on 7 November 1959, and not on the basis "of any theoretical claims or surreptitious or forcible advances made by Chinese forces since."[51]

The map the Indian Ministry of External Affairs (MEA) was speaking about had been attached to a letter Zhou had written to the leaders of the Asian and African nations in the midst of the war to argue China's case against India. More of a sketch map than anything else, this map is hardly to scale and has few reference points. The MEA's response was basically extrapolating those areas there. This was one of the rare Chinese maps that showed the whole of the Galwan river valley to be on the Chinese side of the LAC. Incidentally, this was only the second official map that the Chinese had provided of what they said was the border, the first being the map attached to the *Officials' Report*. The differences between the two are evident.

The dialogue between the two sides now descended into a welter of cross-accusations as to who was where and when, in the remote and desolate Aksai Chin region. Since the area is uninhabited, it was the word of the Chinese against that of the Indians, buttressed by past claims and protest notes accusing the other side of encroachment. Yet again, India and China were talking past each other.

There was one last drama, a sad one at that. Through the war, India's *Chargé d'Affaires* in Bejing had been Purnendu Kumar Banerjee who had in the past interacted directly with Zhou Enlai. On 7 January 1963, he summoned Banerjee for a private meeting and asked him to convey a "very personal and verbal message only for Mr Nehru's ears." Zhou proposed that Nehru and he stop negative statements against each other for about three months and thereafter the two should meet quietly with small delegations "at an agreed place" for about two days, to exchange ideas "for an agreed and joint action to defuse the current situation."[52]

Banerjee returned to the embassy and wrote down a summary of the message and took it in a single typed sheet with him to New Delhi in his wallet. He was there for several days and met Nehru officially, as well as other officials. Then, he was summoned for a private meeting with Nehru where he gave him the message. After reading it, Nehru went into a monologue on the Chinese relationship, his efforts to promote goodwill and his relationship with Zhou and his sense of betrayal at what the Chinese had done. After a short discussion, Nehru asked Banerjee if he had shown the message to anyone else. When Banerjee said no, Nehru, a regular smoker, struck a match and burnt the paper over an ashtray saying that it would take the Indian side more than a quarter of a century "to return to any substantive negotiation."[53]

The similarities between the situation in 1962 and 2020 are striking. At both points China has felt the need to assert its claims, and India to resist them. In 1962, China proposed a 20-km buffer zone; in 2020, the disengagement process has involved setting up small no-patrolling areas. This could well be extended in some future arrangement to other areas of the LAC as well.

The differences, too, are marked. In 1962, the Indian Army collapsed in the face of the PLA offensive, while in 2020, the outcome has turned out to be different. Instead of a bloody war, both sides have worked hard to keep peace. But, at the same time, they have substantially enhanced their military presence along the LAC, which may not bode too well for the future.

Between these two points—the end of the war in the autumn of 1962 and the clash in the summer of 2020—is a long story of the two Asian giants seeking to deal with each other as mature nations as they went through their own domestic trials and tribulations and emerged in the 2000s as nations destined to lead the world in the twenty-first century.

3

NINETEEN NINETY-THREE

The year 1993 turned out to be as consequential for the Sino–Indian border issue as the fateful 1962. This was the year in which the two sides agreed to sign an agreement which truly marked the end of that war, with India accepting, for the first time, that the Sino–Indian border was defined currently by a Line of Actual Control (LAC), pending a settlement of their boundary dispute.

Of course, this did not come out of the blue. It was the logical end of a process that began with the ceasefire of November 1962. But it was also a product of its immediate backdrop—the Tiananmen Square massacre and the split in the Communist Party of China in 1989, the stabilizing of a minority government in India, the collapse of the Soviet Union in 1991 and the spectacular US victory in the first Gulf War of August 1990–February 1991.

But the story began as the embers of war cooled in 1962. Despite the intervention of a clutch of non-aligned nations, called the Colombo Powers, India and China did not agree to a common process for the ceasefire and a resumption of border negotiations, but India had little choice but to abide by the LAC imposed by China in the wake of the war. Actually, both sides essentially walked away from the border in the ensuing decade, especially in Ladakh.

Sino–Indian relations remained tentative in the aftermath of the war. In 1965 when India and Pakistan fought a war, the Chinese came out in favour of Islamabad and even conducted some military move-ments to pressure India to ease Pakistan's self-created predicament. It was not entirely a coincidence that India agreed to a ceasefire by the time designated by a Chinese ultimatum. When India and Pakistan fought yet another war in December 1971, China more or less stayed out, whether it was because of the weather, which would have closed the Himalayan passes, the threat of Soviet intervention, or its own policy decision, is not clear.

In 1967, the two sides clashed near Nathu La in Sikkim, with mor-tars, artillery and machine guns being used; scores of personnel died on both sides. That year, Red Guards stormed the Indian Embassy in Beijing and assaulted Indian diplomats, sending ties between the two countries to a new low.

In the 1970s, the two countries tried to put the pieces of their rela-tionship back together again. It began with Mao's smile and greetings to the Indian *Charge d'affairs*, Brajesh Mishra, who was lined up with other diplomats on the ramparts of Tiananmen Gate on May Day 1970. Mao famously told Mishra, "How long are we going to keep quarreling like this? Let us be friends again."[1]

In 1971, the US and China became friends and Beijing succeeded Taipei's seat in the UN Security Council. India's decisive military vic-tory over Pakistan in the war which, later that year, gave birth to Bangladesh, pitted it against the US and China. But with the Soviets in India's geopolitical corner, India quickly and skilfully dealt with the Pakistan Army in the east.

This was a period of turmoil in China. Lin Biao, Mao's putative number two, died mysteriously in September 1971, but the Cultural Revolution rampaged on till Mao's own death in 1976 and, a month later, the collapse of the Gang of Four. For a while the Chinese were worried that India could do to Tibet what it had done in East Pakistan—forcibly detach it from China. However, Mao's passing and the rise of Deng Xiaoping dramatically altered the trajectory of China.

In this period, India went through its own turmoil that led to the declaration of a National Emergency in 1975, leading to the suspen-sion of civil liberties. In 1976, the government had constituted a China Study Group, comprising of senior officers dealing with China. They ordered the relevant departments to use satellite imagery and other modern cartographic means to work out just where the border lay with China. Thereafter, they authorized the border security personnel to move forward, carefully calibrating their patrolling limits in each sector and numbering them from Patrolling Point (PP) 1 near Karakoram Pass, to PPs 10, 11, 12 and 13 in Depsang, down to that fateful PP 14 in the Galwan River valley, PP 15, 16, 17 and 17A in the Kugrang river valley and so on along the LAC till its terminus point in the eastern sector.

Domestically, things returned to normal in India after Indira Gandhi's defeat in the 1977 general election. The new prime minister Morarji Desai wanted to improve relations with China and distance India from the policy of close friendship with the Soviet Union.

In February 1979, Atal Bihari Vajpayee, who was foreign minister, visited Beijing. Vajpayee, a veteran parliamentarian with an interest in foreign affairs, had in his time barracked Nehru on his China policy. But now he realized that there was a need to restore normal relations with India's two antagonistic neighbours, Pakistan and China. Vajpayee had had to cut short his visit following China's invasion of Vietnam, but the trip was successful. China committed itself to stop support to insurgents in north-eastern India, and allowed pilgrims to once again visit the holy sites of Kailash and Manasarovar in Tibet. Vajpayee also hinted that maybe India and China could set aside the border issue and yet normalize ties. But the coalition government, of which he was part, collapsed.

The swap formula

Indira Gandhi returned to power in 1980 with a comfortable majority. Till that point in time, domestic political turmoil had prevented India from giving shape to an effective China policy. But geopolitical shifts were taking place, pulling both the Chinese and the Indians in different directions. Primary among these was what was happening in the Soviet Union, which had invaded Afghanistan in 1979. The Chinese supporting the American jihad against the Soviets were worried about the Soviet troops massed on their border. Though India had formally supported the Soviets in Afghanistan, it was deeply concerned over the instability in its neighbourhood. Yet it was not easy for New Delhi to move beyond its formal position that to move ahead with China, the border dispute needed to be settled.

Deng Xiaoping who became China's supreme leader in 1977 sought to provide a way out by hinting at a revival of the package deal, essentially a *"talis qualis"* (such as it is) settlement. In June 1980, in an interview with Krishan Kumar, editor of *Vikrant*, a now defunct defence journal, he wondered if China could recognize the McMahon Line if India was willing to also recognize the existing *status quo*. The problem was that the issue had been frozen in New Delhi's mind as a situation where China was seeking to trade one chunk of Indian territory for another.

But the issue was clearly in Deng's mind because he raised it again in 1982 with the former ambassador to China, G. Parthasarathi, who was at that time Chairman of the Policy Planning Committee and a key foreign policy adviser to Indira Gandhi. But Parthasarathi ignored it.

In 1983, former Foreign Secretary Shyam Saran, later recounted how he, a junior officer, brought a proposal from Beijing which may have led to what he termed as an "LAC plus" proposal. Here, India would get to keep Arunachal Pradesh and the Chinese would also agree to vacate the area they had occupied in their 1962 campaign. He took it to Parthasarathi, who refused to put this proposition before Prime Minister Indira Gandhi.[2]

The Chinese offer was spurned by New Delhi again, in the main because those who were in decision-making positions like Parthasarthi were Nehru loyalists and had never forgiven the Chinese for what they saw as a betrayal.

It was only after the election and return of Indira Gandhi that talks between Indian and Chinese officials resumed with the first round in December 1981, but they went round and round. There were differences on procedure, as well as conceptual issues. The Indians wanted the border to be discussed "sector by sector," and the Chinese wanted to push their package, which would have more or less regularized the Line of Actual Control. But there was no meeting of minds here, and neither side seemed ready to move forward in a decisive manner. And given the particular problem of a disputed border, the two countries needed to move together, in lockstep, as it were.

The LAC and the LAC Plus formulas were spoken about, though not discussed. India also began to see the value of developing relations in "other" areas, even while the two sides negotiated a border settlement. By the fifth round in September 1984, it appeared that the two sides would be willing to discuss the border in a "sector by sector" approach, provided the agreement reached for one sector would hold only till an agreement was reached for the entire boundary. And India's position remained that unless there was a fair and satisfactory resolution to the border issue, full normalization was not possible.

Expectations were that negotiations would now begin in earnest. The Chinese had agreed to begin discussions on the eastern sector. The Indian side was quite sanguine: China had long been willing to settle this *"talis qualis"*, provided the eastern boundary was not described by the McMahon Line. But equally, the Chinese could not have been unaware that once they resolved the eastern sector in these terms, the Indians would then press for some concessions in the west. But once again the Indians misread the Chinese.

Even as the sixth round began in November 1985, Chinese Vice-Minister Liu Shuqing informed his Indian counterpart, Secretary (East) A.P. Venkateswaran, that actually there was a bigger dispute in the eastern sector, and that India would have to make unspecified concessions here for the Chinese to be able to give concessions in the west.

After twenty-five years of hinting they were willing to live with the McMahon Line, if India conceded their claim in Ladakh, Beijing suddenly shifted the goalposts. The Indian side was baffled because this represented a 180-degree change in the Chinese position that had been hinted at in 1960 by Zhou, more recently by Deng, and in the earlier rounds of the border talks. The Chinese side seems to have decided that there was nothing to gain from persisting in negotiations, and that hereafter, the issue could be put on the back-burner and relations be allowed to develop in other areas.

The Wangdung incident

But an unsettled border always has room for springing surprises and so, too, did this one. After she had returned to power in 1980, Indira Gandhi had ordered a major security review covering virtually all areas from border management to defence research & development. The long trauma was wearing off and the Indian forces, now flush with new

Russian-supplied systems, began to flex their muscles. Among their important tasks was to defend the Sino–Indian border. Given the difficulties of the terrain on the Indian side, the decision was taken to adopt a string of strong defensive positions along the border under a concept called "dissuasive defence." Among the places that the army was asked to focus on again was the defence of the monastery town of Tawang, built in accordance with the wishes of the 5th Dalai Lama, Ngwang Lobsang Gyatso, the Great Fifth, in the late 17th century.

Prior to this, the Indian Army plans had more or less determined to abandon Tawang in the event of another Chinese attack, and planned to hold them at the Se La massif, that connects the Tawang region to Bomdila near the Assam plains. This had also been the site of a defensive bastion in 1962, but for a variety of reasons, the Indian defence there came apart.

Simultaneously, a decision was taken to have intelligence teams of the Subsidiary Intelligence Bureau (SIB) move up to the Indian claim line and establish their presence. One such place was the Wangdung pasturage south of the Sumdorong Chu rivulet, adjacent to the site that saw the fierce opening battle of the 1962 war. This area is east of the trijunction between India, China and Bhutan. Given the climate, the team went in summer along with the nomadic herdsmen, and returned by winter. (See Map 6)

They did this in 1983, 1984 and 1985. But when they went in the summer of 1986, they found the place occupied by the PLA who were constructing permanent structures there. Within days, the Indians lodged a complaint in Beijing, and the latter rejected it. The seventh round of talks held in Beijing in July was consumed by the issue. The difference of opinion was the old one about the McMahon Line. The Chinese extrapolated the exact coordinates from the map attached to the agreement, while the Indian side maintained that the line ran along the highest crest of the mountains, and in that sense, Wangdung was south of the line. This was an important difference in their respective approaches and, in 1962, it had led India to claim the Thag La ridge as the boundary. War broke out when the Indian side was readying to cross the Namka Chu to occupy the Thag La ridge.

In response to the PLA move, the division commander on the Indian side ordered precautionary deployments and asked his forces to occupy the Longro La Pass overlooking Wangdung. Attempts by Chinese patrols to rush the Indians in their newly occupied posts were defeated and, in some instances, the Indians opened fire over the heads of the approaching Chinese troops.

The Indian Army HQ now acted proactively and the then Chief General Krishnaswamy Sundarji himself arrived to assess the situation in August and brought the deployment under the scope of the ongoing Operation Falcon. Under this, between 18 and 20 October, an entire brigade was helicoptered into Zemithang, behind the ridgeline and they moved to occupy forward positions along the Hathung La ridge facing the Chinese. These were areas from which Indian forces had been evicted in 1962. Indeed, when the Indian troops occupied the ridge, they found the remains of their comrades who had died fighting on it a quarter century earlier.[3]

There is a side-story to this that was retailed to me by Sundarji's aides. Rajiv Gandhi only came to know about the seriousness of these moves on 4 December 1986, when he was attending a Navy Day reception at the residence of the Naval Chief. He had some notion of issues there, but now he was told that a crisis was on hand. He ordered all the relevant people, including Army Chief Sundarji, to proceed from the reception to the nearby Operations Room in the main South Block Headquarters of the army and the Ministry of Defence.

Asked as to why the army had not taken permission to make its moves, the army officers told him that they were merely acting upon instructions that had been issued as far back as 1983 to occupy positions that would enable an effective defence of Tawang. In the heated discussion that followed, a senior civilian official suggested that the army could perhaps site their Tawang defences by occupying ridges further south, away from the Chinese positions. Thereupon Sundarji dramatically offered the pointer to him saying, "If you think you are not getting the best advice on this, you're welcome to get alternative [advice]." The civilians backed off and the prime minister upheld Sundarji.[4]

Additional forces were airlifted to the border, first in this region, and then across the entire LAC. The Indians even emplaced T-72 tanks and BMP-1 Infantry Combat Vehicles in Ladakh and northern Sikkim. The Chinese also rushed their forces forward to the border. Both sides were now eyeball-to-eyeball. The Indians contemplated a local offensive to take the Thag La ridge. The Chinese, for their part, threatened to teach the Indians another lesson after 1962. But for the first time since the disaster of 1962, Indian forces had the tactical advantage over their Chinese counterparts.

The army now rapidly reinforced its positions and there was talk of war in the summer of 1987, though through a flag meeting in mid-November 1986, Indian and Chinese forces had agreed to avoid using force and keep a distance between their forces.

But the political rhetoric did not quite die down. Indeed it went up a couple of decibels when later in December, the Indian Parliament passed an act to elevate the Union Territory of Arunachal (North East Frontier Agency till 1972), into a full state called Arunachal Pradesh. The Chinese went ballistic, but they had been out-maneuvered politically and militarily. Along the LAC, the Chinese were confronting an Indian Army which had been re-equipped with Soviet tanks, BMPs, helicopters and transport aircraft, more advanced than anything they had. Politically, they were caught in the midst of their effort to normalize ties with the Soviet Union and rebuild their country ruined by Maoist excesses.

It was a signal to China that it could no longer treat India as a defeated country. The capabilities of the Indian military, leavened by the latest Soviet equipment and led by aggressive generals like K. Sundarji, required a change of approach. Interestingly, the Chinese invited Sundarji to visit China after the crisis had died down. But the government did not permit him to go. After he retired, the invitation was renewed and Sundarji did make his visit.

Rajiv Gandhi goes to China

In the end, diplomacy was able to do its work and the relationship took another turn. Even while standing firm with the army, Prime Minister Rajiv Gandhi dispatched Defence Minister K. C. Pant to Beijing, a visit that was followed in May by External Affairs Minister N. D. Tiwari, who made a transit visit while on his way back from Pyongyang. At this point, building on discussion within the Indian government for a while, Rajiv Gandhi agreed to visit Beijing in 1988, in return for Zhou Enlai's 1960 visit. This visit, in a sense, marked the end of the 1962 war.

Going to China in 1988 was not an easy decision for Rajiv Gandhi. But it was quite in keeping with his style of bold leadership and, certainly, the ability of the Indian Army to stand firm during the Wangdung/Sumdorong Chu crisis helped. Through 1988, the government undertook wide consultations among experts and opinion makers, as well as the Congress Party. There were worries that in a bid to show success, Rajiv Gandhi may offer concessions such as a withdrawal in the Wangdung area. Hanging over the issue was the increasing political pressure on the prime minister on account of the Bofors scandal, which alleged that bribes had been taken for clearing the Bofors howitzers for the army in 1986.

One of the significant outcomes of Rajiv Gandhi's December 1988 visit to Beijing was that India and China agreed to resume negotiations on the border dispute but, pending the settlement, they would maintain peace and tranquility along the border and ensure that their differences did not escalate into clashes, or near clashes, as they had in 1967 and 1986–1987. An important consequence of this decision was that the two would begin the process of developing relations in other areas.

Asked by Juergen Kahl, a German journalist, as to whether India was now subscribing to the Chinese formula of "mutual understanding and mutual accommodation" (MUMA), Rajiv Gandhi's response was that India had its own formula. This was incorporated in the Joint Statement following his visit that spoke of the two sides undertaking peaceful and friendly consultations for a "fair and reasonable…mutually acceptable solution to this question."[5]

Rajiv Gandhi had made it clear to Deng himself that India was simply not ready to offer concessions in the east in exchange for China offering them in the west. One of the outcomes of the visit had been the establishment of a Joint Working Group (JWG) to deal with the boundary issue. The "joint" in the title was deliberate. Earlier talks were between Indian and Chinese officials; the aim of the JWG was to have them work together to come up with a solution to the border dispute.

By now four discernible lines had emerged in the border negotiations since 1960. The first was the Zhou offer of 1960, essentially willing to accept the McMahon Line in exchange for India accepting Chinese claims in Ladakh. Then there was the Indian "LAC plus" position of the 1980s which spoke of a settlement that would refuse to legitimize the Chinese gains of the 1962 war, but accept a settlement based on "logistic and administrative convenience," which meant accepting the Chinese in Ladakh, with their highway in Aksai Chin and the Chinese accepting India's control of Arunachal Pradesh. With the shift in the mid-1980s demanding concessions in the east, the Chinese position had come with a new acronym—mutual understanding and mutual accommodation (MUMA). This meant that for mutual understanding, both sides needed to accommodate each other by making territorial concessions.[6] In other words, to accept the LAC Plus formula in the west, the Chinese would need significant concessions in the east. And finally by the late 1980s, the Indian position turned it around and said that all that was possible was mutual adjustment and mutual understanding (MAMU), which meant that all that India was willing to consider were "adjustments" to the LAC, not major changes.

Shyam Saran has noted that India formally refused to commit itself to the MUMA formula during the visit. This would have gone against the grain of the Indian position, which was that there was no dispute about where the boundary lay, except for the need for some small adjustments. But he has pointed out that "the Chinese principle [of mutual accommodation] was reportedly conceded in private by Rajiv Gandhi, but not acknowledged in public statements."[7] Rajiv Gandhi, in a sense, sought to finesse the Chinese and Indian acronyms and as a senior officer dealing with China at the time remarked, the Indian position now became that it would seek mutual accommodation, mutual understanding and mutual adjustment (MAMUMA).

* * *

So, from the Indian point of view, the basic political decision to normalize relations with China and bypass the insistence on settling the border dispute, was taken in 1988. But now many domestic developments intervened—Rajiv Gandhi lost the general election of 1989. In the next two years, India had an unstable coalition in charge in New Delhi, while the economy sank and large parts of the country saw terrorism, separatist insurgency, social and political turmoil. Internationally, too, the scene was none too good for India. Its most trusted ally the Soviet Union collapsed, hitting India with a double whammy—the loss of a diplomatic partner with a veto in the UN

Security Council, as well as the disruption of spares and equipment for 80 per cent of India's armed forces that had come from the erstwhile Soviet Union.

The ultimate ignominy was when India went bankrupt in early 1991, and had to physically ship its gold reserve to London to keep creditors at bay. And all this happened even as the country went through a general election which Rajiv Gandhi may have lost again, but on 21 May 1991 he was assassinated by a Liberation Tigers of Tamil Eelam (LTTE) suicide bomber.

Rajiv Gandhi's assassination boosted his Congress Party in the second phase of the election, enabling it to reach a number at which it could form a minority government. Senior Congress leader P.V. Narasimha Rao stepped in to form the government in mid-1991. His immediate focus was to address the deep economic crisis in India, which he sought to do by undertaking major reforms and opening up the Indian economy to the world. He was aware, too, of the dire situation of the country, with Punjab and Kashmir in the grip of separatist movements aided by Pakistan. And then, there was pressure from the sole surviving superpower, the US, on the non-proliferation front. So, making peace with China was a logical step.

In turn, China had gone through the Tiananmen incident in 1989 and its ensuing global fallout in the midst of its opening out to the world. The arms embargo imposed by the US and EU was a major setback to Chinese military modernization plans. Meantime, in 1987, border negotiations which had been resumed with the Soviet Union under Mikhail Gorbachev yielded an agreement in May 1991, several months after the collapse of the USSR. The Soviet withdrawal from Afghanistan in 1989 had eased another set of Chinese worries. But Soviet armies hadn't quite been pulled back from the Chinese border.

The Chinese were worried about the situation in Xinjiang and Tibet and wanted to stabilize their south-western border. The military issues with India were nowhere as risky as they had been with the Soviets, but China wanted peace to unroll its reform agenda, and for that needed to stabilize the situation on the border to prevent a recurrence of the Wangdung-like crises. The Chinese saw the Soviet collapse as a fraught lesson on the consequences of military over-reach in attempting to militarily outdo the US. As if to underscore this, the US military put in a virtuoso performance to defeat Saddam Hussein in the first Gulf War. China couldn't but have realized that it needed to focus on rebuilding the country, and keeping its head low.

Change was already in the air. On the eve of the Gulf War in 1990, India's Ministry of Defence hosted an Indo–US strategic symposium at the splendid facilities of the National Defence Academy in Pune which trains young cadets to become military officers. Present on the occasion was a high-level delegation headed by the chief of the US Pacific Command, Admiral Huntington Hardisty. The occasion was a high-level retreat which featured a seminar and parallel official talks. I attended the seminar end of the discussions, which were a portent of the post-Cold War geopolitical shift. Building on the ties that had begun during the Rajiv Gandhi government (1984–1989), India and the US moved towards closer military cooperation. In 1991, General Claude Kicklighter, the Army Chief in the US Pacific Command, came to India with a series of proposals for closer military contact. In 1992, India and the US initiated the Malabar naval exercises which continue to this day.

In early 1992 another Indo–US strategic symposium was convened at Airlie Hall outside Washington DC. The discussion was fairly standard, except for a luncheon speech by our host, James R. Lilley, the US Assistant Secretary of Defense for International Security Affairs, whose message was that with the Tiananmen massacre and the Soviet collapse, whatever strategic cooperation China and the US may have had was at an end. Prior to this appointment, Lilley, an old China hand with the CIA, had been the US ambassador in Beijing at the time of the Tiananmen massacre. He did not have to say it, given the occasion, that Washington was now looking at India, which had begun the process of economic liberalization as its reborn Great White Hope in Asia again.

Having seen that New Delhi now had a stable government, Chinese Premier Li Peng came calling at the end of December 1991; this was the first visit by a Chinese prime minister since that of his foster-father, Zhou Enlai, in 1960. Prime Minister Rao sought to bring up the 1982 Deng offer, but Li indicated it was no longer on the table. In his speeches in India, Li retailed the MUMA formula and spoke about "mutual understanding" which meant taking into account history and taking into account the status quo, though what "mutual accommodation" involved was never quite spelt out.

Six rounds of talks of the Joint Working Group on the border issue were held between December 1988 and June 1993. In the second JWG meeting, India had taken the giant step of, first, accepting that there was a dispute over the border, and, second, moving away from its earlier position of arguing its case for the border on historico-legal grounds. It was at the meeting held at the end of August 1990, that New Delhi had hinted that a settlement could be worked out on the basis of "logistic and administrative convenience"—India accepting China's control of Aksai Chin, in exchange for the Chinese conceding the Indian claim over Arunachal.[8]

In the border negotiations, the Chinese first laid down three conditions—the forward posts set up by India in Wangdung should be withdrawn, the Sikkim-Tibet boundary should be treated separately from the LAC, and that the maintenance of peace and tranquility on the LAC and the clarification of its alignment should not freeze into a boundary settlement.[9]

The Indian response was that would be no unilateral withdrawal in Wangdung. On Sikkim, India refused outright, and on the third issue it noted that there was need for a precise demarcation of the LAC on the ground, without prejudice to the territorial claims of either side. Four posts were withdrawn in the Wangdung area to provide for a kilometre distance between the two sides, but final agreement came only in April 1995, five years later. As for Sikkim, it was subsumed in the rubric of "all" sectors of the Sino–Indian boundary and the third issue, that of the LAC, was addressed in the agreement itself.

The two sides now also got the military into the dialogue process and at the fourth meeting, in February 1992, there was agreement that military commanders would regularly meet at Bum La, north of Tawang, and the Chushul-Moldo border point near the Spanggur Tso. Border trade resumed in July 1992 after a gap of more than thirty years, consulates reopened in Mumbai and Shanghai in December 1992 and in June 1993, and the two sides agreed to open an additional border trading post. During the July 1992 visit of Sharad Pawar to Beijing, the first ever by an Indian defence minister, the two defence establishments agreed to develop academic, military, scientific and technological exchanges and schedule port calls by each other's navies.

The Border Peace and Tranquillity Agreement of 1993

In the summer of 1993, along with two other journalists I was invited to visit China. This was my first visit to the country and it was unquestionably an eye-opener. Everywhere we looked you could see frenetic activity. The skylines of Beijing and Shanghai were a veritable forest of construction cranes. I reported on the trip for India's premier newspaper, *The Times of India*, and the reportage could not but have been tinged by a sense of envy and some dismay. For someone born in the years the Republic of India and People's Republic of China were set up, it was difficult not to be a bit jealous of the decisive direction that the latter was taking, even as India seemed to be stuck in a rut.

The visit had no connection to the disputed border. It was organized very much to show case the new China that Deng Xiaoping was creating. But a routine briefing by the foreign ministry official dealing with India triggered the connection.

Before setting off, I had visited the senior Indian official dealing with China, at the time Joint Secretary (East Asia) Shivshankar Menon. That Prime Minister P. V. Narasimha Rao planned to visit Beijing in September was known. There was talk of an agreement to be signed and, like a good journalist, I was trying to figure out just what it would be about.

Having followed the Sino–India border issue closely, I had a rough idea as to what any agreement between India and China would look like at that stage. But when I quizzed Menon, I got the runaround. He said, probably honestly, that it was yet to be finalized and talks were still on. After all, no official is about to hand a journalist a scoop on the eve of his prime minister's big visit.

Now in Beijing the penny dropped. Unlike the practice of his Indian counterpart in those days, the Chinese deputy director at the Asian desk, Zhang Chengli, briefed out of a book to ensure that he got the facts straight. He gave us a fair summary of the view from Beijing and then he said apropos something I cannot recall now, "…after the agreement is signed." That was a definitive statement and I was jubilant. The other two journalists did not follow border issues: one was a science writer and the other specialized in domestic politics. I knew that the Chinese official would not provide any more information, so I patiently went through the trip, and filed my copy on the changes we were witnessing. After returning to New Delhi, I did a little more digging and my report on the border treaty was ready.

I am not the kind of journalist inclined to score a scoop regardless of the consequences. This could be a sensitive report and have consequences much bigger than I could anticipate and a good reporter doesn't unnecessarily burn his connections with the establishment. So, armed with a printout, I visited Menon in his office and told him, "Shankar, I am filing this for tomorrow's paper. If you have violent objections, please tell me." Menon went through the report, and with a half smile said, "Wait a minute." He walked out into the corridor several doors down to the office of then Foreign Secretary J. N. (Mani) Dixit. He returned ten minutes later, handed me the printout and with a broader smile said, "No comment."

To my chagrin, I learnt that evening that Dixit had held the press briefing for the prime minister's forthcoming visit to China, and virtually gave away the story. He told the journalists that there was a "possibility" at arriving at a pact on the Line of Actual Control during the prime ministerial visit, if a couple of issues that were being discussed at the Joint Working Group could be ironed out.

Fortunately, none of my colleagues saw through the obfuscation. So, the next day, my scoop ran as the first lead of the *The Times of India* of 4 September 1993: "Sino–Indian pact on LAC likely."[10] My report may not have had the agreement clause wise, but it did have its broad contours and noted that the agreement's centerpiece would be the defining of the LAC which could thereafter lead to a thinning of forces along it.

Six days later, the prime minister left for Beijing.

Both countries were agreed that there was need to set aside the boundary dispute, even while maintaining peace and tranquility on the disputed border. But the problem that the negotiators had to deal with was the Line of Actual Control. As we have shown in the previous chapter it was, in the ultimate analysis, a means of describing a border that, in India's opinion, had been forcibly created in the western sector. In the east, even the Chinese agreed that it was approximately the "illegal" McMahon Line, which had been described on a map, albeit with a thick pen, leaving some local ambiguity in places.

As Menon had put it during the negotiations, "the Chinese insisted they would respect the LAC of November 7, 1959 and that if there were any doubts, they would tell the Indians where the LAC lay." Needless to say, the Indians rejected this patronizing approach. Finally, it was decided that the agreement would incorporate the need to clarify the Line of Actual Control (LAC) in its very first clause.[11]

The 7 November 1959 LAC is an item of faith with the Chinese, but as we have shown earlier, this was merely a declaration and a somewhat tautological one at that, where Zhou told Nehru that it was "the line up to which each side exercises actual control" and that it basically conformed to a map published in 1956. At various times, it was both the "traditional and customary line," as well as the line to which China exercised "actual control."

Now, to aid the process of clarifying the LAC, the 1993 agreement created a group of military and civilian expert officials who would work with the existing Joint Working Group to "advise on the resolution of differences between the two sides on the alignment of the Line of Actual Control."

The longer title of the pact was "Agreement on the Maintenance of Peace and Tranquility Along the Line of Actual Control in the India China Border Areas." The shorter form currently used is "Border Peace and Tranquility Agreement" (BPTA) of 1993.

Article I of the BPTA committed the two sides to resolve their boundary issue peacefully through "friendly consultation." Pending a final settlement, the two sides would "strictly respect and observe the line of actual control (LAC) between the two sides." A critical sentence of this article said that "When necessary, the two sides shall jointly check and determine the segments of the line of actual control where they have different views as to its alignment." This was the first time the Indian side accepted the concept of LAC in a formal document.

Article II committed them to keep "military forces in the areas along the line of actual control to a minimum level compatible with the friendly and good neighbourly relations between the two countries." To this end, the two sides would reduce their forces on the LAC on the principle of "mutual and equal security" to mutually agreed ceilings. This was significant since this meant that the two sides could work out ways through which they could equalize any terrain advantages or disadvantage that either side may have at any point in the LAC. The "extent, depth and timing" of this force reduction would be done through mutual consultation.

Article III addressed the issue of military exercises and said that both sides would provide prior notification of such exercises and, further, ensure that they would not undertake certain levels of exercises in "mutually identified zones."

Article IV inaugurated an era of consultation between military personnel on the border to deal with issues and contingencies relating to the border.

Article V committed both sides to avoid air intrusions and brought in restrictions in air exercises in certain zones.

Article VI made it clear that references to the LAC in the agreement would not prejudice their respective positions on the final boundary settlement.

A reading of the agreement reveals the trendline that had led to it. First, was the fact that the two sides had not moved an inch in resolving their border dispute through direct negotiations or talks between the mid-1950s and the 1980s. Second, was the reality that the Indian military was now capable of challenging the Chinese across the LAC and that shaped the need for Article II.

A look at Articles III, IV and V shows that while the Chinese were discomfited by the new Indian posture, they did not necessarily feel threatened. But wanting to ensure stability they felt that the time had come to adjust to the new realities and hence their agreement to sign the BPTA, which spoke of reducing the forces along the border, giving prior notification for exercises, checking air intrusions and so on. They probably had good enough intelligence to know that while the Indians could launch tactical offensives in local areas, they lacked the capability of a strategic strike into Tibet.

This was actually reflected in the prevailing Operational Directive issued by the Indian minister of defence to the armed forces in the early 1980s. This apex-level directive enjoined them to maintain a posture of "dissuasive deterrence" with regard to Pakistan, and one of "dissuasive defence" in relation to China. As one senior officer explained to me, in ordinary language it meant that the army needed to have the capability of launching an offensive deep into Pakistan in one case, whilst on the other, it was to avoid any offensive planning and instead adopt a posture of strong defence-in-depth as a means of deterring China.

The BPTA committed both countries to seek a negotiated settlement to their boundary dispute. This was, as Menon points out, a huge step, because till then India had basically demanded that the Chinese pull back from every inch of Indian territory occupied by China. Furthermore, the agreement, if implemented fully, would be a major factor for peace along the border. It introduced the important concept of "mutual and equal" security through which India's terrain disadvantages would be taken into account in the possible redeployment and thinning of forces that the agreement envisaged.

* * *

At the eighth meeting of the Joint Working Group (JWG) in August 1995, the two sides had agreed that there were twelve areas where there was a difference of perception over where the Line of Actual Control(LAC) ran—Trig Heights, near Daulat Beg Oldi, and Demchok in the western sector; Shipki La, Kaurik, Barahoti and Pulam Sumda in the central sector; and Namka Chu, Wangdung/Sumdorong Chu, Yangtse, Asaphi La, Longju and Dichu in the eastern sector.[12] Note, Pangong Tso, Kugrang river valley, Depsang and Galwan did not figure in the list.

In the run up to the BPTA and in its aftermath, senior Indian and Chinese officials began to interact regularly. The agreement had itself also spelt out many steps requiring them to be in touch regularly. Following the Rao visit, contacts at all levels were enhanced but there was a special interest in promoting military-to-military links. Almost immediately after the 1993 agreement was signed, a high-level tri-Services PLA delegation visited India. In July 1994, General Bipin Joshi became the first serving Indian Army chief, to visit China.

Though Bipin Joshi and I were from the same neck of woods in the mountain state of Uttarakhand, we are not related, but we were friends till the general's untimely death of a heart attack in November 1994. Two months or so before his departure, he called me, asking for my views on the visit. He was not aware of the earlier invite to General Sundarji, and I told him that the Chinese were keen to interact with the new generation of Indian generals. I also gave him a suggestion. In

1900, Indian troops of the British contingent were involved in the eight-nation effort to relieve the Beijing Legation Quarter during the Boxer Rebellion. The alliance forces defeated the Chinese army and then assaulted Beijing. Thereafter the city was subdued and systematic looting began, with each army accusing the other of doing it, but all were involved. The Indian units came back with trophies, the most noteworthy being a set of Ming-era plates that change colour if poisoned food is placed on them. No one I know, had really tested this because the plates had been framed and hung above the bar in the officer's mess of a prominent tank regiment.

I suggested to General Joshi, that it would be a dramatic gesture if he were to give back those plates to the Chinese. The general, himself a tank man, was quite struck by this. When I met him on his return, I asked him how the visit had gone. He was quite over the top with the reception that he and his delegation had got. He said he had modified my suggestion because the tank regiment had not been inclined to give up its precious booty, so he persuaded another regiment to offer up a huge temple bell that had been taken away in the sacking of the Summer Palace in Beijing. When the Chinese were presented with this, they were clearly taken aback by the gesture, but they made a brilliant come-back. Before the general took his flight home, they had cast a replica of the bell for him to take back to the unit.

In the mid-1990s, Sino–Indian ties were affected by reports of Chinese assistance to Pakistan's nuclear programme, as well as by its supply of M-11 short-range missiles. In official talks, the Chinese predictably denied these charges. Remarkably, however, when India had approached the Chinese in 1993 for the supply of nuclear fuel for the Tarapur Atomic Power Plant, they had obliged. The US had stopped supplying fuel for this plant to conform to its own non-proliferation laws. So, the French had stepped in and done the needful in 1983, but when they halted the supply, India was in trouble till the Chinese agreed. The first shipment arrived in 1995.

In 1996, the Congress Party had lost the general elections and the country was once again governed by an unstable coalition headed by Prime Minister H.D. Deve Gowda. What was becoming increasingly apparent was that China had managed to restore its own stability following Tiananmen, but though India had recovered its control of

Punjab, which had been wracked by a terrorist movement between 1983 and 1993, it was still mired in Jammu & Kashmir where a rebellion had broken out in 1990. Worse, with unstable coalitions, the economic liberalization initiated by Narasimha Rao had lost steam.

But ties between India and China remained stable enough to have Chinese President Jiang Zemin, accompanied by Foreign Minister Qian Qichen and Chairman of the Tibetan Autonomous Region, Jiangcun Luobu, come to India on 28 November 1996 for a four-day visit. This was the first visit to India by a Chinese leader who was both the head of the Communist Party of China and the President of the People's Republic. Both countries were focusing on rebuilding their economy and one of the decisions taken was for the two sides to work on a "cooperative and constructive partnership" for the twenty-first century.

It was no surprise, then, that on Indian soil President Jiang also called on Pakistan to set aside the Kashmir issue and move towards normalization of relations with India. This went four-square against the Pakistani notion that India needed to address the "core" Kashmir issue before any normalization. Coming as it did, when the Pakistan-backed Kashmir insurgency was raging, it was a pleasant surprise for New Delhi, but a shock to Islamabad.

Some unfinished business had been left on the military confidence-building side in the BPTA and this was addressed by an Agreement on Confidence Building Measures in the Military Field Along the Line of Actual Control in the China-India Border Areas, which was signed on 29 November 1996. This was essentially a companion agreement to the BPTA and, given the Sino–Indian border dispute, it is quite a remarkable document.

Article I enjoined the two sides to avoid using the military capability to attack or threaten the other side. Article II noted that, even as the two worked towards a "fair, reasonable and mutually acceptable settlement," they would "strictly respect and observe the line of actual control...no. activities of either side shall overstep the line of actual control."

Article III committed both sides to limit to the minimum their respective forces in specified and mutually agreed geographical areas. They were to reduce combat tanks, infantry combat vehicles, field guns and howitzers, heavy mortars, surface-to-surface missiles, and other weapons systems mutually agreed upon. They would also exchange data on the forces and equipment on the LAC.

Under Article IV both sides agreed not to hold large-scale military exercises near the LAC and to provide advanced notification for all exercises above a brigade/regimental level.

Article V was aimed at avoiding air intrusions across the LAC and it prohibited the flight of combat aircraft within 10 km of the LAC. Unarmed transports and helicopters were allowed to fly up to the LAC.

Article VI is important because it had implications for the June 2020 incident. Under this, both sides had agreed that neither shall open fire, or even hunt with guns, within 2 km of the LAC. If personnel came face to face, they were enjoined to avoid escalation and enter into immediate consultation.

Article VII committed the two sides to expand the regime of their scheduled flag meetings between border personnel as well as create telecommunication links at designated places in the LAC.

But everything hinged on Article X, and the agreement said so in as many words. The Article noted: "recognizing that the full implementation of some of the provisions of the present Agreement will depend on the two sides arriving at a common understanding of the alignment of the line of actual control…the two sides agree to speed up the process of clarification and confirmation of the line of actual control."

Further, as an initial step in that process, "they are clarifying the alignment of the line of actual control in those segments where they have different perceptions." And, equally significantly, "they agree to exchange maps indicating their respective perception of the entire alignment of the line of actual control as soon as possible."

All other measures spelt out in the agreement would, therefore, be on an "interim basis" and the detailed implementation measures would be worked out by the Joint Working Group that was already looking at the boundary question.

What was evident from the provisions of the agreement was that the Chinese had, indeed, been quite shaken by the 1986–1987 experience and were keen to ensure that they were not taken by surprise again. Hence the elaborate CBMs addressing issues of troop and heavy weapons reduction, notification of exercises and movements, conflict avoidance and communications. But, in retrospect, we could say that the Chinese did not want a permanent fix, just something that would stabilize the situation, rather than deal with the problem.

4

THE SEARCH FOR STABILITY

With the detailed agreement on military confidence-building measures signed at the end of 1996, both countries could feel a sense of satisfaction. They were both embarked on a journey which they hoped would transform their respective countries. Deng Xiaoping had told Rajiv Gandhi in his Beijing visit of 1988, that the century of Asia would not come without the development of China and India, but he had added, nothing was fore-ordained: they would have to struggle hard to achieve that goal.

Relations between the two had steadily improved since Rajiv Gandhi's visit which was followed by that of Prime Minister Narasimha Rao in 1993. There had been two high-level Chinese visitors to India in this period—Premier Li Peng in 1991 and President Jiang Zemin in 1996—and two major agreements to promote peace and tranquility on the border. There was also a steady flow of other visitors—journalists, businessmen, officials and ministers—between China and India. It looked as though the two were, indeed, developing a constructive partnership and that though the border settlement was a pre-condition for it, it appeared that it could be just a matter of time before that happened.

But it soon became apparent that the process had only been skindeep although the process of stabilization of the LAC, as per the 1993 and 1996 agreements, continued. At the eighth Joint Working Group (JWG) meeting held in New Delhi in August 1995, there had been a final agreement on pulling back the four forwardmost posts in the Wangdung/Sumdorong Chu area by 50–100 metres. In the next meeting, a year later, the two sides agreed to enhance military-to-military relations through reciprocal visits by major-general level officers. Two more meeting points were created in the eastern part of the Line of Actual Control (LAC).

The process of normalizing economic ties was also begun. Border trade had been recognized across six passes in the central sector in the 1954 agreement, but that had not been renewed after its first eight-year tranche.

Since Sikkim was an Indian protectorate, it did not figure in the agreement. But actually, it was the most important point for India-Tibet trade and its importance grew with the Chinese occupation of Tibet. In the early 1950s the Chinese had even formally requested India for transport facilities from Kolkata through Nathu La and Jelep La, to Yadong and Lhasa.[1] The Indian trade agent issued the licences for trading and among the items exported to Tibet were commodities like petrol, diesel, auto parts, liquor, rice, sugar, watches, construction materials and so on. In turn, the Chinese side supplied silk and wool and also paid for the imports with silver currency.[2]

However, following the Tibetan uprising this route remained disturbed and was shut following the 1962 war. Though the Chinese considered the border with Sikkim to have been settled by the Anglo-Chinese Convention of 1890, they refused to recognize India's 1977 annexation of the princely state. In the Sino–Indian border dialogue, Sikkim was carefully skirted because of Chinese sensitivities.

However, trade across some other Himalayan passes had begun in 1992 with the opening up of the old trade route of Lipu Lekh in Uttarakhand, followed by Shipki La in Himachal Pradesh. But this was more token than anything else, with wool, silk, goat and sheep skins, horses and borax being bought by the Indian side, and food by the Tibetans. (See Map 5) The more significant trade over the seas had resumed in 1977, but it actually took off in 1988 following the Rajiv Gandhi visit, and by 1999 it amounted to some $2 billion.

In the mid-1990s, India went through one of its periodic bouts of political instability. The Congress had been voted out of power in the elections held in April–May 1996, and a government headed by Atal

Bihari Vajpayee of the BJP lasted just thirteen days, another headed by H.D. Deve Gowda, eleven months till April 1997, and its successor headed by I. K. Gujral, too, lasted for about a year. General elections had to be held again in February 1998. Vajpayee emerged as the leader of a coalition anchored by his Bharatiya Janata Party (BJP) and took office again in March 1998.

One of his top appointments was that of George Fernandes, leader of the Samata Party, as the defence minister. Fernandes was a known supporter of the Dalai Lama and an advocate of "Free Tibet." He immediately began to focus on China and accused the PLA of intruding into Arunachal Pradesh. He then charged Beijing of being "the mother of (Pakistan's) Ghauri missile," that had been tested on 10 April 1998 and which had, for the first time, brought all parts of India within the range of a Pakistani missile system. Later that month, in an interview with TV personality Karan Thapar, he tried to be somewhat discrete when quizzed on China. But he couldn't resist the host's formulation that "China was the *potential* threat number one" (emphasis added) for India. This formulation, minus the qualifier "potential", made the headlines and he was attacked from the right and the left in India, though Beijing deemed his comment unworthy of comment. Finally, the government let it be known that Fernandes' remarks were "not the considered view of the government."[3]

Coincidentally, at the end April 1998, India had hosted General Fu Quanyou, Chief of the General Staff of the PLA in India. There were protests by Tibetan exiles, and a 60-year old monk immolated himself. But the visit went well. Fernandes had been on his best behaviour, though he did raise the recent Pakistani missile test with the visiting Chinese brass. Prime Minister Vajpayee, too, spoke of the problems between the two countries that needed to be resolved. What Fernandes had done was to have subtly shifted the focus of India's security concerns to China, which was now growing at a frenetic pace. Mired in Kashmir, the Indian defence establishment continued to obsessively view Pakistan as its main enemy, yet its main challenge remained China. Despite all the talk about "a constructive and cooperative relationship" with India, Beijing was Islamabad's principal arms supplier and continued to supply material for making both nuclear weapons and missiles.

India, Pakistan go nuclear

While this controversy was raging, unbeknownst to most, as well as Fernandes himself, the prime minister had ordered the country's top scientists to conduct a series of nuclear weapons tests. India had carried out a lone nuclear test in May 1974 in an underground facility near Pokhran village in Rajasthan, close to the Pakistan border. At the time, seeking to fudge the issue, India had claimed it was merely testing the concept of underground nuclear explosion for peaceful purposes. But after this lone test created a furore around the world, New Delhi had stopped work on the programme.

Now, on 11 and 13 May, a little more than a week after General Fu had returned to China, India carried out five tests at the same Pokhran range in the desert of Rajasthan. There is some ambiguity as to how successful the tests were. But certainly, the test of a basic fission device, of the kind India had tested in 1974, was successful. The event was wildly applauded in the country, but abroad was a different matter. The US almost immediately imposed stringent sanctions on India, which was followed by other countries. Millions of dollars of American aid was halted, as well as loan guarantees for US exports to India. President Bill Clinton termed India's action as "a great betrayal." The US also said it would oppose loans from the World Bank, Asian Development Bank and other multilateral agencies to India.

New Delhi claimed that the tests were "security driven" and occasioned by Pakistan's testing the Ghauri. But actually, Vajpayee had also authorized a test in May of 1996 as well, and the devices had been emplaced in the underground shafts when news of his government's fall after just 13 days, led to their cancellation. The Ghauri excuse didn't quite wash.

But soon the true story came out. After the tests, Prime Minister Vajpayee wrote letters to leaders of the US, UK, France, Russia, Japan, Canada and Germany. The letters were fairly innocuous and sought to explain the Indian rationale. In any case, India did get support from France and Russia.

But the letter sent to President Bill Clinton was promptly leaked to *The New York Times* by the administration itself. In the letter, Prime Minister Vajpayee spoke of the "deteriorating security environment, especially nuclear environment faced by India." He went on to add that "We have an overt nuclear state on our borders, a state which committed armed aggression against India in 1962." Though relations had improved in recent years, Vajpayee noted, "an atmosphere of distrust persists mainly due to the unresolved border problem." To add to this, "that country" had aided another of India's neighbours "to become a covert nuclear weapons state."[4] Not surprisingly, the letter enraged Beijing. If the Chinese thought that time would dull India's memories of 1962, and the new CBMs would enhance trust, they had been proven wrong.

After the 11 May set of tests, the Chinese reaction had been quite mild. Indeed, they did not even make a direct comment and merely published a news item on page 6 of the *People's Daily*. However, after *The New York Times* disclosure of May 13, the reaction to the second set of tests was strong and even bitter. On 14 May, the Chinese foreign ministry attacked India for "undermining the international effort in banning nuclear tests so as to obtain hegemony in South Asia" and said that it had "maliciously accused China of posing a nuclear threat to India." This "gratuitous accusation" was aimed at justifying its development of nuclear weapons.

The Indian response was blunt. India, said it could not "but take into account the offensive nuclear weapon and missile capability in our region, nor the well documented history of proliferation through clandestine acquisition." It referred to China's July 1996 test saying that this was its forty-fifth test, as compared to the six done by India.

The next month, the United Nations Security Council (UNSC), under the chairmanship of China, unanimously passed Resolution 1172 that called on India and Pakistan to refrain from further tests, stop the processes of weaponization, cease the production of fissile material, join the negotiations for a fissile material cut-off treaty (FMCT), sign the Comprehensive Test Ban Treaty (CTBT) and the Nuclear Non-Proliferation Treaty (NPT) unconditionally. Formally then, this became not just the position of China, but the US, France, the UK and Russia as well.

India now came under considerable pressure as Bill Clinton scrapped a visit to New Delhi and travelled to China instead at the end of June 1998. Here both countries reiterated their support for the draconian

UNSC Resolution 1172. Indeed, the US asked China to contribute to South Asian stability and issued a joint statement on the "South Asian question." The statement declared that the recent tests in South Asia were a matter of "deep and lasting concern to both of us." The US and China pledged to not just prevent a nuclear and arms race in South Asia, but also promote reconciliation and a peaceful resolution of differences between India and Pakistan. They endorsed the UNSCR 1172 and said they were committed to assisting the resolution of India-Pakistan differences, including that on Kashmir. Clearly, the US had come to see the Indian tests as being motivated by its Pakistani concerns, rather than those of China.[5]

This was certainly most unpalatable to India: its aspirations were to be seen in the league of China and the big powers, not Pakistan. Now it seemed that the US and China wanted some kind of a condominium over South Asia. There was an echo here from an earlier proposal of the George H.W. Bush administration in 1991 to pin down India and Pakistan into a nuclear restraint regime, to be guaranteed by China, the Soviet Union and the US. At that time, New Delhi desperately needed to keep on the right side of the US on account of its distressed economic situation and so India had fobbed off Washington by engaging it in a bilateral dialogue on nuclear non-proliferation issues. In 1992, Bush lost the election and the pressure on India eased off.

The China–US South Asia statement of June 1998 was especially galling, given India's difficulties in Kashmir, and the government of India protested against what it said was interference in its domestic affairs. In a press note, the government of India accused the US and China of seeking to "carve out a supervisory role for themselves in this part of the world."[6]

Indian diplomacy now went into overdrive to soften the fallout of its actions. On one hand, India declared a voluntary moratorium on further testing, on the other, it offered a "no first use" (NFU) pledge and declared that India will only seek a "credible, minimum deterrent."

During the nuclear tests and its fallout, Jaswant Singh, a trusted confidante of Prime Minister Vajpayee was the deputy chairman of the Planning Commission (the PM being the chairman). He had played a key role in articulating India's response in the aftermath of the tests. In early June, Singh flew into the US, engaged think tanks and newspapers and then initiated a dialogue with US Deputy Secretary of State Strobe Talbott. This was before the US–China South Asia statement, but the dialogue process did not falter. Jaswant Singh (who became minister of external affairs in December 1998) and Talbott held 14 meetings in ten locations around the world to conduct an extensive dialogue on a range of issues: Pakistan, Kashmir, China, the US interest in non-proliferation. Before the dialogue, the Clinton administration had followed the George H. W. Bush administration's policy of wanting to "cap, rollback and eliminate" the Indian nuclear programme. But soon it became clear to the Clinton administration that that was not a doable deal.[7]

Beijing got the drift of these developments early enough. The US was showing no interest in pushing the implementation of the drastic UNSCR 1172. Then, came a meeting between Jaswant Singh and Chinese Foreign Minister Tang Jiaxuan in Manila, at the sidelines of the ministerial meeting of the ASEAN Regional Forum (ARF) in July 1998. Singh recounted the meeting in his book, *A Call to Honour*. After Singh's comment, Tang launched his tirade, attacking India in all the familiar terms that had been used by Chinese spokesmen in the past months. Tang suggested "that as India 'had tied the knot it had better untie it also.'" Instead of rising to the Chinese bait and responding by table-thumping, Singh neatly pivoted: "you actually need two hands to untie a knot" he told Tang. Adding: "It is very difficult to do it single-handed. You give your hand, I will give mine. And together, with two hands, we will untie that knot."[8]

This was the beginning of the thaw in the post-Pokhran Sino–Indian relationship. In October, the Prime Minister's Office in India issued a formal statement declaring that it did not see China as an 'enemy' and had no intention of getting into an arms race with it. From the outset the issue really had been not so much about nuclear weapons, but about the loss of face, and, once this was satisfied, the relationship moved back to its engagement track. It was announced that the next Joint Working Group (JWG), postponed because of the tests, would now be held in July 1999.

The Kargil War

But in that year, came another development that had the potential to further strain Sino–Indian ties, but did not. The year began well, even brilliantly, when Prime Minister Vajpayee visited Pakistan and sought to kick-start a major India—Pakistan reconciliation. As part of the visit, he inaugurated a new India-Pakistan bus service and also paid a visit to the Minar-e-Pakistan, a monument in Lahore dedicated to the founding of the country. This was a special gesture from a prime minister of a party which had long opposed partition and had even called for a Greater India (Akhand Bharat). Among the important achievements of the visit was a decision to initiate a dialogue on nuclear issues.

But things started unravelling fast. First, domestically, the Vajpayee government lost an important ally and a vote of confidence in parliament and was forced to resign on 17 April 1999. But within weeks India discovered that the Pakistan Army had launched a covert operation to occupy positions across the northern parts of the Line of Control, in an area near Kargil in western Ladakh. When discovered, Pakistan claimed it was an action undertaken by the Kashmiri freedom fighters. But soon it became clear that it was a Pakistan Army move, using the Northern Light Infantry, a military unit specific to the Gilgit-Baltistan area. The aim of the operation was not clear. In the circumstances of the recent nuclear tests, the logic probably went, the world community would be hugely alarmed over the development and would compel India to make a deal with Islamabad on Kashmir.

Though the operation could have cut off India's principal road to Ladakh, by this time the alternate route via Manali in Himachal Pradesh had come into operation, though both the military and civilian logistic chains remained overwhelmingly oriented to using the one passing through Kargil.

As is well known, it is easy to start a war but very difficult to predict how it will unfold. And so it happened. India decided on a smart, but expensive strategy of not hitting Pakistan outside the area Islamabad had itself chosen in Kargil. This did require the Indian Army to pay a heavy price in terms of casualties, because it had to mount frontal attacks against the well entrenched Pakistani forces in the heights. The Indian Army rose to the occasion and launched a campaign across the front, with the air force in a supporting role.

But the more important role was diplomatic. The Indian decision not to widen the conflict was welcomed by the international community, especially the US, because it avoided a larger war and reduced the risk of escalation. Pakistan had hoped that the threat of escalation would bring the US and China into resolving the issue. It certainly hoped that China would pull its irons out of the fire.

The Chinese could not but have known what was happening. The Pakistan Army Chief General Pervez Musharraf had arrived in Beijing on 24 May and was in constant touch from his hotel room with his Chief of General Staff Lt Gen. Muhammad Aziz Khan in Rawalpindi as the Kargil operation was unfolding. Unbeknownst to the two, the Indians were listening in, and, no doubt, the Chinese as well.

Pakistan Foreign Minister Sartaj Aziz had rushed to Beijing on 11 June but had been disappointed when he was told by Premier Li Peng that it would be a good idea to settle the dispute through peaceful means. Tang Jiaxuan, the Chinese foreign minister, told Aziz that Pakistan should hold negotiations and consultations to resolve the Kashmir issue politically. Having got little comfort, Aziz flew out the same day and landed in New Delhi to meet Jaswant Singh.

But the Indians had a surprise for him as well. Just before his arrival his Indian counterpart Jaswant Singh released the text of two conversations to the media. Here, the Pakistani generals more or less confirmed their role in the Kargil operation and the manner in which they were obfuscating issues in their discussions with their own prime minister, Nawaz Sharif.[9]

Aziz was followed to Beijing, at the end of the month, by Prime Minister Nawaz Sharif himself. But while there was a lot of talk of the "all weather friendship" between the two countries, in practical terms Beijing conceded little to Pakistan. The Chinese were simply not willing to commit themselves to what was clearly a foolish and adventurist action on the part of the Pakistan Army.

President Jiang Zemin was cited by the Chinese media as saying that "China hopes Pakistan and India would jointly ease the current tension in Kashmir and settle existing problems through dialogue in the interest of the people of South Asia." Finding little support, Sharif cut short his originally announced six-day visit and returned home and then set off to the United States, seeking help. He landed in Washington DC for a meeting with President Clinton on 4 July, the anniversary of US independence. But Clinton agreed to meet him anyway and read the riot act to him. This led to an agreement put forward through a joint statement through which Pakistan agreed to "restore" the LoC, in other words pull back to its side.[10] The combination of US pressure and Indian military action finally compelled Pakistan to abandon its Kargil operation.[11]

But there was an enigmatic Chinese action which may, or may not, have been related to the Kargil developments, or it could have been the PLA acting on its own. Indian border forces detected a distinct increase in Chinese military activity on the LAC just as Indian operations got underway in June 1999. In the long-contested Trig Heights area near DBO, the Chinese began constructing a natural surface road to an area disputed by both sides. At the same time, they rapidly built a track from Spanggur Tso to the southern bank of Pangong Tso so as to better coordinate patrolling of their boats on the lake with their foot patrols in the area. In one area, east of Bum La pass near Tawang, Chinese forces came closer than usual to the Indian forces and stayed there for the next 40 days or so, building a permanent encampment which was only dismantled in September.[12] As mentioned earlier, in the Pangong Tso area the Chinese extended a road from Sirijap to Finger 8 and began blocking Indian forces in their attempts to patrol up to Sirijap. Clearly, the Chinese never missed an opportunity to press their claims along the LAC.

The Kargil affair brought out the key difference between the Line of Control (LoC) that India had with Pakistan, and the Line of Actual Control (LAC) with China. In its incursion, Pakistan had sought to fudge the issue by claiming that like the LAC, the LoC was not clear and both sides differed on its interpretation. But this was simply untrue.

The LoC was created through intense negotiations between India and Pakistan and was reproduced in two sets of maps prepared by each side, with local sector commanders and surveyors meeting and identifying features to each other's satisfaction. These were discussed in a series of 9 higher-level meetings between 10 August and 11 December 1972. At each meeting the inputs of the sector commanders were taken up and differences resolved; where a resurvey was needed, it was done. Some of the more intractable points were ironed out by the meeting of the two army chiefs. Besides maps, there were 19 annexes comprising 40 pages giving details of each feature, landmark and the coordinates of the LoC. Through this process, four sets consisting of 27 map sheets were formed into 19 mosaics. Two senior Indian and Pakistani generals signed each individual mosaic of all four sets. These were exchanged, examined and approved by both sides on 11 December 1972.[13]

This detail is relevant to our survey, given the issues with the Line of Actual Control (LAC) between India and China. Nothing like this process has occurred anywhere around the LAC and it is not surprising then that claims and counter-claims have arisen. One additional reason is, of course, that unlike most of the LoC area, which is lower and inhabited, the Sino–Indian LAC, especially in the Ladakh area, lies in a snowy high-altitude desert where some activity like sheep-herding may take place for a limited period of time, but permanent human habitation is limited. Yet, it needs to be pointed out, that the clearly delineated LoC had seen egregious violation—bombardment, cross-border movement of militants and weapons especially since 1990—while the LAC, however fuzzy, had been largely peaceful.

Indeed, what this actually brings out is the key point that the issues between India and China and the LAC are less about its location and lack of precision, and more about the use that is being made of its fuzziness by Beijing to periodically heat up the situation so as to keep New Delhi off-balance.

By accepting the Indian version of events during the Kargil affair, Washington probably confirmed to the Chinese mind that India and the US were now moving to a new level of relationship. In June, after telling Pakistan foreign minister, Shaukat Aziz, to resolve the issue through negotiations, Tang had pointedly avoided any reference to the UN resolutions on Kashmir, or said anything that could be construed to be support for Pakistan's actions.

Following the eleventh meeting of the JWG, which was held in April 1999, the decision was taken to normalize Sino–Indian ties again. Jaswant Singh visited Beijing in mid-June, even as the Kargil war was reaching its peak. This was the first visit by an Indian external affairs minister in eight years and, besides Foreign Minister Tang, Singh met Premier Zhu Rongji. The Chinese had, as we noted, self-consciously stayed away from the Kargil issue and were happy with Singh's official reiteration that India did not consider China a threat. A decision was taken to move ahead with the clarification of the LAC and, finally, to hold a strategic security dialogue.

As a measure of the improved ties, China invited President K. R. Narayanan for a visit in May–June 2000. This was the second visit by an Indian head of state in fifty years. Early that year in April, the decision was taken at the JWG to show and exchange maps of the Line of Actual Control (LAC), and later that year, in November 2000, maps of the 545-km long central sector were exchanged at the meeting of the expert group. An Indian official spokesman had said on the eve of the Joint Working Group (JWG) talks that as long as the "mutual accommodation, mutual understanding and mutual adjustment"(MAMUMA) process was followed, there was no reason why a "just and reasonable settlement" of the dispute was not possible in quick time.

That year, a PLA delegation led by Lieutenant General Tian Shugen, Vice President Academy of Military Sciences, visited India in August, while two Indian Navy ships paid a goodwill visit to China in September. There were visits by ministers, official delegations and cultural exchanges, all signs that Sino–Indian relations were on an even track.

This process continued through 2001, with the visit to India of Li Peng, now chairman of the National People's Congress (NPC), and a year later with the thirteenth meeting of the JWG, where the counterpart of Indian Foreign Secretary Chokila Iyer was Vice-Minister Wang Yi, who is still dealing with India issues, among his other responsibilities as foreign minister now.

The year 2002 began with the usual round of ministerial visits, with the new Chinese Premier Zhu Rongji coming to New Delhi in January, followed by Jaswant Singh going to Beijing in March. Premier Zhu's visit was the first by a Chinese prime minister in ten years. It had originally been proposed for November 2001, but was postponed on account of the 9/11 attack on the US. The focus of the visit was on establishing a sound economic relationship and for China to capitalize on its recent membership of the WTO.

What was remarkable was that all this was happening even as the Indian and Pakistani armies were fully mobilized along their border ready for war as a consequence of a terrorist attack on India's Parliament House on 13 December 2001. Zhu's visit was itself a message of sorts and, during the visit, Beijing made it clear that they were not party to India–Pakistan tensions. China simply took a backseat, leaving the crisis management to the US. As one US official put it,

China was "the dog that did not bark" through what is now known as the "twin peaks crisis." All they did was to counsel moderation and let the US handle things.[14]

However, whether it was in the wake of Kargil, or the "twin peaks crisis" it did not prevent Beijing from continuing to back Pakistan by supplying missiles and other war material. After the nuclear tests, Beijing increased shipments of special steel, guidance systems and motors, to Pakistan. In 2000, it began a major programme for enhancing Islamabad's armoured forces. It also agreed to sell Pakistan 50 F-7MG fighter aircraft. In September, the US had embargoed Chinese companies for delivering 12 shipments of components for Islamabad's Shaheen missile.

But the border issue did not quite die down as was evident from an item in *The Times of India* on 21 November 2000 which said that the Chinese had built a track on a part of the north bank of the Pangong Tso claimed by India. This news item had triggered a query by a member of parliament. The government's reply was anodyne: it said that the two sides had been trying to clarify the LAC, but "pending clarification of the LAC, both India and China have been carrying out normal border management activities including patrolling upto their respective perception of the LAC in the area." This was the track we referred to earlier between Sirijap and Finger 8.

But in its response, the government did acknowledge that the Chinese had, indeed, built a track "upto their perception" of the LAC in the area. The government reply said they had registered a protest at various levels and the response was denial and counter protests "against our activities in the area." For good measure the response also retailed the Indian formula that through border talks, it was "seeking a fair, reasonable and mutually acceptable settlement to the boundary question through a dialogue."[15] But the response played down the fact that the building of the track had led to a restriction on India's ability to patrol up to its perception of the LAC in the same area.

Another Parliamentary question in early 2001, based on the army chief's comment on Chinese activities along the LAC, got a similar response that, pending clarification of the LAC, the two sides have been carrying out normal border management activities "including construction of tracks and patrolling upto their respective perception of the LAC." It referred to the recent visit of Li Peng to New Delhi and said that in the official talks with the Indian prime minister, "both sides expressed satisfaction at the progress made on LAC clarification exercise."[16]

This was, of course, an important conjuncture. The US had faced a terrorist attack in September 2001 and was now rampant and ready for war, which would involve Afghanistan and, indirectly, Pakistan. China was not going to get in the way. Having got into the WTO just a week before the Indian Parliament attack, Beijing was fully focussed on the enormous economic opportunities that had just opened up for it.

Overall the positive trend in Sino–Indian relations was the cumulative effect of the process that had begun with Rajiv Gandhi's visit and led to the two important agreements of 1993 and 1996. The process had grown institutional teeth through the creation of the Joint Working Group (JWG) and its sub-group, the India–China Expert Group, and had led to an extensive process of meetings between border military personnel, the thinning down of forces in some areas, and so on. But already, as the Pangong Tso episode revealed, things were fraying at the edge. This became apparent when the key process of clarifying the LAC ground to a halt.

* * *

During Jaswant Singh's visit in March 2002, I happened to be in Beijing and took the opportunity to meet Singh at the official Diaoyutai Guest House in Beijing. He told me that the two sides now virtually had a timetable with which to complete the first phase of their efforts to resolve the border issue. This was to "clarify and confirm" the LAC. That the Chinese, too, were on the same page became apparent when the then vice foreign minister Wang Yi used identical language: "clarify and confirm" the LAC to a visiting Indian delegation at the time. Wang said that thereafter substantive negotiations could take place on settling the dispute in the spirit of "mutual accommodation, mutual understanding and mutual adjustment [MAMUMA]."[17]

Based on this, efforts to clarify and confirm the LAC were stepped up. It was decided that maps of the western sector would now be exchanged in June 2002. The process having taken one step forward, with the exchange of maps of the central sector in 2000, now went back two steps. When the expert group of the two sides met on 17 June 2002, maps of the western sector were exchanged. Both sides looked at the maps for around 20 minutes and then the Chinese side hastily returned the maps and took back theirs. Even now it is not quite clear as to why.

According to Kalha, the maps had showed the maximalist position of both sides and these were not palatable to the Chinese.[18] India had shown its claimed boundary all the way up to the Afghanistan trijunction, while the Chinese dealt with the Indian boundary as beginning from the Karakoram Pass. Adding that extra element from the trijunction to the Karakoram Pass not only involved taking a position on the India-Pakistan dispute on Kashmir, but also questioned the Pakistan-China boundary pact of 1963, through which China gained the Shaksgam valley. The valley, a strip of land some 5,000 sq. km, lies to the west of Karakoram Pass and is north of K-2, the world's second highest peak. This has been ceded provisionally by Pakistan to China as part of the China-Pakistan agreement of 1963. This cession is subject to confirmation after India and Pakistan can work out a final settlement of the Jammu & Kashmir dispute.

Even the short peek of the Chinese map had brought out to the Indian side the differences of perception as to where the Line of Actual Control (LAC) lay in the western sector. Running from north to south, there were differences, minor and significant, at Samar Lungpa (176 sq. km), a little north-east of Daulat Beg Oldi, the Trig Heights a little south-east of it, the Depsang Plains (972 sq. km), Hot Springs (38 sq. km), Changlung (13 sq. km), Kongka La (5 sq. km), the north bank of Pangong Tso (212 sq. km), Spanggur Tso (24 sq. km), Mount Sajum, Dumchele (25 sq. km), Demchok and Chumar (80 sq. km).[19] Not surprisingly, perhaps, the number of friction points had increased from the two that had been identified for the western sector at the Joint Working Group (JWG) in 1995.

Looking back from 2021 and taking into account the increased friction along the Line of Actual Control in the last decade, it would seem that the Chinese were not particularly comfortable with the notion of a mutually accepted LAC since they felt that this could well freeze into the final boundary and would deny Beijing the ability to use the differences over the LAC to periodically unbalance India. As it is, minus a mutually recognized border or an LAC, it was simply not possible to implement the goals laid out by the ambitious 1993 and 1996 agreements for building down the military forces along the LAC, a process that could have taken the relationship of the two countries into a completely different trajectory. But, as we will see, the two countries now decided to move their border discussions onto a completely different track.

5

POLITICAL BARGAIN

As noted in earlier chapters, Sino–Indian relations were on a positive trajectory since the Rajiv Gandhi visit to Beijing in 1988. The bad blood in the period May 1998–1999, after India carried out its nuclear tests, was a temporary blip, and the relations continued to improve thereafter. While there was no major agreement of the kind the two had signed in 1993 and 1996, there were a number of smaller, practical agreements and memorandums of understanding on a range of issues from setting phytosanitary standards, to cooperation in vocational education, outer space, technology and agriculture and so on. Direct passenger flights to New Delhi and Beijing were also inaugurated.

Both countries had other distractions—India was involved in untangling its relations with the US, even while being stalked by Pakistan. Yet ties with China were intrinsically linked to these developments as well. Its sophisticated handling of the Kargil attack by Pakistan prevented any spillover into its improving ties with China. Likewise, it aided the process of India's rapprochement with the United States. Likewise, the Chinese played a low-key role in the so-called "twin peaks crisis" of 2002 in the wake of the terrorist attack on the Indian Parliament House in December 2001.

For both, ties with the United States were an important pivot. The enhanced US-India understanding arising from the Jaswant Singh–Strobe Talbott talks had been a major factor in getting Beijing to repair its relations with India as well. As Garver has pointed out, in an article in 2001, "Chinese and Indian leaders are extremely sensitive to the alignment of the other vis-à-vis the United States." This is a factor in the relationship of China and India since the 1950s and holds good even today.[1]

China was busy with its economic reform agenda which was manifested by the appointment of Zhu Rongji as the prime minister after Li Peng. Besides structural changes in the way the economy was managed, China also sold off many unprofitable state-owned enterprises. It began the long process of negotiating its entry into the World Trade Organization, a process which was only completed by the end of 2001. Though China entered the WTO with much tougher conditions than other developing countries, in the ultimate analysis, the changes it made to its economy benefited the country and set the stage for an intensification of its economic growth and integration into the world economy.

Things were not all that smooth in the US–China relationship. First, in January 1999, came the 3-volume report of a Congressional Select Committee, chaired by Christopher Cox on Chinese commercial and military espionage in the US in the 1990s. The most damaging parts of the report dealt with China's theft of US thermonuclear weapons design information. The report charged that the PRC had stolen US missile technology and proliferated it to other countries and also gotten US satellite manufacturers to part with missile design information without legal sanction. The thrust of the report was that the loosening of technology control regimes in the wake of the collapse of the USSR had been partly responsible for some of the lapses like enabling China to obtain high-performance computers that could be used for design, modelling, testing and maintaining advanced nuclear weapons as well as for R&D relating to missiles, satellites, submarines and aircraft. The report concluded that the PRC had "mounted a widespread effort to obtain US military technologies by any means—legal or illegal."[2]

Then, came the bombing of the Chinese embassy in Belgrade in May 1999 which created a major rift in their relationship. The Belgrade bombing triggered a major Chinese effort to develop high-technology strategic weapons. The "995 High Technology Plan", a reference to the date of the bombing—the year (99) and the month (5)—is not publicly acknowledged but is mentioned indirectly in Chinese journals and media.[3]

This was followed by a more serious incident of 1 April 2001 when a collision between a US Navy EP-3 reconnaissance aircraft and a PLA F-8 fighter resulted in the death of the Chinese pilot. The damaged US plane landed in Hainan Island and the Chinese demanded a cessation of US flights along the Chinese coast and an apology from the US. Twenty-four members of the crew were held for over a week and the incident created a great deal of bad blood between the two countries.

Then came the 9/11 terror attacks on the US in September 2001. Islamist terrorism now emerged as the biggest challenge before the US, which sought global support, and Beijing was supportive, whether it was in Operation Enduring Freedom in Afghanistan or the invasion of Iraq. Even as the US got involved in wars that cost trillions of dollars, China focused relentlessly on economic growth. They toned down their hostility to the US and went along with Washington as it asserted its military power around the world.

Having pushed back the Pakistanis in Kargil, won the general election of October 1999 and established a working majority, the National Democratic Alliance government led by Atal Bihari Vajpayee and the BJP began to focus on issues of economic transformation as well. Ambitious plans for infrastructure construction and privatization of state-owned enterprises were rolled out.

India had discovered its software mojo in the years leading up to the new millennium when the world's information technology industry was focusing on the so-called 'millennium bug.' Indian companies like Infosys, Satyam and TCS had played a significant role in debugging computers that had been programmed to use only two digits to signify the year. Hyderabad, Pune and Bangalore, which had provided the manpower to deal with the millennium bug, now emerged as centres that could provide software solutions across the board.

* * *

In 2002, around the same time as External Affairs Minister Jaswant Singh made his first official visit to Beijing, I had an opportunity to visit several places that I had been to in China in 1993. What was astonishing was the transformation. In 1993, Pudong was a gleam in the

Chinese eye, very much a rural backwater when we had been taken there to be briefed on the plans for the future. Now, it was transformed: several skyscrapers had been built, others were under construction. There was a gigantic new airport, high-tech zone and a sparkling new finance and trade district.

Equally striking was the transformation around the Xijiao State Guest House built around a huge garden. In 1993, walking out of the garden-like ambience where our guest facility was located, I found that we were surrounded by single storied workers' tenements on either side. But when I walked out the gates in 2002, I was stunned to see all of them gone and in their place a diplomatic quarter had been built with expensive villas and houses.

But that year, China was to undergo another crisis which has its echoes today. This was the outbreak at the end of the year of severe acute respiratory syndrome (SARS), beginning in Guangdong in November 2002. Then, as now, the Chinese leadership stumbled. Details of the virus were investigated and reported by the local authorities and sent up to Beijing on 27 January 2003, though their report did not note how contagious the disease was. However, the official announcement of the pandemic came only on 11 February and even then the danger of the illness was played down, even as the system was focused on the National People's Congress (NPC) meeting in March. The Communist Party of China now became worried about the SARS' potential for causing economic instability and damaging the image of the party.

For a couple of months there was panic in China: the main worry was that the epidemic would bring its headlong growth to a halt. It was only after the NPC session finished in mid-March that the authorities began to take SARS seriously. But if China's Leninist government with its obsession for secrecy delayed in effectively communicating its dangers in the beginning, it used the instruments from its political tool-kit—mass mobilization—to bring it under control by June. By that time some 349 people had died in China and 299 in Hong Kong.

The reason for this digression into a pandemic is occasioned not because it was a prelude to what was to come in 2020, but that at this time plans had been in motion for Prime Minister Atal Bihari Vajpayee to visit Beijing. In April 2003, in the midst of the SARS epidemic, China's *bête noire*, Defence Minister George Fernandes, arrived in Beijing and Shanghai for an official visit which was also his first visit to China.

In February 2020 Beijing's current ambassador to New Delhi, Sun Weidong, recounted Fernandes' criticism of the media for exaggerating the dangers of the epidemic. Sun, who was then director of the Asian Department in the Ministry of Foreign Affairs, said that the Chinese side appreciated the gesture, coming as it did from a long-time critic of China. Through the visit Fernandes said all the right things and called for closer trade, economic and even military cooperation between India and China. He met his Chinese counterpart, Cao Gangchuan, and the vice chairman of the powerful Central Military Commission(CMC), Guo Boxiong, who was later purged and jailed for life in the Xi Jinping era for corruption. He called on Premier Wen Jiabao and President Jiang Zemin, who, of course, was also chairman of the CMC.

Fernandes coming to China during the SARS epidemic was not an unusual step for the well known political maverick. But the Prime Minister's Office didn't take SARS lightly and wanted to postpone the June visit. But Vajpayee, ever the leader, took the decision to press on to Beijing, regardless of the warnings.

Vajpayee visits China

I was part of the media delegation accompanying the prime minister on his week-long visit to Beijing and Shanghai between 22 and 27 June 2003. The Chinese appreciated the Indian gesture of coming through SARS and this was apparent in our warm welcome as we landed in Beijing. The country was still in a serious funk, the streets were empty, as were the malls and hotels. The prime minister was put up at the official guest house, but the rest of his party was at the Peking Hotel near the Tiananmen gate. There was no one else in the hotel but the Indian party and we were first "shot" at with temperature guns and then allowed to enter. Every morning while entering the breakfast area, the temperature gun was deployed, as it was in virtually every place you went to in Beijing.

But the political agenda in Beijing was more expansive. Atal Bihari Vajpayee had followed the Sino–Indian dispute since the days he was the Jana Sangh (the forerunner of the BJP) Member of the Lok Sabha, the lower house of parliament, in the period 1957–1962. Those were the years in which China policy was first debated, with the parliament taking an increasingly truculent stand against any deal with China. Vajpayee's oratory contributed a great deal to creating the situation that virtually tied Nehru's hands in 1960.

In 1979, Vajpayee became external affairs minister (EAM) of the short-lived government headed by Morarji Desai in the aftermath of Indira Gandhi's defeat in the 1977 general elections, an event that the Chinese rejoiced in because they saw her as an instrument of Soviet policy. As the EAM, Vajpayee made it clear that his job was to normalize ties with China and Pakistan that had been frozen by conflicts in 1962 and 1971. As part of this venture, he reached out to China in 1979 by being the first Indian minister to visit the country since the war of 1962. In his meeting with Deng Xiaoping, the Chinese leader repeated his offer of a package deal. But Vajpayee was not authorized to respond so he didn't. But the whole initiative got messed up when the Chinese attacked Vietnam during the visit and spoke of "teaching a lesson" to the country, using the same language they had used against India in 1962. There was an uproar in parliament and the whole issue went back into the deep freeze.

Now, as prime minister, Vajpayee took up the challenge again in very different circumstances. First, he was the prime minister of a stable government that looked like it was going to be around for a while. Second, both India and China appeared to be on an upward growth trajectory and the complementarities in their relationship were becoming more apparent by the day. Third, Vajpayee felt he had unfinished business left over from 1979—working out a border settlement with China.

The 2002 visits of Chinese Premier Zhu Rongji to India and External Affairs Minister Jaswant Singh to China, and that of Defence Minister George Fernandes, had set the stage for the Vajpayee visit which was piloted by Principal Secretary and National Security Adviser Brajesh Mishra, who had been the recipient of Mao's smile in 1970. It had become clear to Mishra from those visits, as well as the interaction of other senior leaders with their Chinese counterparts, that the mood in Beijing was receptive towards cooperation. An important barometer was the visit of Fernandes himself, an ardent supporter of Free Tibet and who had just some years ago called China a "potential enemy Number One."

Another measure of the relationship came from the fact that Sino–Indian trade was booming. In one decade it had grown from USD 265 million in 1991 to nearly USD 3.6 billion in 2001. And it was still continuing to grow. It expanded 37.5 per cent in 2002 to a figure of nearly USD 5 billion as compared to the previous year. The growth was fairly balanced with a tilt of about USD 398 million in China's favour.

Indian and Chinese companies had also begun investing in each other's country. China's investments in India since 1991 totalled some USD 225 million. On the other hand, Indian investment in China was also growing and had reached some USD 63 million. An early entrant in those days was Huawei, which had recognized India's potential as a provider of software and invested in an R&D centre in Bangalore, its first outside China.

But the centerpoint of Vajpayee's visit was political. Its most important outcome was to take up the settlement of the boundary dispute anew. The process had gone from negotiations between prime ministers in the 1950s to package deals and sterile talks between officials in the 1960s and 1980s. We have seen how, finally, in 1993, the two set aside the efforts to settle their boundary dispute and sought to firm up a mutually acceptable Line of Actual Control, even while developing normal relations in other areas. But by this time, even the process of clarifying the LAC had ground to a halt, though it remained officially on the agenda.

To clear the decks as it were, the two sides made a bargain on the status of Sikkim and Tibet. India accepted that the "Tibet Autonomous Region (TAR)" was part of the territory of the People's Republic of China. The earlier formulation that "Tibet was an autonomous region of China," implied, according to Kalha, that there was no invasion in 1951, since TAR was part of the PRC established in 1949. Also, this meant that India recognized that Tibet was TAR, not the regions which had been lopped off from Tibet and linked to other provinces like Qinghai, Szechuan, Gansu and Yunnan.[4]

The negotiations on the Tibet and Sikkim issue went down to the wire and finally it was negotiations between an Indian team led by Mishra and the Chinese Vice Minister Wang Yi that cleared it. The

115

Chinese held out till the end for India declaring that Tibet was an inalienable part of China, while the Indians insisted that they would only recognize that Tibet Autonomous Region (TAR) was a part of the People's Republic of China.[5]

There was criticism of this move among many policy analysts in India. But Vajpayee felt that this was a reflection of the situation on the ground. This step was only an acknowledgement of the existing reality and the change had been discussed with the Dalai Lama and his representatives in India. Indeed, delegations from the Dalai Lama had been received in Beijing in December 2002 and June 2003 indicating that there was the possibility of a negotiated settlement between the Chinese and the Tibetans. There had been a similar cycle of talks between the Chinese and the Dalai Lama's representatives in the 1980s as well, as described by the Dalai Lama's brother Gyalo Thondup.[6]

In exchange, as it were, the Chinese agreed to recognize the Indian annexation of Sikkim. In 1977, the Chinese had strongly criticized the Indian action and had said that India had forcibly occupied Sikkim.[7] They had continued to recognize Sikkim as an independent entity and refused to consider its border as being linked in the Sino–Indian context. To an extent, this was also an outcome of the fact that, in 1890, the Qing and the British empires had signed the Anglo-Chinese Convention which laid out the borders between Tibet and Sikkim.

Reluctantly, however, the Chinese, too, agreed to accept the ground reality. But they did not do so immediately. All they did during the visit was to designate a place called "Changgu of Sikkim State" and the Renqunnggang on the Chinese side, as sites for a border trade market, which are actually adjacent to the Nathu La pass through which Tibet and India had traded for long and which marks the boundary between Sikkim and Tibet. They also promised to change the map in their foreign ministry's annual report the next time around, and that was indeed done for the 2004 report.

Special Representatives

In his talks, Vajpayee told his counterparts that there had been enough of trying to approach the issue through legal-historic principles, the time had come to make a straightforward political deal. So, he sprang the idea again at a dinner organized in his honour by Premier Wen Jiabao. Somewhat reluctantly, the Chinese went along with it. The final formulation was contained in the joint declaration which noted, "the two sides agreed to each appoint a Special Representative (SR) to explore from the political perspective of the overall bilateral relationship the framework of a boundary settlement."

Many of the other issues, too, were incorporated into the carefully drafted joint declaration, "On Principles for Relations and Comprehensive Cooperation between China and India," which also took into account the intense diplomacy of the period after the nuclear tests and declared that "the common interests of the two sides outweigh their differences." Further, that they were not a threat to each other and would not threaten to use force against the other. And that their development trajectories stood to benefit from their collaboration.

But the crowning achievement was the appointment of Special Representatives who would report to the two prime ministers themselves, and their principal job was to explore a settlement from "the political perspective." Some details of the behind-the-scenes developments have come through the memoir of Dai Bingguo, who served as the first Chinese SR and dealt with a succession of his Indian counterparts till 2014, beginning with Brajesh Mishra. According to Dai, Vajpayee had mooted the idea in his 1979 visit as the external affairs minister, and subsequently, in the runup to the 2003 visit, the Indian side had put out some ideas through diplomatic channels. Among these were that the SRs would not be involved in specific negotiation or poring over maps and historical claims. They would be tasked to work out the guiding principles and come up with a framework for a settlement.

The Chinese side made a quick decision to accept Vajpayee's offer and Dai claims that his appointment came to him with little warning. Till that point in time he had been a top-level party functionary dealing with a range of issues from SARS to North Korea.[8] But perhaps Dai is being a little less than candid here. After all, he was present during Vajpayee's meeting with President Hu Jintao.

From the Chinese point of view this was a hugely positive development. The Vajpayee proposal meant that India had at last abandoned its position that the Sino–Indian boundary had been established by treaty, custom and usage and agreed with the Chinese that it needed to be negotiated through the process of "mutual accommodation, mutual adjustment and mutual understanding."

In a statement at the conclusion of his visit, Vajpayee spoke of the importance of "exploring the framework of a boundary settlement from the political perspective." He also defended the Indian acceptance of TAR as an autonomous region of China.

Though the expert group meetings seeking to clarify the Line of Actual Control, as per the 1993 and 1996 agreements, had deadlocked in 2002, and an entirely new process of seeking a border settlement had been initiated, the two sides made it clear that the confidence-building measures regime to maintain peace and tranquility on the LAC would continue, including the process of clarifying the LAC.

The two sides also began to lay the foundation of the new relationship by promoting their economic ties. This was evident from the huge business delegation that had accompanied the Vajpayee visit. In the Shanghai leg of the visit the interactions were primarily in the realm of economic relations. The Chinese showcased their gleaming new city across the Whangpu river, called Pudong when they organised a boat ride up river for the visiting prime minister.

By now, as pointed out, trade between the two countries was booming. At this point the trade imbalance, which became a problem later, was not so visible and the relationship appeared to have a strong complementarity. So, India exported iron ore, plastics, iron and steel products, organic chemicals, precious stones, electrical machinery. China supplied India with electrical machinery and equipment, organic chemicals, silk, machinery, optical and medical instruments, fabrics and textiles. Border trade, which at this point was through just Lipu Lekh and Shipki La passes in the central sector (though a third point through Nathu La in Sikkim had just been approved), had also grown, though it was quite insignificant compared to ship-borne trade. A great deal of the border trade was also happening through the smuggling of Chinese goods like electronics and consumer goods through Nepal and even across border points like Dumchele in Ladakh.

In the meeting in Shanghai, Vajpayee spoke of the partnership between Indian software and Chinese hardware. As a mark of this, Indian companies were already providing software for companies like Huawei, Air China, ZTE. Ratan Tata, chairman of Tata Sons, had been appointed Honorary Economic Adviser to the Chinese city of Hangzhou, where Tata Consultancy Services had set up a software development centre to service its international clients, and IT companies like Satyam and Infosys had also made their entry. An engaging feature of the connection was the entry of educational software services being provided through companies like Aptech and NIIT.

But for all the bonhomie and the claim that they did not represent a threat to each other, the one topic that was not touched upon was that relating to nuclear weapons. While it was India's 1998 nuclear tests which had played a catalytic role in bringing the relationship between the two countries to this point, there was no mention of nuclear issues in the documents, speeches and declarations associated with the visit. China has refused to discuss nuclear issues with India, let alone risk-reduction measures.

At this time in 2003, India's nuclear capability was limited. On the other hand, in relation to India, China held a substantial threat in terms of weapons and their delivery systems, principally missiles. Besides, by supplying Pakistan with nuclear weapons designs, material and missiles, China has already done the worst it could by India. China does have a "No First Use" declaration, as did India. But there was an element of ambiguity there as to whether it applied to India as well, since India possessed nuclear weapons. Formally, at least, China continues to abide by the UNSC Resolution 1172, and therefore it refuses to recognize India as a nuclear weapons state and hence feels it has no reason to have a dialogue on nuclear weapons issues with India.

* * *

On our way back to New Delhi from Shanghai, I had occasion to have a word with Principal Secretary Brajesh Mishra. I wondered aloud how much more time the long negotiation on the boundary settlement would take. Mishra's laconic answer was "Three years." I felt he was being facetious and left it at that.

Later, in 2008 or so, after he had retired I would often run into him at the bar at the India International Centre in New Delhi where he came for a drink and a chat with friends every Saturday afternoon. On one occasion I picked up the conversation again. And he repeated the answer. "We had given ourselves the time frame of three years," he told me, "if it could not be settled in that period, it would not be settled in another fifty years."

As much has been confirmed by Dai Bingguo in his memoir. During the first and second meetings, Dai told Mishra that it would take 3–5 years to address the issues. At the end of the second meeting, Mishra took Dai aside and said Vajpayee was 79 years old and he himself was 75, and both were keen to settle the dispute as early as possible.

Dai's analysis was that India had finally realized that it could neither forcibly impose its "unilateral territorial claims on China," and nor could the issue be resolved by "demanding unilateral concessions from China." Second, it was aware that China's economic growth had picked up enormously, and if India was not to be left behind, it needed to accelerate its own economic growth, something that required a stable and peaceful external environment. And then, of course, was the personality and vision of Prime Minister Vajpayee himself, who had shown a steadfast commitment to resolve issues with China during his term in office.

The China episode was not a flash in the pan. Just how focused Vajpayee was in his belief that for economic advance India needed peaceful borders emerged from his January 2004 visit to Islamabad where he signed a far-reaching agreement with President Pervez Musharraf of Pakistan. The agreement, which sought to resolve the Jammu & Kashmir issue in quick time, came close to success. Unfortunately, events in Pakistan undermined its principal Pakistani interlocutor, Musharraf, who was forced out of office in 2008.

The BJP suffered an unexpected loss in the general election of 2004 and left office. By this time, Dai and Mishra had held two meetings and formulated the broad guiding principles for their discussion. But that speed was of essence became apparent when the momentum of the Special Representatives (SRs) carried onto the incoming Congress Party-led government that had appointed former foreign secretary J. N. (Mani) Dixit as the National Security Adviser and the Special Representative for talks with China. By this time, as Dai recounted, the two sides had worked out the basic path they were to follow. First, develop political guiding principles in a short time frame, then work out the framework agreement and then finally put it down on the ground to demarcate the border.

The third round of talks was held within a month of the new government taking office, and the fourth round in November 2004. Then, shockingly, in January 2005, Dixit suffered a heart attack and passed away. So, in March, the government of India appointed the new National Security Adviser M. K. Narayanan, who also became the new SR, and the next round of talks took place in New Delhi during Prime Minister Wen Jiabao's 9–12 April 2005 visit to India.

The Political Parameters Agreement

This meeting essentially put the final touches to an agreement which I again scooped, two weeks before it was actually signed. On 26 March, my lead story in *The Hindustan Times*, the paper I worked for at the time, declared: "Delhi, Beijing close to settling border dispute," and that a "10 or 12 point agreement incorporating the 'political parameters and guiding principles' of resolving the boundary dispute" was expected to be signed next month during Wen's visit. I then listed the key guiding principle from the Indian point of view, which would be of not disturbing "settled populations," and the need to take into account each other's security concerns.[9]

The report was accurate, except that the agreement had 11 clauses. Also, in hindsight, I was somewhat more upbeat than I should have been. Once again, the reason I managed to get the story was a combination of sheer luck, as well as the fact that I tracked the Sino–Indian border issues closely. Luck came my way in meeting the new Chinese ambassador Sun Yuxi at an outdoor cocktail party, at an embassy of a country that I cannot now recall, sometime in the second half of March 2005. He essentially laid out the story for me. I doubt if it was out of naivete; perhaps the basic work in the agreement had been done during a visit of Foreign Secretary Shyam Saran to Beijing earlier in the month and he thought that what he was telling me was common knowledge. Or maybe he mistook me for someone else. But whatever it was, for me it was a bonanza. It was a measure of the positive climate of Sino–Indian relations that I didn't bother to check this time with the Ministry of External Affairs since it was unlikely that running such an item could create any problems.

To begin with there was some unfinished business. As part of the Vajpayee visit, the Chinese had promised that they would recognize

Sikkim to be a part of India. They had already changed the map in their Ministry of Foreign Affairs annual report of 2004. Now they came through in a classic diplomatic fashion when, in the Joint Statement adopted on 11 April the two sides agreed on the language that spoke of border trade through "Nathu La pass between the Tibet Autonomous Region of the People's Republic of China and the Sikkim State of the Republic of India."

The next day, before his departure, Wen Jiabao presented Prime Minister Manmohan Singh a revised official map showing Sikkim as a part of India. In this heady atmosphere, it was not surprising that the two sides signed an India–China Strategic and Cooperative Partnership for Peace and Prosperity, though when I quizzed a senior official on the bonhomie of a strategic partnership, he replied, somewhat drolly, that it was specific to achieving "peace and prosperity." And who can quarrel with that?

It was no accident that Wen's first stop had been Bangalore, the major centre for India's digital industry. He repeated the formulation that I first heard in Shanghai during the Vajpayee visit of 2003 about Indian software and Chinese hardware combining to make world-beating products. In just three years, trade had ballooned from around USD 5 billion in 2002 to USD 13 billion by the time of Wen's visit. The two sides had also established a minister-level Joint Economic Group to promote economic engagement between the two countries and there was talk of an India–China regional trade agreement that would cover trade in goods, and services and investment as well as a Bilateral Investment Promotion and Protection Agreement.

But by far the more significant achievement was the agreement on the "Political Parameters and Guiding Principles for the Settlement of the India–China Boundary Question" signed on 11 April 2005 (hereinafter Political Parameters agreement). It underscored the fact that India had moved on from the Nehruvian notion that India's borders, defined by custom, usage and history, had already been fixed, with nothing left to discuss except minor adjustments. The preamble of the new agreement noted that the two sides were convinced that "an early settlement of the boundary question will advance basic interests of the two countries and should therefore be pursued as a strategic objective." Here, very clearly, the boundary issue was taken from the backburner and placed on the front one.

Article II stated that the solution would proceed "from the political perspective of overall bilateral relations." So, they would not be looking at historico-legal or technical solutions.

Article III was quite explicit committing the two to "make meaningful and mutually acceptable adjustments to their respective positions on the boundary question, so as to arrive at a package settlement to the boundary question."

The centerpiece of the agreement were articles IV and VII. Article IV said that the two sides would give due consideration "to each other's strategic and reasonable interests" within the framework of their commitment to "mutual and equal security". Article VII declared that in arriving at a settlement, "the two sides shall safeguard due interests of their settled populations in the border areas."

Article VI said that "the boundary should be along well-defined and easily identifiable natural geographical features" that the two sides agree on. This was the issue on which the 1980s talks had bogged down.

The task for the Special Representatives was now to move forward to arrive at "an agreed framework" that could provide the basis for the "delineation and demarcation" of the Sino–Indian boundary. This process, which continues to this day, was aimed at discussing the specifics of adjustments that they were willing to undertake.

A common-sense reading of these two articles suggested that the two sides were likely to strike a deal on a largely *talis qualis* basis. After all, was not the Aksai Chin's real strategic importance to China alone, not India? And was not the issue of settled populations specific to India in Arunachal Pradesh? But the devil was in the detail of those "adjustments" which the two sides have not yet agreed on.

The Political Parameters agreement has, so far, been the only negotiated document between the two sides on their boundary dispute. When it was signed, it generated enormous enthusiasm and optimism. But note that the two sides had been moving in this direction for a while. As we have pointed out, at the Joint Working Group meeting in August 1990 the Indian side had suggested a resolution of the boundary issue based on "logistic and administrative convenience." This was code for the so-called "LAC plus formula" wherein the two sides would settle on the Line of Actual Control (LAC), with China agreeing to give up the gains it had made and retained during the war in the western sector.

Briefing the media, after the agreement was signed, Foreign Secretary Shyam Saran said that India had made it clear that it had the political will to push through the agreement, notwithstanding the parliament resolution calling for the reclaiming of Aksai Chin. Saran also noted that with the agreement, the SR's talks had established the political principles and guidelines for the boundary settlement, and now it would move to phase two in which the two SRs would work to create a framework agreement for the purpose.

The positive trend in the relationship between the two countries was underscored by another protocol signed on the same day on the implementation of the military confidence-building measures. This protocol basically updated, refined and expanded the measures that had been agreed to in the 1996 agreement. Article IV of the protocol, for example, said that should the two sides get into a face-to-face situation on the LAC, they shall "cease their activities" and "simultaneously return to their bases." And of course, they should not use force or threaten to use it. It also expanded the schedule of border meetings at Chushul-Moldo in Ladakh, Nathu La in Sikkim, and Bum La, north-east of Tawang. Additional border meeting points were added at Kibithu-Damai, the eastern extremity of India and the Lipu Lekh pass in the central sector.[10]

This protocol also set up the quaint banner drill that was followed, at least till the summer of 2020, by the two sides when their patrols met in contested territory. One or the other side would whip out a banner saying, "This is Indian/Chinese territory." The second banner read, "Turn around and go back to your side." Incidents where such banners were flashed came to be known as "face-offs" in army terminology.

The Joint Statement at the end of Wen's visit repeated the language of the Political Parameters agreement when it noted that an early settlement of the boundary issue was in their interest and "should therefore be pursued as a strategic objective." Remarkably, the ghost of "Line of Actual Control (LAC) clarification" had even now not yet been laid since the agreement also spoke of the need for the JWG to continue its work to obtain an "early clarification and confirmation" of the LAC. Further, that the two sides had agreed to "complete the process of exchanging maps indicating their respective perceptions of the entire alignment of the LAC on the basis of already agreed parameters, with the objective of arriving at a common understanding of the alignment, as soon as possible." This, despite the failure to exchange maps of the western sector in 2002.

In March 2005, on the eve of his visit to India, Premier Wen had addressed his annual customary press conference in Beijing on the occasion of the National People's Congress annual session. He said that he would be visiting India soon with a three-point agenda of enhancing bilateral ties to strategic levels, and to seek a fair resolution to the boundary issue through a "fair, reasonable and mutually acceptable plan" which would be based on "mutual accommodation and accommodation of reality."

And then, displaying an uncommon emotional touch, he quoted a well-known phrase from the Hindu religious text, the *Upanishads*: May God protect us both together/May God nourish us both together/ May we work conjointly with great energy/May our study be vigorous and effective/ May we not hate any/ Let there be peace in me and my environment and the forces that act on me.[11]

His visit suggested that things were going swimmingly well for the two Asian giants, but then, as it often happens in human affairs, things began to come apart. The reasons were probably bigger than just the India–China issues.

6

THE CRACKS BEGIN TO SHOW

Germany was the unlikely spot to deliver tough news on the Sino–Indian border issue. So it was something of a surprise for the Indian Foreign Minister (later President of India) Pranab Mukherjee when, in the course of a meeting at the sidelines of the Asia-Europe (ASEM) meeting in Hamburg in May 2007, his Chinese counterpart, Yang Jichei, informed him that the clause in the Political Parameters agreement on not disturbing settled populations did not apply to the Tawang tract, or for that matter to Arunachal Pradesh. The message, almost exactly two years after the far-reaching agreement on Political Parameters, came in the wake of a perceptibly changed Chinese behaviour in relation to Arunachal Pradesh. A few days earlier, Beijing denied a visa to an Arunachal Pradesh-born Indian Administrative Service (IAS) officer, on the grounds that the state was actually a part of China. As a result the government of India cancelled a mid-level training programme that would have had 107 officers of India's premier administrative service, the IAS, visiting China.[1]

The Indian response came a week later in early June 2007, when Prime Minister Manmohan Singh met Chinese President Hu Jintao at the coastal resort of Heiligendamm, on the Baltic Sea, at the sidelines of the G8 meeting. He emphasized to his Chinese counterpart that the border should be settled through a "pragmatic solution" which will not require large-scale displacement of people. This was as broad a hint

India could give that the Chinese should not walk back from the 2005 agreement. During the talks, the Indian side tried to prod Hu on the issue of "settled populations," but he did not respond.[2]

New Delhi was dismayed, but it should not have been. In November 2006, the government had welcomed President Hu Jintao on a state visit to India. A week earlier, the Chinese Ambassador New Delhi, Sun Yuxi, said in an interview that the Chinese position was that "the whole of the state of Arunachal Pradesh is Chinese territory. And Tawang is only one of the places in it. We are claiming all of that." While he was, stating the obvious, it was grating to Indian ears, given the expectation that they were on track to settle the border broadly along the alignment of the existing Line of Actual Control. Speaking in the Lok Sabha (lower house of parliament) External Affairs Minister Pranab Mukherjee termed the comment "uncalled for and objectionable" and declared that the issue of Arunachal Pradesh's status was simply "not debatable."

Why did the Chinese enter into an agreement in April 2005, only to walk back from it? The answers lay in what was happening parallel to these developments between the US and India. A month before Wen's visit, US Secretary of State Condoleezza Rice had been in New Delhi to prepare for Prime Minister Manmohan's visit to Washington DC in summer that year. It was on the eve of this visit that an unnamed US official (widely known to be Philip Zelikow, key aide of Rice) had let it be known in a background briefing that Rice had presented India with the Bush administration's outline for a "decisively broader strategic relationship" whose goal "is to help India become a major world power in the 21st century." Adding in parenthesis, as it were, "We understand fully the implications, including the military implications, of that statement." This comment was, of course, played out in the media as it was meant to.

Then, weeks after Wen's visit, Japanese Prime Minister Junichiro Koizumi had come calling. He was the first Japanese head of government to visit in half a decade. During the visit, the two sides signed a document on the "Strategic Orientation of a Japan-India Global Partnership."

More important than the visit, was the context, something that became apparent only later. The Japanese prime minister's visit came shortly after anti-Japanese protests had taken place in China, triggered by the approval of a new edition of a controversial text book whitewashing Japanese war crimes during the Sino-Japanese war of 1937–1945. It morphed into a larger movement of boycotting Japanese goods and opposing Japan's bid for a permanent seat in a reformed UN Security Council. Across China businesses connected with Japan were vandalized and several Japanese were injured. There is little doubt that the Chinese authorities, who prize "social stability," were deliberately lax.

What the events did was to push Japan towards India. War guilt had persuaded Tokyo to play a major role in providing official development assistance (ODA) to China in the early 1980s and 1990s. This, and Japanese companies in search of business opportunities, helped China kick off its economic growth. By the mid-2000s, with China emerging as a world manufacturing powerhouse, Japan's relative importance to it had declined. But the Japanese had not quite caught on, till the events of 2005.

There was a sharp uptick in Japanese interest on India: several prominent Japanese companies, which had generally avoided the country, began to consider investing there. And there was a perceptible rise in Japanese ODA to New Delhi. Given the scale of Japanese investments in China, this was hedging more than anything else, but over the next decade Indo-Japanese relations showed a dramatic improvement and took on a strategic content even as China suddenly began to turn up the heat over its claim to the Senkaku Islands in the East Sea, which it calls Diayou.

Of greater significance was the July 2005 visit of Prime Minister Manmohan Singh to Washington DC, within months of the departure of Premier Wen and the signing of the Political Parameters agreement, and the visit of US Secretary of State Condoleezza Rice. The visit marked a strategic shift in Indo-US relations.

The Jaswant Singh-Strobe Talbott dialogue had yielded a commitment for "strategic partnership" between India and the US in 2001. The two countries had begun working along an action plan called "Next Steps in Strategic Partnership (NSSP)" and then, in January 2004, they announced a new series of steps to focus on three areas: civilian nuclear activities, civilian space programmes and high-technology trade. In addition, they began a dialogue on ballistic missile defence (BMD). The process involved an expanded engagement on nuclear regulatory and safety issues, the peaceful uses of space and strengthening laws against nuclear proliferation. The idea was to reach a point where the US would be comfortable with India's nuclear behaviour so that it could not just overlook the 1998 tests, but be open to wider high-technology development and transfer ties.

So, it should not have been a surprise when in the course of Manmohan Singh's visit, India and the US announced a US-India civilian nuclear cooperation agreement on 22 July 2005. Under this, India agreed to separate its nuclear and civilian reactors and place the latter under International Atomic Energy Agency (IAEA) safeguards, continue its moratorium on nuclear testing, pledge not to transfer nuclear technologies to states that didn't have them. In turn, the US would adjust its laws and policies to enable civilian nuclear trade with India, and also push the Nuclear Suppliers Group(NSG) to give India a special exemption on its nuclear trade restrictions.

Ostensibly the deal was about promoting clean energy to a country which had hugely growing energy needs. But there was little doubt that it was a major strategic move. By removing the "mother" sanctions on India on account of its refusal to sign the Nuclear Nonproliferation Treaty (NPT), the US was laying the stage for the rapid development of strategic ties with India. The Chinese understood this well.

Nevertheless, at least till 2006, the Chinese continued to see India as a country with which they could do geopolitical business. This is evident in President Hu Jintao's November 2006 visit. Significantly, among the various agreements, both sides also said they would advance cooperation in the area of civilian nuclear energy and in the use of space-based technologies. In the Joint Declaration, the two sides upheld the Political Parameters agreement and repeated the formulation that "an early settlement of the boundary question" needed to be "pursued as a strategic objective."

Just as the Indians could not ignore the increasing presence of China in world affairs, so, too, could Beijing not ignore the fact that India had the size and economic potential to possibly even best China, and in the 2000s entered into a period of fast economic growth. In a lecture to the Asia Society in Hong Kong in mid-2008, the then Chinese ambassador to India Zhang Yan was relentlessly positive. He said China-India relations were "on a fast track" and both had had a number of high-level visits, such as Prime Minister Manmohan Singh in January 2008. Both economies were growing and there was "a global convergence in international and regional affairs." The depth of the ties was evident from the many mechanisms for strategic dialogue, foreign policy consultation, anti-terrorism, as well as military-to-military relations having been established. As for the border, "both are mature enough to handle the differences in the best possible manner."[3]

In June 2006, the two Special Representatives (SR) had had their seventh round of talks in New Delhi, and this was followed within months with the eighth round in Beijing. Trade was growing and the two sides celebrated a "Year of Friendship" along with several cultural exchanges. Following the seventh round, India's SR M.K. Narayanan said that he was hopeful of arriving at a basic framework agreement for resolution "within the next two to three rounds." A sign of the quickening pace of negotiations became evident with the ninth round of talks in New Delhi in January 2007 followed by two more rounds that year—the tenth in Coonoor in April 2007, and the eleventh in Beijing in September 2007.

However, even as Indo-US negotiations for the nuclear deal wound their way to conclusion by sequential actions on the part of India and the US by October 2008, Sino–Indian relations were hit by two other developments.

The first was the sudden uprising in Tibet. The summer Olympics scheduled to be held in Beijing in August 2008 were the rallying point of the protests against the Chinese repression of Tibetans. It began in March 2008 with protests by monks and nuns and other Tibetans to commemorate the 49th anniversary of the 1959 Tibetan Uprising. They rapidly spread to monasteries across Tibet Autonomous Region and, more significantly, to regions of Tibet that had been merged with Chinese provinces such as Qinghai, Sichuan, Yunan and Gansu. Protests also took place in India, Nepal, Australia, North America and Europe where communities of Tibetan exiles lived.

The uprising took the Chinese aback. After all, they reasoned, they had transformed Tibet from a place which didn't have the industry to make even match-sticks to one which was now crisscrossed by highways, modern houses, safe drinking water and had more than 300 modern industrial enterprises.[4] The Chinese authorities were convinced that the Dalai Lama and the Tibetan government-in-exile, also known as the Central Tibetan Administration, based in India, had a hand in the protests. The Dalai Lama denied this and said that the protests were an outcome of "deep seated disillusionment and despair" felt by the Tibetans. Ironically, at this time, the Chinese were also carrying on a dialogue with representatives of the Dalai Lama over the future of Tibet. There is little doubt that the developments in Tibet would have made the Chinese much more wary of any kind of deal with the exiled Tibetans and, by extension, India.

China rises

The second development was the outbreak of the global financial crisis (GFC), which began in late 2007 and culminated in the collapse of Lehman Brothers in the US. It enveloped countries like the US, the European Union and Japan, which went into a recession. But because of China, many Asian countries managed to escape the crisis relatively unscathed. China was affected, with its GDP growth rate plunging from 13 per cent in 2007 to 9 per cent in the third quarter of 2008, and 6.8 per cent in the fourth quarter and continuing downward to 6.1 per cent in the first quarter of 2009. But the Chinese provided a massive monetary stimulus to the economy, which not only revived the Chinese but also other Asian economies.[5]

While China now had to reckon with the issue of debt and structural instability and industrial over-capacity, the fact that its growth revived when the other developed countries fumbled had important geopolitical consequences. Domestically, too, the stimulus helped fund infrastructure growth, especially in the area of railways and its national electricity grid.

But the 2008 GFC for the first time showed up the relative weaknesses of the US economy and the growing strength of the Chinese. It began the phase in which the US began to turn more inward and the Chinese began to look outward more. Where the US began to question its own policies and model, China began to be seen as the world's most dynamic and successful society. The effects of the crisis were long lasting. Writing in 2014, Jonathan Kirshner, a professor of economics at Cornell, noted that the crisis accelerated two pre-existing trends: "the relative erosion of the power and political influence of the US and the increased political influence of other states, most notably, but not exclusively, China."[6]

There was a lot of commentary about the end of the 'unipolar moment' and the arrival of the 'post-American' era. There was talk about how the Washington Consensus would soon give way to the Beijing Consensus. A lot of it was alarmist and premature, but there could be little doubt that the GFC had taken China up a couple of notches in the global geopolitical order. Where India had once been seen as almost a near peer, it now went down a couple of notches and began to appear smaller in Beijing's calculations. Inevitably in the aftermath as China developed a bigger economic footprint, its interests and capabilities also grew and so did its geopolitical assertiveness.

This was manifested in places as diverse as the Ladakh border, the Senkaku Islands and the South China Sea. Along the Line of Actual Control in 2007–2008, India noticed increased Chinese "transgressions," which meant aggressive Chinese patrolling into areas which were claimed by both sides. Significantly, they took place along the Pangong Tso's north bank, at Trig Heights, near Daulat Beg Oldi in the north, and Demchok in southern Ladakh. Similar incursions were noted in northern Sikkim, in particular the northernmost tip which juts into Tibet like a kilometre-long finger. China had been claiming this area for some time, even though the Sikkim border was supposed to be a done deal since the British times. As a result of this, the Indian Army had to set up a permanent post in the area. There were similar transgressions in Arunachal Pradesh at the Asaphi La, as well at the Dichu/Madan Ridge area.[7]

This became the standard pattern in the ensuing years. What is interesting was the decided Chinese focus on Ladakh, rather than in the eastern sector where, since the mid-1980s, China began to claim more serious disputes existed and where there were also similar pockets claimed by both sides.

In October 2010 Chinese personnel blocked the construction of a road in Demchok being undertaken as part of an employment generating scheme. The previous year, too, they had done the same by waving guns at the workers. Even more dramatic were events in Chumar, at the southernmost point of Ladakh in August 2011: PLA personnel landed by two helicopters and destroyed seventeen stone 'sangars' or bunkers used by the Indian Army patrols when they visited the area. According to the Indian district administration, this area was distinctly within the Indian border.

There were similar incidents, some even bizarre, to go by the reports appearing in the Indian media. In one the Chinese entered 1.5 km into Indian territory near Mount Gya, at the trijunction of Ladakh, Himachal Pradesh and Tibet, and painted a rock with the symbol of China. In another they air-dropped cans of food in the same area which, according to the report, were past their "use-by" date. In turn, according to a report, the Indian administration painted over the rocks and inscribed "India" on them.

Some of these reflected breathless reporting by the media. Such tactics, including leaving empty cigarette packets, wrappers and writing "India" or "China" have been par for the course on the LAC for some time. Both sides left these so-called "tell-tale signs" in the contested area they patrolled. The other side diligently picked them up and took them back as evidence and even displayed them in formal briefings such as one I attended while accompanying an Indian Army chief to the Tawang area. The Indian Army had routinely dealt with them, but what began to happen at this time was that some diligent reporters also got in on the act and started filing reports making the situation sound more alarming than warranted.

In fact, in 2010, at the end of his three-day visit to India, Chinese Premier Wen Jiabao had appealed to the Indian media not to sensationalize the boundary question. He pointed out that not a single shot had been fired on that border in recent years, but the "media war" compelled leaders "to come out and do something to repair the harm," he complained.[8] Facebook and Twitter had not quite gained the popularity there were to have later in India. But there was an explosion of private TV channels noisily competing with each other, that were becoming a power unto themselves.

But there were manifestations of a shift in the Chinese approach to India as well. One was the implicit questioning of Jammu & Kashmir's status by giving Indians living in the state a loose-leafed stapled visa instead of a regular one. Then, China began to insistently describe Arunachal Pradesh as "Southern Tibet." In 2008, two weeks after his visit to China, Prime Minister Singh visited Arunachal Pradesh. This visit, the first by a prime minister in a decade, was clearly aimed as a message to Beijing; predictably it led to a formal protest.

The next year, in 2009, China opposed an Asian Development Bank loan of USD 60 million to Arunachal Pradesh since the area was disputed, though India eventually managed to convince the ADB to approve it. China protested a repeat visit by Prime Minister Singh to the Arunachal in 2009, but what raised the temperatures higher in Beijing was the visit of the Dalai Lama to Tawang monastery, where he received a delirious reception.

Finally, tempers boiled over in New Delhi when, in August 2010, the Chinese denied a normal visa to Lt Gen. B.S. Jaswal, the head of its Northern Army Command, headquartered in Udhampur in Jammu & Kashmir, and which also looks after Ladakh. As part of the recent high-level military exchanges between the two countries, the general had been selected to be part of a military delegation to visit China. But Beijing declared that since Jammu & Kashmir was a disputed state, it would not give him a normal visa. An angry New Delhi called off the visit and scrapped all military-to-military exchanges.

For the first time, too, India also began to raise the issue of Chinese activities in Pakistani-held Kashmir, which is claimed in its entirety by India. This is the region through which the Chinese highway linking Pakistan with Xinjiang runs.[9]

Elsewhere, Beijing began taking an interest in the Senkaku Islands, claimed as the Diayou by the Chinese, in the East Sea. In September 2010, a Chinese fishing trawler rammed a Japanese coast guard vessel leading to the detention of the boat and the arrest of its captain by the Japanese authorities. This became a major point of contention between the two countries which also played itself out in the hyper-nationalistic fringes of both countries.

In 2009, China first began to assert its "Nine-Dash Line" claim in the South China Sea, though the line, as such, goes back to a KMT map published in 1947.[10] In response to a Vietnamese submission on a claim of a continental shelf beyond 200 nautical miles, China told the UN in a *note verbale*, that "China has indisputable sovereignty over the islands in the South China Sea and adjacent waters." They said that the Vietnamese claim had infringed Chinese rights and jurisdiction. A map was attached which enclosed the entire South China Sea within a line that had nine dashes spread from Taiwan, going past the Philippines, past Brunei and Malaysia and then turning up along the Vietnamese coast to China.[11]

Efforts to moderate the dispute had been under way since 2002 when the ASEAN signed a Declaration of Conduct of Parties in the South China Sea. But as in the case of India, this agreement was only the prelude to yet another agreement, the Code of Conduct of Parties in the South China Sea, which has been in negotiation since. In 2012, China wrested the Scarborough Reef from the Philippines, and began construction in seven features that it occupied on the Spratly islands.

In 2013, the Philippines sought arbitration with China on several issues relating to the South China Sea, including the legality of the Nine-Dash Line under the United Nations Convention on the Law of the Sea (UNCLOS). The verdict in 2016 was quite categorical—there was no cause for China to claim "historic rights" to the area within the Nine Dash-Line; there was no basis for rocks and low-tide elevations in the South China Sea to be termed as "islands" and hence generating maritime zones as a unit. China and Taiwan have both rejected the ruling.

Even while the arbitration was on, China intensified its island construction programmme. Though Xi Jinping personally pledged that China will not militarize these artificial islands, soon the Chinese were stationing fighters and anti-ship missiles on them. It is only with some hindsight that we can see something common between what was happening in the South China Sea and the Himalayan border.

The world community did not quite recognize it at once. But since the GFC of 2008, there has been a consistent shift in Chinese attitudes. Prior to this, it followed Deng Xiaoping's 24-character strategy of "hiding one's capacities and biding one's time," but increasingly the Chinese became insistent that they would not under any circumstances compromise their self-proclaimed core interests. This was the ambience which led to the emergence of Xi Jinping as the Communist Party of China's supreme leader in 2012.

Speaking at the party politburo study session in January 2013, Xi had spoken of following the path of cooperation and peaceful development, but he had also emphasized that "We will never give up our legitimate rights and will never sacrifice our core national interests. No country should presume that we will engage in trade involving our core interests or that we will swallow the 'bitter fruit' of harming our sovereignty, security and development interests." By now it was clear that far from hiding its capacity, China was using it to safeguard what it claimed were its legitimate rights and core interests.[12]

But the impact of these developments—the Tibet imbroglio, the Indo-US Nuclear Agreement and the GFC 2008 outcome—was visible in Sino–Indian ties soon enough. Its obvious manifestation was on their border negotiations being conducted by their Special Representatives. From the beginning of 2006 till the end of 2007, a space of two years, the two sides had held five rounds of SR talks. Now, they went into a pause. The next round, the twelfth, was only held in September 2008, a year later, and likewise the thirteenth round in August 2009. The difference of views on the Political Parameters agreement made it clear that there was going to be little further progress on that track. So, beginning with the thirteenth round, the two Special Representatives also took on additional items of agenda in their ambit. These included issues of political and strategic concern to the two countries, effectively making them the point persons for the political relationship between the two countries.

Of course, neither side acknowledged that the talks were going nowhere. They maintained their formal dialogue. But a telegram from July 2009 later released by Wikileaks provided an assessment based on conversations between US diplomats in Beijing and Chinese scholars. All commented on the increased tensions arising from the Indian military build up in the eastern part of the LAC. And all appeared to be pessimistic about the state of the border talks. CICIR South Asia specialist Hu Shisheng told the US diplomats that "both sides' position appeared irreconcilable." Referring to the Chinese negotiating stance, Hu noted that Tawang's ties to Tibetan Buddhism "had sharpened its cultural and historical resonance for China." According to him India had "betrayed" China by occupying it at a time it was busy in the Korean war.[13]

China's western strategy

Even as the political moves and counter-moves between New Delhi, Beijing, Tokyo and Washington DC were the focus of attention in the

2005–2010 period, the Chinese had embarked on a significant domestic programme which had major implications for India. This was its so-called "Western Development Campaign" which led to a sharp upgradation of its infrastructure in Tibet, something which had important military implications for India, which was embarked on a similar course, but was slower to get its plans off the ground.

The poor state of the Chinese infrastructure in Tibet, as of the 1980s, has been brought out well by the writer Vikram Seth's travelogue *From Heaven Lake*. A Mandarin speaker from Stanford University, who had spent two years as a student of Chinese language in Nanjing University, Seth decided to hitch-hike from Xinjiang across Tibet and make his way to India via Nepal in the summer of 1981. He travelled largely along what were Highways 109 and 219 and his description of the difficulties, the terrible roads, the danger of floods and so on is compelling.[14]

However, after the Chinese economic reforms took off, Beijing embarked on the so-called "Western Development Campaign" aimed at ensuring that regions like Tibet and Xinjiang did not get left too far behind the mainland. The campaign was kicked off by Jiang Zemin in 2000 and it pledged to build 35,000 km of roads, 4,000 km of railways and dozens of new factories along with oil and gas pipelines. The slogan given was "Go West," though in this case "west" meant everything from Sichuan to Xinjiang.

The campaign had a mixed set of objectives. First, it sought to promote economic growth in areas that were being left behind in the Chinese opening up, so as to ensure political stability there. Second, it was aimed at exploiting the natural resources of the far western regions of Tibet and Xinjiang, and third, at promoting cultural consolidation by encouraging the movement of Han migrants to minority areas in Tibet and Xinjiang.[15]

Besides three pipeline projects leading out of Tibet and Xinjiang and connecting Sichuan to Wuhan, there was what was termed a three-dimensional infrastructure development plan for Xinjiang and Tibet based on promoting rail, road and air connectivity. Most of the road systems were built to military specifications. To begin with these were the Qinghai-Tibet Central Highway (No. 109) running from Xining in Qinghai to Lhasa, which is the principal road carrying cargo and people in and out of Tibet. The second was the Sichuan—Tibet Eastern

Highway (No. 318) from Chengdu to Linzhi and Lhasa. The third, was the Lhasa—Kasghar Western Highway (No. 219) going through Aksai Chin, with one branch leading to the Khunjerab Pass and thence into Pakistan. The first two had been opened in 1954, a the third in 1957.

These original highways are now integrated into the national highway system, the 109, with a length of 3,901 km, running all the way to Beijing. Highway 318 from Shanghai to Zhangmu on the Nepal— border, runs a length of 5,476 km, from where it connects to the Nepal-Tibet Friendship Highway. The 219, which passes through Aksai Chin, is expected to be more spectacular as its development plan is to extend it to Guangxi, on the east coast of China, 10,000 km away from its eastern extremity at an obscure town near the Mongolia—Xinjiang border.

By 2012, the length of the expressways in Tibet totalled 97,800 km, and it had five airports linked to 38 cities in China. In 2012 the entire Western Highway (219) going through Aksai Chin was repaved for the first time in fifty years, and work was initiated in re-paving and upgrading older highways and building new feeder roads and rail links.[16]

Within Tibet, too, roads and expressways linked virtually every village and town to the highway system. Besides upgrading the roads leading into Tibet, China ramped up the building of internal highways and feeder roads within Tibet to service the strategically significant border areas with India, Nepal, Bhutan and Pakistan. According to one estimate, between 2001 and 2005 some 42,700 km of highways were opened to traffic and the process of connecting Tibet's towns and villages continued through the decade.

When the last Tibetan county, Medog, in eastern Tibet, was connected to the highway system in December 2010, it was front-page news in *China Daily*. Even *The New York Times* took notice of the event in linking up the village where snow and rain made the narrow roads difficult to traverse. The road required tunnelling 3 km through a mountain and rebuilding portions of an old road.

Perhaps the most ambitious project has been the railway to link Golmud in Qinghai province to Lhasa in Tibet. In 2006, the 1,432-km-Qinghai—Tibet railway line, traversing extremely forbidding terrain, some at an altitude of 4,000 metres, became operational.[17] The Lhasa airport at Gonggar was built in the 1960s and upgraded in the mid-

1990s, while other airports came under the tenth Five Year Plan (2000–2005) at Nyingchi, Ngari-Gunsa, Shigatse and Qamdo.[18]

The Tibetan uprising of 2008 persuaded the Chinese government to double down on its Western Development Strategy. In 2010, China began a major effort to upgrade this infrastructure by investing billions of dollars more in Tibet and Xinjiang. Besides the development of two backward regions, the aim was to enhance the capabilities of enabling forces from other regions to reach the remote border areas. This would add 8,000 km of railway lines and create seven new airports. By this time China had already completed a fibre optic network to improve the PLA's communications in Tibet and Xinjiang.[19]

In 2014, the Chinese completed the 33-km Xinguanjiao tunnel on the Qinghai—Tibet Railway. Also, according to *China Daily*, the Lhasa railway had been extended to Shigatse. In June 2021, Xi Jinping inaugurated the Lhasa-Nyingchi section of the Sichuan Tibet line. Now it is working on the 1,011-km section to Ya'an near Chengdu scheduled to be completed by 2030. By 2022 railways will be built to link Shigatse to Gyirong on the Nepal border, as well as to Hotan in Xinjiang, which may follow Highway 219 and go through Aksai Chin. Both these lines run parallel to the Indian border and have obvious military implications: Nyingchi, for example, is just 15 km from the border with India. The Sichuan–Tibet line will shorten the distance between the Chinese mainland and Tibet consderiably.

Most cargo comes into Tibet through highways, but the railways have a huge psychological role in breaching the mental barriers about Tibet being isolated. All these developments have had social and political consequences in Tibet, but they have also served hugely to strengthen the PLA's posture vis-à-vis the Indian Army ranged across the LAC.

The Tibetan policy was not just about infrastructure and development. An important item in the agenda was the tightening of political and social control. The Chinese appointed more hard-line cadres in Tibet, even while boosting the economic aid. President Hu Jintao was, himself, an experienced Tibet hand, having been party secretary of the Tibet Autonomous Region (TAR) in the period 1988–1992.

One part of this was developing a register of all living Buddhas, monks and nuns in TAR and the Tibetan areas of the neighbouring provinces. As part of this it terminated negotiations with the representatives of the Dalai Lama.[20] Given that the threat the Chinese confronted there was from monks and peaceful protestors, the effort was to assimilate Tibet into the Chinese fold through economic development.

India shifts gears

In March 2011, reviewing a report on the construction of border roads in the country, a committee of India's Lok Sabha (lower house of parliament) was provided data by the Ministry of Defence on the state of road infrastructure in Tibet. The government agreed to part with the data, having earlier denied that they had it. The ministry noted that all major highways in Tibet had been upgraded to two-way, black-top all-weather roads open to traffic through out the year. This included the Western Highway (219) through Aksai Chin with three alignments crossing the Tibetan plateau to Lhasa, the Central Highway (109), and the Eastern Highway (318).

In addition, the report said, China had built feeder roads linking to these highways, logistic centres and defence installations to all the passes and military positions along the Line of Actual Control (LAC). Thus Dambuguru, Khurnak Fort and Sirijap were linked by black-top roads. The passes in the area around Pangong Tso, like Ane La, Charding La and Kongka La were also connected by roads. Similar details were provided for roads in the central and the eastern sectors.[21] (See Map 1)

Around the time the Chinese stepped up the construction and upgradation of their infrastructure in Tibet, India, too was getting a measure of what it needed to do in the areas bordering the LAC. Given the physical difficulties of the terrain, shortage of money and, to an extent, complacency generated by the 1993 and 1996 agreements, India had once again slackened the pace of its border infrastructure construction that had intensified in the wake of the 1986–1987 crisis.

Though India had been in the business of building border roads since the 1950s, their pace had been painfully slow. In great measure it was an outcome of bureaucratic lassitude and lack of resources. In addition, the Indian challenge was orders of magnitude greater. Though the band of territory that needs to be serviced is just around 200–300 km wide (with the exception of Ladakh) it comprises one of the highest mountain chains in the world, the Himalayas. Even on a good two-lane, black-topped highway, the time taken to reach the border from the Himalayan foothills could be two to three days by a car or bus.

These mountains also form a barrier to the Tibetan plateau and get the full blast of the monsoon for several months, at least in the central and eastern portions. Thereafter the moisture in the air ensures heavy snowfall in the higher reaches, blocking roads and passes for six months in the Ladakh region. The Himalayas, being the youngest mountain chain in the world, are also extremely fragile. Entire sections of road are often wiped out by landslides during the monsoon and, after heavy snow, roads need to be re-laid every summer in many places. Indian infrastructure construction has been fitful. India got its first road to Ladakh (which closes for winter for 5–6 months anyway) only by 1965. In the east, the road to Tawang came up 1962 and the one to Walong in the 1990s.

There was another issue: based on the doctrine that India would adopt a defensive posture across the Himalayas in the event of another Chinese attack, the roads were left well short, anywhere from 25 to 50 km, of the LAC itself. The soldiers in the forward-most posts were supplied by air in the case of places like Daulat Beg Oldi and Chongtash in Ladakh, or by trains of specially bred mules, whose original stock had actually been imported from the US in the 1960s. The air force had made landing grounds in Along, Pasighat, Daporijo, Tuting, Walong, Mechuka, Tezu and Ziro, in the east and places like Leh, Thoise, Nyoma, Hot Springs, Fukche, Daulat Beg Oldi and Chushul. Only some could take heavier transports. Flying in Arunachal was a difficult process, as testified by the US casualties flying over the Hump in World War II. Wrecks of old Caribou planes that serviced some of the ALGs can still be seen next to some advanced landing grounds (ALGs) in Arunachal Pradesh.

From the mid-2000s, India had become sensitive to the need to orient its policy with an eye on rising China. Part of this had been articulated in the "Look East" policy of Prime Minister P. V. Narasimha Rao in the early 1990s. But that had more to do with trade and commerce. Now, India needed to be alert as China sought to expand its political influence in the neighbourhood, in countries like Nepal, Myanmar and Sri Lanka.

Fortunately, it had the services of two outstanding foreign service officers, both China specialists and Mandarin speakers. Shyam Saran became the foreign secretary along with the new government headed by Manmohan Singh. On his retirement in 2006, he was succeeded by Shivshankar Menon, who was ambassador to China during the Vajpayee visit, and who was appointed National Security Adviser in January 2010 shortly after his retirement. He was succeeded as foreign secretary by yet another officer specializing on China, Nirupama Rao. As the NSA, Menon also became the Special Representative for the boundary talks with China. His counterpart, however, remained the same, Dai Bingguo, and the two met in Beijing in November 2010 for the fourteenth meeting of the SRs. The press release after the meeting was anodyne and suggested that the meeting had been routine.

Saran, a trekking buff, was familiar with the poor state of infrastructure in the mountains, and as someone who had been ambassador to Nepal and Myanmar, and had served in Beijing in the early 1980s. As foreign secretary, Saran toured Arunachal Pradesh and in a report to the prime minister at the end of 2004, recommended the construction of several strategic roads in both Arunachal and Ladakh. He also proposed the revival of the landing grounds that had been lying defunct since the 1962 war.

The generally creaky government machinery began to get energised, not only by the top officials but also by the fact that the country was doing well economically, and budgetary constraints that had normally slowed things down were not there.[22]

After he retired in 2006, Saran was appointed a special envoy of the prime minister. Though formally his job was to deal with the new US nuclear deal, he also looked at the border infrastructure. In the summer of 2007, he again toured the Ladakh area, with Defence Minister A.K. Antony, and found that little had been done regarding the revival of the advanced landing grounds. Back in New Delhi, Saran again pressed the government to revive the ALGs in DBO, Chushul, Fukche and Demchok. Later he carried out an aerial survey of the Manali–Leh Highway to see whether it could be made accessible through the year.[23]

This route from Himachal Pradesh to Ladakh had been developed with the help of the US and was for a long time termed a Charlie II road, which would kick in in the event of a blockage of the Srinagar–Leh Highway. Till the 1980s, the only traffic it saw was an annual test convoy sent to check the condition of the road after the snows had melted. Now it was opened to tourist traffic. The problem with it was that, at Rohtang, Baralacha La (pass), Nakee La, Lachung La and Tanglang La, snow would block the highway and the only way out was to tunnel through them.

But it was not just Menon or Saran, but the entire government headed by Manmohan Singh which was riposting to the increasing capabilities of China in the region and in Tibet. The key incentive was India's economic performance, which had reached a point where it could undertake measures it had been contemplating for a while, such as the construction of certain roads, activating advanced landing grounds proximate to the LAC or the raising of additional forces to police the border. On a visit to Arunachal Pradesh in 2008, one that was protested by China, Prime Minister Manmohan Singh announced a INR 24,000-crore (INR 240-billion) special package for the state. Priority, he said, was to be given to road construction, in particular the 1,811-km Trans-Arunachal Highway which would run from Tawang in the west, in a semi-circular manner to the south-eastern tip of the state without touching Assam. This highway has now been completed.

However, by 2010, an accounting for the previous decade showed that work had begun on 277 roads, totalling 13,100 km of which only 29 roads amounting to 823 km had been completed although the deadline for completion was 2012. Bureaucracy, environmental protection rules, and strained resources, made the process slow and painful, but the direction of India's endeavour was clear: it was determined, sooner or later, to match China's impressive road infrastructure on its side of the Himalaya.

Plans were put in place to add another 15,000 km of roads over the next decade to 2022. The government also began to think of tunnelling as an option. A good measure of the sense of purpose of a government in building mountain infrastructure is its decision to tunnel sections of a road. This requires both resources and effective project management. Strategic compulsions had pushed India to build a 3-km tunnel under the Banihal pass within just two years in the mid-1950s to ensure all-weather connectivity with the Kashmir valley. But after that, tunnelling as an option to promote all-weather, or even simple connectivity to the mountain regions, was considered only in the 2000s, when the project for a tunnel through the Rohtang pass and another two on the

Srinagar–Leh Highway at Zoji La pass and the nearby Z-Morh (Z-turn) were approved.

Getting the air force to move was obviously easier than building the roads, though sending supplies by air was prohibitively expensive. In May 2008, an Indian Air Force AN-32 transport aircraft landed at the Daulat Beg Oldi airstrip for the first time since 1966 when a specially configured Fairchild Packet had done so. Later in 2008, the Fukche ALG, virtually adjacent to the LAC, was also opened up. In 2009, Nyoma, just 23 km from the LAC, was reactivated. In the east, the ALGs were opened up, being promoted for civilian as well as military use.

In 2008, boosted by the growing capabilities of the Indian military and the deepening of the "iron friendship" of Pakistan and China, the Indian defence minister revised his longstanding Operational Directive (Op. Directive) to the military to cater for what was beginning to look like a two-front challenge to Indian security. In other words, the military were now told to be prepared to take on a war which could possibly simultaneously involve both Pakistan and China. Till this point in time, they had worked along an Op. Directive of the 1980s vintage, which called for a capability to launch an offensive against Pakistan but maintain a defensive posture with regard to China.

As an outcome of the new directive, India took another meaningful step in 2008 when the government approved the raising of two new divisions for its army. These were the first new raisings in decades, and the defence ministry was clear that they were aimed at redressing what New Delhi thought was a growing adverse balance against India along the Line of Actual Control (LAC). These combat formations, each some 23,000 strong, would supplement the existing 10 divisions, already arrayed along the LAC. The original idea was to raise these divisions over the next five years in a two-phased plan. But the army felt that the forces were needed urgently and so it dipped into what are called "war wastage reserves" (equipment and munitions stored for use in the event of a war) and skimmed off personnel from existing army formations and raised the new divisions in just two years. They were deployed in Nagaland and Assam, but designed for use on the Tibetan front.

Along with this development, India began to strengthen its air-force posture in the north-east as well. Given India's Pakistan obsession, for long the centre of gravity of its deployments has been westwards, aimed at fighting a war with Pakistan. Its best assets, fighters like the Russian-made Su-30MKI or the French Mirage 2000s, were based in western states like Maharashtra, Rajasthan, Punjab, Haryana and Madhya Pradesh. In mid-June 2009, a squadron (18 aircraft) of Su-30MKI, which is currently the frontline fighter of the IAF, was shifted to Tezpur in Assam, near the foothills of Arunachal Pradesh. And in March 2011, a second squadron was shifted to the Chabua air base also in Assam.

This was the time when the growing ties with the US began to kick in. Among the first purchases India made from the US in 2008 was the C-130 transport aircraft, whose older versions had flown in US assistance to India in the wake of the 1962 war. This was followed by the acquisition of C-17 heavy lift transport aircraft in 2009. In the same year, India made another important purchase, the advanced P-8I maritime reconnaissance aircraft. Another important purchase initiated was that of 140 M777 ultralight howitzers, which were easily transportable in helicopters, specifically for use in the mountain areas. India was, by this time, also conducting annual Yudh Abhyas (war experience) exercises with the US.

By 2011 or so, India began to become more confident of the effort it was putting in, and the impact it was having. Speaking to the Lok Sabha in early March 2011, Defence Minister A.K. Antony lamented the lack of a commonly accepted Line of Actual Control, even as he informed the members of the steps China was taking to enhance its infrastructure in Tibet. He said India's infrastructure development and force modernization was in consonance with the Chinese build up.[24]

Having pulled back from the far-reaching Political Parameters agreement, and raised questions about their stand on Jammu & Kashmir and Arunachal Pradesh, the Chinese now went on to another track. This was to thwart the ambitious Indian programme of building up its border infrastructure along the Line of Actual Control and the raising of additional forces facing Tibet. This began to surface in the Chinese conversations with the Indian side with regularity.

The Chinese attitude to Indian border construction was most obviously manifested in Demchok, one of the few areas in Ladakh where the Indians occupy a tiny bit of Chinese-claimed territory. A small stream separates the two Demchoks—the Indian and the Chinese. On the Chinese side there is impressive infrastructure, including a large store house and residential facilities. But the Chinese have blocked any effort by the Indian side to construct anything on its Demchok, because they claim this is contested territory, though evidence that it is at the border between Ladakh and Tibet is quite clear. The reason for the Chinese insistence is also apparent: Demchok, on the old trade route to Tibet, is also proximate to the 219 Highway.

In meeting after meeting, whether routine border talks or higher level exchanges, the Chinese kept on hammering the issue without a trace of irony: Why don't you freeze your border construction programmes? Why do you want to push infrastructure construction in this region? It could destabilize the situation and so on. The Indian response was obvious: We are only playing catch up to what you have already done in Tibet. But that could not assuage the Chinese concerns because catch up meant that the dominance they had had on the border would be affected and could impact the larger Sino–Indian relationship where, since by 2010, the Chinese saw themselves as a world power in a category quite different from India.

The Chinese side didn't seem to realize that the two countries were now involved in a classic security dilemma. China's military modernization and infrastructure construction began to be viewed as a threat by India. In turn, New Delhi's response in developing its infrastructure and plugging perceived loopholes in its defences began to be viewed the same way by China.[25] There was, perhaps, a way India could have responded better, that is by saying that the infrastructure was not aimed at China, but at enhancing the quality of life of the citizens living in the inhospitable mountain region. Somehow, New Delhi never thought of this because in reality its infrastructure programme was aimed at military goals.

Soon it became apparent that this line was actually being pushed by the PLA. Over the decade, the Chinese had been paying close attention to the growing capabilities, especially those related to nuclear strike. The first test of India's Agni 3 (3,000–5,000 km range) ballistic missile in 2006 was accompanied by media commentary as to how this would bring into range all of China. This, in a way, reinforced in the Chinese mind the issue that arose when India blamed problems with China for going nuclear in 1998. Chinese analyses of Indian military modernization in the mid-2000s depicted India as an expansionistic and hegemonic power which was projecting offensive military doctrines like Cold Start. Though Cold Start was merely aimed at changing the Indian Army's culture of undertaking lumbering mobilizations that were useless against the quick developing crises in the era of terrorism, the Chinese saw in it a potential doctrine that could be used against China.[26]

Cold Start was soon put onto the backburner as India found that it could not afford the kind of capital costs it would have to incur if it restructured its army the way the doctrine demanded. But its strategic programmes continued to grow, and since these were really aimed at China, they alarmed them. In 2009, India launched its first ballistic missile submarine, the *Arihant*. Even though it was to use a missile of a very limited range, the programme had a built-in capability of enhancing the product over time. Equally important was the test-firing of a 5,000-km range Agni V missile in April 2013.

But the Chinese were not too concerned about the strategic leg of the Indian programmes, which were relatively backward and being developed at a leisurely pace compared to their own effforts. In any case, they were carefully monitoring India's activities. In 2008, the Federation of American Scientists revealed a huge Chinese missile launch facility in Delingha in the Tibetan plateau in the Qinghai province of China. These included launch pads and command centres for nuclear capable medium-range missiles like the DF-21 and the DF-31, capable of reaching northern India and southern Russia.

In 2009, for the first time the PLA began to shift its focus away from its "Taiwan contingency" and focus on other areas. For the first time their largest ever Kuayue (Stride) exercise focused on trans-regional mobility and overland military operations against potential adversaries like India and Vietnam. The next year it held its first live fire drills in Tibet involving fighter aircraft, attack helicopters, artillery, tanks and electronic warfare units.

* * *

Formal relations between the two countries remained excellent. Economic cooperation, bilateral political and social and cultural exchanges between them were at an all-time high. China soon became India's largest trading partner with trade totalling USD 60 billion in

2010. At the global level, the two sides worked together on climate change, trade negotiations and calling for the restructuring of global financial institutions to give developing countries a voice. The Russia–India–China trilateral grouping had been around since the 1990s, and in October 2009 they held a scheduled ministerial summit in Bangalore with the joint communique focusing on the positive areas of cooperation between the three sides such as international organization reform, climate change, economic cooperation and so on.

That year, the three countries took a larger step in formalizing their global outlook by giving shape to the Brazil, Russia, India, China and South Africa (BRICS) grouping whose aim was to improve the global situation in the wake of the 2008 GFC and reform financial institutions.

Despite, or perhaps because of, the infrastructure construction on both sides of the Sino–Indian border, border trade was booming. In Nathu La, by 2010 trade had risen more than ten times since it had been opened in 2006. Tibet's cross-Himalayan trade was up 88 per cent though driven more by trade with and through Nepal.

Yet, there were signs of wariness. In September 2008 the Nuclear Supplier's Group met to consider giving India a waiver for civil nuclear trade based on its commitments to the US. It was no secret that China did not want to support the Indian case, and if it had formally objected, the proposal would, indeed, have fallen through. But it did not do so because of US pressure. Beijing conducted an indirect, and even covert, campaign through countries like the Netherlands, Norway, Austria, Ireland and Switzerland to see if they could derail the exemption. Eventually, President George W. Bush himself leaned on Chinese President Hu Jintao to get Chinese acquiescence.

In 2011, the two sides resumed high-level military exchanges that had been curtailed since the episode of the refusal of a visa to Lt Gen. Jaswal. This was announced at the sidelines of Prime Minister Manmohan Singh's meeting with President Hu Jintao during his visit to Sanya in Hainan Island to attend the BRICS summit. Another outcome of this meeting was the decision to create a Working Mechanism on Consultation and Coordination(WMCC) on India–China Border Affairs, headed by joint secretary-level foreign ministry officers, to aid in the everyday management of issues relating to the border, such as trade and mail delivery, etc. They were not, however, empowered to discuss the resolution of the border issue, which remained in the remit of the Special Representatives.

Later that year, in September, the two countries announced that they would resume joint military exercises after a four-year gap. The decision was announced following talks between Indian Defence Minister A.K. Antony and his Chinese counterpart General Liang Guanglie, who became the first Chinese defence minister to visit India in eight years. The process hit another minor bump when, in January 2012, India called off the visit of a 30-member military delegation to Beijing, after it had refused to issue a visa to a senior Indian Air Force officer who hailed from Arunachal Pradesh.

In November, there was another contretemps when the Chinese began issuing passports where on the eighth page there was a watermark map of China which depicted most of South China Sea as part of China, as well as the territory disputed with India—Arunachal Pradesh and Aksai Chin. Vietnam refused to stamp the passport, while India began stamping its own map on visas issued to Chinese citizens.

In January 2012, at the sidelines of the fifteenth round of the Special Representatives' meeting, the new WMCC was formally inaugurated. This was the last official meeting that Dai Bingguo attended as the Chinese SR, though he and his Indian counterpart Shivshankar Menon met in an informal meeting in December 2012 as well. These meetings were important because Dai wanted to record and summarize the consensus the two sides had reached in their negotiations to establish a framework for a border demarcation. Menon and he sat together and sorted out the consensus points they had arrived at. In his autobiography, *Strategic Dialogues* published in 2016, Dai mentions this fact but provides little or no details as to what those points were. However, during the Doklam crisis, which we will describe in a later chapter, both sides revealed some of these points of agreement they had arrived at.

In May 2013, just after the termination of the Depsang crisis, which will be described in the next chapter, Wei Wei, the Chinse ambassador in New Delhi, wrote that in the Special Representatives talks since the 2005 Political Parameters agreement the two sides had "reached an 18-point consensus on the resolution framework."[27] As much as was confirmed by Shivshankar Menon in an interview in 2015 after he retired. He said that by 2012, the two sides had reached a point where the only thing missing was the political will to settle the boundary issue. "We have done whatever technical work has to be done.... We have brought it to a point where we know what our respective stands are...Now it is a question of a political decision."[28]

One of the pieces of prescient advice that Dai had in his overview, at the end of the chapter dealing with India, was that "in the current stage, before the final settlement of the border issue, the two sides must have good border control, and make sure that there are no border skirmishes."[29]

That's the advice that seems to have been ignored by the Chinese side after his retirement.

7

FOUR TENTS, NINE MEN AND A DOG

The incident that took place in the Depsang Plains in the spring of 2013 was a curious one. The region lies at the very northernmost end of the Sino–Indian border, adjacent to Aksai Chin. It features two bulges, one into Indian territory in the area adjacent to the Chip Chap river, which, in a sense creates a bulge south of that into the Chinese-held Aksai Chin. Bulges are always the fodder for war planners, and so are these. Both sides try to equalize the bulges by pushing them back and this makes for a fraught situation. (See Map 4)

At mid-morning on 15 April, an Indian observation post detected a group of Chinese personnel headed into the Indian side of the Line of Actual Control (LAC). This was not unusual: there were, as we have pointed out, many places along the LAC where the border was really marked by a Line of Perception—the Chinese had one and the Indians another. In this case the Lines of Perception had been some 10–15 km apart.

The Chinese patrolled to their line and the Indians theirs. By agreement neither side could build structures or camp in this area. The Depsang Plains, some 900 sq. km in size and at an altitude of 16,000 ft (5,000 m), lie between high mountains on the Indian side and the Laktsang range in the east, adjacent to which runs the Chinese Aksai Chin Highway (G-219). To its north is the undisputed Sino–Indian border point—the Karakoram Pass, and to the south a knot of mountain territory which includes the Galwan river, the site of the June 2020 incident.

To their surprise, the Indians were confronted by something unusual next morning. The Chinese had pitched tents and had not gone back. Neither did they do so the day after. Their encampment, comprising four tents, some nine men and a dog, was 19 km inside the Indian perception of the LAC. And while Chinese patrolling in the area was not unusual, their establishing a camp there was. And soon we had a full-blown crisis in hand. New Delhi immediately ordered the Indo-Tibetan Border Police to advance up to the Chinese positions and also pitch their tents there. They set up their encampment of eight tents eyeball to eyeball with the Chinese. Both sides displayed banners advising the other side to pull back because they were on the other's side of the LAC.

This area is clearly sensitive for both India and China and has long been fought over by India and China. In the case of India, it abuts its northernmost post of Daulat Beg Oldi which was just about 30 km away. For the Chinese the flat terrain provides no easily defensible obstacle till the Laktsang range, 40 km to the east, and that much closer to the 219 Xinjiang–Tibet Highway. Not surprisingly, the Chinese side denied that they had crossed the LAC. The official spokeswoman of the Foreign Ministry, Hua Chunying, declared that the Chinese patrol had not gone across the LAC "by even one step." As per protocol, the Indian complaint triggered meetings at the official level and the Indian External Affairs Ministry called in the Chinese ambassador to protest.

The genesis of the deployments of the two sides here goes back to the 1962 war. The Indian official history of the 1962 war recounts that the 14 Indian posts spread out from the mountains north of the Chip Chap river and the Depsang Plains to it south near the Jeong Nala were wiped out in a matter of days. And the remaining posts in DBO, Track Junction and Sultan Chushku abandoned.[1] It is perhaps not a coincidence that the most serious Chinese action in 2020 is the blockade of Indian patrols in the the the Depsang plains. More than a decade after the war New Delhi reasserted the claim to the southern part of this area and established PP 10, 11, 11A, 12 and 13 as its patrollling route.[2] This seems to confirm the belief in some circles that the Chinese are belatedly seeking to re-establish themselves to the points they had reached in 1962.

According to Major General P. J. S. Sandhu, who has edited a study of the war from the Chinese point of view, in the western sector their aim was to remove 43 Indian posts out of 72, which they felt were on their side of their 1960 claim line. He has cited a Chinese Central Military Commission (CMC) directive of 14 November 1962 ordering the PLA to strictly limit their attack to the 1960 claim line. Even returning Indian fire from across that line required the approval of the General Headquarters.

But, in the Depsang Plains and the Chip Chap river valley, after eliminating more than a dozen Indian posts, they did not go back to their claim line, but occupied additional territory. The problem, he says, was that the Indians had withdrawn all along the line, even from positions that had not been attacked since they were mainly there for showing the flag and not for fighting. Even the Daulat Beg Oldi post, which was "neither attacked, nor contacted by attacking troops, was abandoned."[3] But subsequently, while the Chinese maintained their hold along the Chip Chap river, in the southern part, the Indians began to once again patrol to the limits of their 1962 claim.

The site of the PLA encampment of 2013 had been carefully chosen. It lay on the banks of a rivulet called Raki Nala, south of the Chip Chap river, at a point 7 km north-west of the Burtse camp from where paths branched out to the north and the south where lay India's Patrolling Points (PP) 10, 11, 11A, 12 and 13 that indicated the limits of patrolling for Indian border forces. For historical reasons, this 20-odd km frontage was actually short of the LAC which was several kilometres further east. Within the Indian military and border police establishment, this was known as the Y-Junction or Bottleneck. As the name suggests, the Chinese blockade effectively prevented India from patrolling a large part of its claimed LAC. (See Map 4)

This is an area where the Indian-claimed LAC bulges out eastwards covering an area of some 900 sq. km. Equally, from the Indian point of view, it is a Chinese bulge westward where the Chinese-claimed LAC comes within kilometres of the Darbuk-Shyok Daulat Beg Oldi (DS-DBO) road.

Chinese pressure had been steadily building up in this area. In September 2008, the PLA carried out several patrols there and dismantled the Indian patrol hut at Y-Junction and destroyed the stored rations and fuel there. This action was repeated in May 2009 and June 2009 when they penetrated even further in and destroyed rations and construction material at the Burtse patrol base.

On 18 April 2013, Indian and Chinese military officials met at Chushul-Moldo, near Pangong Tso and Spanggur lakes, where they usually held their flag meetings. The Indian side told the Chinese that they were in breach of the various agreements in setting up camp at the Y-Junction. For their part, the Chinese produced a map, which was attached to the 15 November letter of Zhou Enlai to Afro-Asian leaders. This is essentially a sketch map, but even a glance at it will show that it is not useful in explaining the Chinese case, considering its scale.

At this point came a riposte intended to convey its own message. Some 800 km down the LAC, is a place called Chumar, at the point where the Indian state of Himachal Pradesh meets Jammu & Kashmir. On 18 April the Indian Army put up a tin shed at a Patrolling Point overlooking the Chinese side of the LAC, and since the Chinese have claims in the Chumar area, and a structure was on the LAC, it drew their attention. (See Map 1)

The Indian ambassador to China, S. Jaishankar, had been discussing the Depsang issue with the Chinese foreign ministry official responsible for the border, Deng Zhenghua. As soon as the shed came up, Deng protested to Jaishankar who told him that he had no mandate to discuss Chumar. The issue on hand, from India's point of view, was the Chinese encampments in the Depsang area, which constituted a change in ground positions there.

The official Indian position was restrained. Prime Minister Manmohan Singh said that this was a localized situation and talks were on to resolve it. External Affairs Minister Salman Khurshid compared the incursion to acne that would vanish after an ointment was applied to it. But the Opposition raised a huge alarm accusing the government of complacency and inaction.

The Chinese move was somewhat puzzling. Relations between the two countries were good. In 2012, China had emerged as India's largest trading partner with trade touching USD 66 billion. Even more curious was the timing of the incident: a little more than a month later their new premier, Li Keqiang, was to visit New Delhi for his first official foreign visit after having been appointed in March as prime minister of the PRC in the annual session of China's parliament, the National People's Congress (NPC).

This was the same NPC that had formalized the appointment of Xi Jinping as president. Five months earlier, at the 18th Party Congress in

November 2012, Xi had been elected General Secretary of the Communist Party of China. His meeting with Indian Prime Minister Manmohan Singh in Durban at the sidelines of the BRICS summit on 27 March 2013 had gone well. Speaking to the media after the meeting, Xinhua quoted Xi as saying that on the border issue "China and India should improve and make good use of the mechanism of special representatives to strive for a fair, rational solution framework acceptable to both sides as soon as possible." That phrase "as soon as possible" was new and seemed to presage something.

A little earlier, on19 March, speaking to reporters in Beijing, Xi had reeled off the standard formulation that the boundary question was left over from history and its resolution would not be easy, and in the meantime, the two sides should maintain peace and tranquillity in the border areas.

The Indians were perplexed by these statements. But they were clear that the Li visit would not go through if the situation in Depsang remained deadlocked. Perhaps the Chinese had calculated that India would not publicize the incident, which was in a remote area far from the prying eyes and ears of the media. Instead, the Indian media, obviously briefed by the government, went hammer and tongs on the issue. Whatever be the case, the ball was in the Chinese court.

Beijing's message was soothing. The foreign ministry spokeswoman, Hua Chunying, had to bat questions on the issue repeatedly. Her basic response was that "China-India relations are in good shape," that the border problem was something left over from history, and since it was not demarcated, there were bound to be situations like the current one. But, she maintained, there was adequate communication on the issue between the two sides, and existing mechanisms were being deployed to deal with it. She maintained that there had been no violation of existing agreements and that the Chinese forces scrupulously patrolled only their own side of the LAC.

Initially, on 22 April, the Chinese rejected reports that the PLA had even set up a tented post in the Indian territory. This was probably a technical sleight of hand, since China claimed that area and, in their view, it was their territory. On 25 April, the Ministry of Defence in Beijing made their first comment on the issue in response to questions from an Indian newspaper. They said that the PLA had not violated

any bilateral agreements. They blamed the row for differing perceptions of the LAC and ignored the query as to why a tented post had
been set up.

At the 23 April border meeting, the PLA sought a deal. They would
back off if India stopped its infrastructure development work in the
Daulat Beg Oldi area, the construction of bunkers near the reactivated
advanced landing ground at Fukche, near Demchok, and dismantled
the shed put up in Chumar. Now the message became clear. By their
action in Depsang, which they knew would get India's attention, they
were signalling that Indian border construction was the issue causing
them a lot of concern. Implicit in their message was the view that in
the current circumstances, because of their better infrastructure, they
had a dominating position along the Line of Actual Control and they
wanted India to cooperate in ensuring that things remained that way.

There was therefore concern at the tone and tenor of the freewheeling Indian media. In an editorial the CPC daily, *Global Times*,
excoriated them saying that it was difficult to ignore "their malicious
impact." The editorial wanted the government of India to clarify the
situation, namely, acknowledge that both sides patrol their claimed
borders. But there was no reference to the changed nature of the current intrusion.[4]

For its part, India sought to dampen some of the more exaggerated
reporting. On 25 April, Prime Minister Manmohan Singh played
down the situation saying it was a "localized problem" and that talks
were on to resolve it. External Affairs Minister Salman Khurshid, too
felt that it was best left to the local authorities and that he would step
in, if needed. In two weeks, on 9 May, Khurshid was scheduled to
travel to Beijing on an official visit, but there were hints that it could
be called off if the problem was not resolved. The Chinese said the
next day that they had taken note of the PM's statement and that, in
any case, the two sides had been in communication through border
meetings and diplomatic channels such as the Working Mechanism
for Consultation and Coordination (WMCC) on boundary affairs.

With the Chinese premier's upcoming visit looming, the Indian side
refused to blink when, in the 30 April meeting at Chushul-Moldo, the
PLA attacked India for breaching the agreement in Chumar. Then
three days later, the tone suddenly changed. They called the Indian side

for an unschedulled border meeting and said they would be willing to disengage unconditionally, although there was an unstated understanding that the Indians would dismantle the shed in Chumar after the Chinese broke camp and returned to their side of the border in Depsang. The agreement was activated the very next day on 6 May.

What was remarkable in hindsight, is that the face-off did not escalate at any stage. From the outset, the two sides established tented camps on two sides of the Raki Nala, but there was no belligerence; indeed, the two sides even shared tea with each other and no weapons were brandished. Instead, the mechanisms worked out in the confidence-building measures kicked in, especially the WMCC that had been set up in 2012, and which handled the prolonged negotiations between the two sides which led to its resolution. But it was a warning bell, considering that it was clearly initiated by a violation of the 1993 BPTA, and the most serious incident since the Sumdorong Chu incident of 1986–1987.

A paper by Isabelle Saint-Mézard in 2013, amongst other things, compared the Indian and Chinese reactions to the incident. The Indian response was low profile, with ministers and the prime minister himself playing down the incident. That could not be said of the media, which went into a frenzy following the report of the intrusion on 20 April. In contrast, notes Saint-Mézard, in China there was "silence and opacity." There was outright denial that the incident had taken place at all since the position was that China always upheld the LAC's sanctity. No official explanation of the incident was made available. In the paper, which was written after interviews in Beijing, Saint-Mézard says that this in part reflected the Chinese assigning a low priority to ties with India. It also marked a deterioration in the manner in which the two sides viewed each other. And, in the ultimate analysis, it revealed that the effort to put aside the dispute and develop normal ties had been "played out and revealed its limitations." In other words, the border had returned to centre stage in Sino–Indian relations.[5]

As events were to prove, Saint-Mézard's analysis was prescient.

In the immediate aftermath of the incident on 13 May, Director General of the Information Department of the Chinese Ministry of Foreign Affairs Qin Gang was in New Delhi to prepare for Li's visit. He told reporters that the Depsang incident was an "isolated" event and that there was need now to "redouble efforts to push forward negotiations for a framework agreement on the boundary settlement."

Writing at the end of the month, a Chinese scholar, Liu Zongyi, noted that the two countries had a "competitive symbiotic relationship." The economies of the two countries complemented each other, but India and the US were moving closer together because of the mistrust engendered by "the Indian mass media and some strategic Indian scholars." As for the recent standoff in Depsang, Liu noted that despite the hype, "China would not wish to provoke simultaneous conflicts with Japan and China." He was referring to the developments in the Senkaku/Diayou Islands arising out of the Japanese nationalization of the islands in December 2012 and the Chinese creation of an Air Defense Identification Zone (ADIZ) in November 2013.[6]

After the standoff, India redeployed and created a new patrol base at the Y-Junction to be semi-permanently occupied. Yet in 2015, a Chinese patrol came up to the old patrol point but went back after Indian troops raised a banner asking them to do so. Later in August, they bypassed the Indian post and came to 1.5 km short of Burtse. They pitched a few tents and held up banners saying, "This is Chinese territory, go back." They were there for some 24 hours and returned, indicating that this was a flag-showing expedition, rather than something more serious.

The Border Defence Cooperation Agreement

Since mid-2005, India and China had been having an annual defence cooperation dialogue. At the annual dialogue in January 2013 China had formally mooted the idea of a freeze or limits on the troop levels on the LAC. The two sides had also discussed other suggestions for keeping peace along the LAC, such as avoiding tailing the other side's patrols, avoiding night patrols, having more flag meetings between local commanders and so on.

Then, a month before the Depsang incursion in early March, visiting Lt Gen. Qi Jianguo had come with a draft Border Defence Cooperation Agreement (BDCA) which he presented to the Indian side, incorporating these proposals and calling for a freeze in current troop levels on the border. India did not quite reject the freeze idea, it merely conveyed to the Chinese side that it was studying the proposals. At this time, the prospective Li visit had not materialized, since the NPC was yet to formally elect him prime minister.[7]

There was a feeling on the Indian side that the Depsang episode was aimed at signalling the PLA's seriousness about the need for a BDCA. Since the mid-2000s, the Chinese would have known that India had been trying to build its DS-DBO road. Despite a major setback when poorly sited sections of the road were washed away in 2012, the Indians had renewed their efforts.

With the Depsang incident behind them, relations between India and China picked up pace again. At the end of June 2013, the National Security Adviser, Shivshankar Menon, visited Beijing for the sixteenth round of the Special Representatives' talks, described as "productive, constructive and forward looking." The new SR was a contrast to Dai, who did not have much diplomatic experience, whereas Yang Jichei had been ambassador to the US and spoke fluent English having begun his career as an interpreter.

Among the things that Menon raised with Yang was the need to clarify the Line of Actual Control (LAC) to prevent the Depsang-like developments. In previous years, the Chinese would reject this request saying that India was trying to use this clarification issue to fix the *status quo* on the border permanently. This time, however, they said they would examine the issue.

In early July, Defence Minister A. K. Antony followed Menon to Beijing for the first visit by an Indian defence minister in seven years, which was described *pro-forma* perhaps, as "cordial and friendly." A future course of bilateral joint exercises and exchanges was worked out, as was the decision to go ahead with the Border Defence Cooperation Agreement. Given the bonhomie, it was not surprising that, later in July, Chinese Foreign Minister Wang Yi said that the two countries were truly "natural strategic partners" after his meeting with his Indian counterpart Salman Khurshid at Bandar Seri Bagawan, at the sidelines of the ASEAN Regional Forum meeting.

Military-to-military ties between the two countries were thus also doing well. Indeed, even while relations became tense in April because of the incursion, a delegation of Indian military officers had spent several days in China on a scheduled visit to coordinate arrangements for a joint defence exercise expected to be held later in the year. The exercise, called "Hand-in-Hand," was held in November near Chengdu, the headquarters of the erstwhile Military Region. The theme of the exercise was counter-terrorism, something that both could live with without too much of a difference of opinion.

A week earlier, in October 2013, on the occasion of Prime Minister Manmohan Singh's visit to China, the two sides signed the Border Defence Cooperation Agreement that the PLA had been pushing for. It was signed by India's defence secretary and Admiral Sun Jianguo, Deputy Chief of General Staff of the PLA. This was the first, and so far only, Sino–Indian agreement which was directly signed by the PLA from the Chinese side and the Ministry of Defence on the Indian. From the Chinese point of view this was not an issue since the PLA did border management. But in the Indian system, the ministry for dealing with foreign countries was the Ministry of External Affairs and it is rare for the MOD to get involved in such matters.

The new and operative part of the agreement was that "they shall not follow or tail patrols of the other side" in areas where there was no common understanding of the Line of Actual Control. Each side had the right to seek clarification about activities in such areas through the various military-to-military dialogue mechanisms. Article IX said that if the forces came face to face with each other in the disputed areas, both should exercise self-restraint, "not use force or threaten to use force against the other side."

This agreement was a marginal advance on previous ones because the main Chinese goal of getting some kind of a freeze on border construction activity had not been conceded by India. Now the Chinese started pursuing that goal through a call for the two sides to conclude a Code of Conduct which would codify a whole range of behaviour and activity, not just the LAC but the border zone as such. Given that past agreements were often being honoured in their breach, shifting goalposts in this way was a tactical move whose aim was to confuse, even while continuing to (a) block movement on a boundary settlement and (b) gain advantage on the border, especially in the west.

The Indian side, too, kept sending its own signals that it was not about to give way easily. At the end of November 2013, President Pranab Mukherjee visited Arunachal Pradesh and hailed the importance of the state to the country's "Look East" policy. The Chinese response was not long in coming and foreign ministry spokesman Qin Gang criticized the visit and urged India to avoid actions that might further complicate the boundary issue.

Meanwhile, lacking the wherewithal to directly take on China, India reached out to important friends like Japan and the US. Shortly after Li Keqiang's visit, in late May, Manmohan Singh travelled to Japan where he received a warm welcome from his counterpart Shinzo Abe. The Japanese had been wooing New Delhi ever since the 2005 anti-Japanese demonstrations in China which Tokyo had no doubt had official sanction. Japanese Official Development Assistance (ODA) to India, as well as private investment, had steadily grown in the ensuing decade and by 2013 India had become its largest recipient. The two countries began with collaboration between their coast guards and then held a joint naval exercise in June 2012. In 2013, Abe and Singh agreed to enhance the frequency of such exercises as well as begin a maritime dialogue. Under its laws Japan could not offer either nuclear or conventional military technology to India, but an effort was initiated to set up the manufacture of the US-2 amphibian aircraft in India to service its navy and maritime interests.

Ties with Washington were also enhanced, if only incrementally. Following an official visit to Washington in September 2013, India was put in the category of "closest partners," a footing that was said to be not dissimilar to that occupied by UK with regard to defence technology exports. A Joint Declaration on Defence Cooperation worked up an ambitious agenda for the two countries to collaborate on technology transfer, trade, research and co-development. The two sides also announced India's participation in the Rim of the Pacific (RIMPAC) naval exercise in 2014.

More important, the government clearly understood that things had changed on the Sino–Indian border. So in July 2014, they approved the creation of a Mountain Strike Corps that would strengthen India's military posture along the Line of Actual Control. Comprising some 40,000–60,000 personnel, the corps would have formations along the LAC and its purpose was, as its name suggested, offensive. For the first time the Indian Army mooted a capability which would be premised on the possibility of launching an offensive across the LAC with China.

163

We referred earlier to the mid-2000s apex-level Operational Directive that the army had got from the political leadership ordering them to prepare for a "two-front collusive threat" from Pakistan and China. Since it is a secret guidance its details have never been revealed. But with the approval of the Mountain Strike Corps, the intention became obvious: India would acquire a capability of launching offensives against both Pakistan and across the LAC against China. The Indian plans to acquire US-made heavy lift aircraft and helicopters and M-777 ultra-lightweight howitzers were linked to this goal.

Providing crucial muscle to this strike corps would be two new armoured brigades, one to be deployed in Ladakh, near Chushul, and the other near Sikkim. It was clear, of course, that these deployments would be premised on the development of roads and other infrastructure which could support the movement of armour.

Election time in India

At this time, India was expecting to hold its next general elections in mid-2014. Domestic political temperatures were already rising as Narendra Modi began to emerge as the BJP's prime ministerial candidate against a Congress Party-led government which was already looking shaky. In early September 2013, a week or so before Modi was formally anointed as the BJP's prime ministerial candidate, a controversy arose over a report by former foreign secretary Shyam Saran on the border in eastern Ladakh. Between 2 and 9 August 2013, Saran, now chairman of the National Security Council's advisory board, had visited Ladakh and given the government an overview of the progress in infrastructure construction projects which he had advised on earlier as foreign secretary and then prime minister's special envoy. Because it was near election time, a report, formally denied by the government, gained currency that the patrolling points in the Depsang region, which had been set a few kilometres to the west of the actual LAC, had now become the LAC itself as the Chinese had moved westwards to dominate the area. As a result India had lost 640 sq. km of area in the LAC in the recent months.

This was an explosive revelation, especially with the general elections due in seven months; predictably the Opposition latched on to the issue. Defence Minister A. K. Antony made a formal statement in parliament:

"I would like to state categorically that Shri Shyam Saran has not stated in this report that China has occupied, or has denied access to India to any part of Indian territory." He said that the thrust of the report was the progress in development of the border infrastructure required "to ensure the connectivity between Ladakh and neighbouring areas."[8]

The controversy related to what we have depicted in Map 4. We noted that the Indian patrolling was done along the tracks between Patrolling Points (PP) 10, 11, 11A, 12 and 13. But as the map shows, the LAC lies generally some kilometres to the east of these tracks. What Saran had said in his report was that there was some risk that the patrolling point path could become a *de facto* LAC, if the Indian personnel did not visit the areas of the LAC which by the Indian reckoning were several kilometres to the east of the line of patrolling points.

Even as election fever rose in India, the two countries held several important meetings. First, on 10 February, was the meeting of the Working Mechanism for Consultation and Coordination (WMCC) on the India–China boundary affairs, the body comprising the key desk officers in the respective foreign ministries. This fifth meeting reviewed the developments on the Sino–Indian border, especially Ladakh. It also discussed the implementation of the Border Defence Cooperation Agreement and additional measures to maintain peace and tranquillity on the border.

The same evening, the two Special Representatives met for the seventeenth round of their dialogue. This would be the last round in which Shivshankar Menon participated with his Chinese counterpart Yang Jichei. In the sixteenth round, both sides had put forward their respective frameworks for the border settlement; this time they examined them in detail. The stumbling blocks remained—China saying that they needed concessions in the east, essentially the Tawang tract, for a workable deal. As to the Code of Conduct, the Indian side told the Chinese that they were supportive of any move that would enforce predictable behaviour on the border and ensure that things did not get out of hand.

Modi in command

This was general election time in India and many of the issues, such as the "lost 640 sq. km" were grist for the election mill. Reports of transgressions, too, tended to get played up. In the May elections, the Bharatiya Janata Party led by Narendra Modi came to power and former police and intelligence officer, Ajit Doval was appointed National Security Adviser. A few months later he was also designated the Special Representative for relations with China.

In June, shortly after the Modi government took office, Chinese Foreign Minister Wang Yi arrived in New Delhi as a Special Envoy of President Xi. He was uncharacteristically forthcoming to the media. He told reporters at the end of his two-day visit: "Through years of negotiation, we have come to an agreement on the basis of a boundary agreement, and we are prepared to reach a final settlement." The Chinese saw an opportunity in India for their companies dealing with infrastructure. Wang characterized India "as a massive buried treasure waiting to be discovered." His discussion with India's new External Affairs Minister Sushma Swaraj focused on the possible increase of Chinese investments, including a possible "Chinese" industrial park in India. What Beijing was looking for, he told his Indian counterpart, was an easing of Indian trade rules.[9] Clearly, the Chinese saw the arrival of Modi in New Delhi as a huge opportunity both on the political and business front.

There was considerable speculation about the positive tone of Wang's remarks towards India. Some observers believed that with China dialling up tensions with Japan, Vietnam and the Philippines on territorial disputes along its eastern coastline, Beijing was seeking to ensure that its western flank remained quiet. But, as we will see, this was not quite the case.

The July 2014 meeting between the newly elected Indian Prime Minister Narendra Modi and Xi at the sidelines of the BRICS summit in Fortaleza, Brazil went off well. A news report said that the two met for 80 minutes, beyond the 40 minutes scheduled. The Chinese agency Xinhua said that Xi had called for "a negotiated solution to the border issues at an early date." In turn, Modi had responded that maintaining peace and tranquillity on the border was important and incidents there should not be allowed to undermine relations. Clearly what Xi, and earlier Wang, were talking about, was resolving the issue on Chinese terms, which meant India conceding Tawang to China. As this was simply not feasible from the Indian point of view, New Delhi was keener to prevent the kind of incidents that had happened the previous year in Depsang.

Within months, the Indian fears proved to be correct when there was a spate of incidents on the Ladakh border. These, curiously, began just before Xi Jinping arrived in India for a state visit in September 2014 and continued through the visit. According to *The Times of India*, responding to a question in parliament in August, the Union Home Ministry said that there had been no "intrusion" into the Indian side of the LAC since 2010. However, it said some "transgressions" had occurred, presumably the patrolling by the PLA of areas along the LAC disputed by both sides. Indeed, it said some 1,612 "transgressions" had occurred, 334 cases till August 2014, 411 in 2013, 426 in 2012 and 228 in 2010.[10]

We need to be clear that the Indian side's reportage would be mirrored by similar complaints by the Chinese of instances of Indian incursions/transgressions, had the Chinese media operated in the same freewheeling style as the Indian media. In 2020, former Army Chief V.K. Singh created a brief flurry when, in exasperation, more than anything else, he declared that India had transgressed more times than China along the LAC. "Let me assure you," he told the media in the southern Indian city of Madurai, "if China has transgressed 10 times, we must have done it at least 50 times."[11]

As India's infrastructure had improved, the army had also rejigged the internal protocols of its formations, asking them to conduct more vigorous patrolling. Where some patrols were going just once a week, they were now going daily and as a result were intercepting similar PLA patrols, well before they came deeper into the Indian side of the LAC in disputed areas. At the same time they were also entering the area that the Chinese had considered theirs for a long time. Besides, both sides now also had set up surveillance devices and optronic equipment to keep an eye on the other side in certain sections of the border.

Call them what you will, but the intrusions/transgressions did not end with the May 2013 agreement. A new problem area had actually already appeared in Chumar in southern Ladakh at the time. (See Map 1) In December 2013 some 22 PLA personnel pitched tents in the Chepzi area, near Chumar in south-eastern Ladakh, and left only after a flag meeting. In March 2014, some 20 PLA soldiers came into the

Indian side of the LAC in Chumar, but Indian border guards formed a chain to block them. In June, there were reports of Chinese boats entering the Indian side of the Pangong Tso, being confronted by Indian boats and asked to go back, as per the banner drill. In July 2014 there were reports of PLA incursions in other parts of southern Ladakh, in the Demchok areas, as well as near Charding La. Some of these were simply shepherds from the other side bringing their flocks and camping on the Indian side. But other actions were official and deliberate.

Xi comes to New Delhi

The chain of events that put the disputed border on the front burner during Xi Jinping's first visit to India in September 2014 began in August when India started building an irrigation canal in Demchok, as part of a rural employment guarantee scheme. Local officials in the Demchok area complained that Chinese officials were blocking the construction of the canal 600 metres from the LAC. The chief district official at Leh confirmed this and said that whenever the workers went to work on the canal, the Chinese civilian officials stopped them. In this area, both sides used their civilians for making the point about their claim, and keeping their respective armies behind the civilians. The Chinese ferried their civilians in PLA trucks and encouraged them to pitch a camp in the area to prevent work on the irrigation channel.

Then, further south, on 8 September, Indian border guards resurrected the old observation hut that gave them an overview of the Chinese positions in Chumar. The disputed area there is in a 14,000 ft (4,250 m) high bowl accessible easily from the Indian side, but with some difficulty from the Chinese. From a high point, India is able to observe Chinese movements easily. They had earlier maintained a post with optronic sensors to monitor Chinese movements but this equipment had been destroyed once by the Chinese, and the post itself was dismantled as part of the 2013 settlement.

Almost immediately, some 200 PLA troops with road-building equipment arrived in the area to build a 5-km road towards Tible, a little short of Chumar, which is a high point where they could put up their own observation post. Indian border guards confronted the Chinese and late in the night they demolished some 20 metres of the new track the Chinese had laid.

By the time Xi landed in India, 1,000 Chinese troops were facing off against an equal number of Indians in the area. Despite two flag meetings, one of them a 12-hour marathon, efforts to resolve the issue proved fruitless. The Indians wanted the Chinese to back off and destroy the road they had already made and the Chinese side wanted the structure the Indians had at the observation point dismantled.

In the run up to Xi's visit, the media narrative had been focusing on resetting the Sino–Indian relationship under two strong leaders. Press reports had spoken of the prospect of massive of Chinese investments worth tens of billions of dollars coming into India and Chinese expertise being used to modernize Indian Railways and help build Indian infrastructure. Modi, who had visited China several times as chief minister of Gujarat, was seen as a leader who would focus on economic growth and provide Chinese businesses opportunities.

A Chinese columnist Qian Feng wrote in the *Global Times* on 18 September, the day Xi landed in Ahmedabad, that Modi's decision to receive Xi in his home state and on his birthday was unprecedented in India's diplomatic history and evidence of the new style, where personal relationships between leaders were a factor in building mutual trust. He welcomed the "much more flexible and pragmatic policies that have been adopted" by the Modi government to promote Chinese investments and boost economic and trade cooperation.

But from the Indian point of view, the Chumar incident became the story, rather than the Sino–Indian bonhomie. The incident had been immediately brought to the attention of President Xi by Prime Minister Modi in Ahmedabad in Gujarat where he began his official tour on 18 September. On day two of Xi's visit, the issue was discussed by India's Foreign Minister Sushma Swaraj with her Chinese counterpart Wang Yi, who was part of Xi's delegation. It was also discussed at the official talks in New Delhi, and thereafter the two armies pulled apart a bit, and began to communicate with each other through loudspeakers.

According to reports, Modi took up the issue of the incursions with Xi, who assured him that he had conveyed the concerns to Beijing, and expected it to be acted upon. Reportedly, Xi said that the PLA transgression was a small incident, to which Modi riposted that "a tooth ache was a small thing, but it could paralyse the whole body."

The Chinese foreign ministry spokesman in Beijing, Hong Lei, said with "immediate and effective communication" the incident had been "effectively controlled and managed." On the ground, however, nothing had changed. Just what Hong meant by "effectively controlled and managed" was not clear.

In subsequent conversations, public and private, with the Chinese leaders, Modi picked up a theme which he repeated thereafter. This was on the importance of clarifying the Line of Actual Control as early as possible so as to prevent these incidents.

On 18 September, speaking at the joint press conference in New Delhi after the official delegation-level talks, Modi said India attached great "importance and priority" to relations with China and referred to the importance of China in his development plans. Then, he came to the border issue:

> I raised our serious concern over repeated incidents along the border. We agreed that peace and tranquillity in the border region constitutes an essential foundation for mutual trust and confidence and for realizing the full potential of our relationship... While our border related agreements and confidence building measures have worked well, I also suggested that clarification of Line of Actual Control would greatly contribute to our efforts to maintain peace and tranquillity and requested President Xi to resume the stalled process of clarifying the LAC. We should also seek an early settlement of the boundary question.[12]

The Chinese would have been chagrined by Modi's direct style which was quite a contrast to his predecessor Manmohan Singh's approach. But Xi did not take the bait. All he said was that "the border has yet to be demarcated, sometimes there may be incidents but both sides are capable of handling the situation with border mechanisms so that these don't have a large impact."[13]

According to a Reuters report, the issue was also taken up in their official talks, where both sides traded charges: the Indians said that the Chinese had "transgressed" across the LAC 334 times in 2014, while the Chinese insisted that the Indians had done so 410 times.

What Modi said sounded reasonable and appropriate to the fact that China had, after all, committed itself to clarifying the Line of Actual Control in the BPTA, as well as the agreements of 1996 and 2005. But, surely by now, the Indians should have gotten the message: the Chinese were not interested in clarifying the LAC because differences over some portions of the LAC were a useful instrument of China's border policy.

India had, after all, a very well defined and delimited Line of Control (LoC) with Pakistan, and yet, that was a "live" line that had over the years featured bombardment, machine gunning and the cross-border activities of jihadi warriors. There was no doubt about the clarity as to where it lay. Had Beijing wanted a stable LAC, they could have ensured one since the areas of contention were fairly insignificant unlike, say, the South China Sea where it was about fisheries, oil and the freedom of navigation.

Notwithstanding the contretemps on 18 September, Xi gave a lengthy speech at the Indian Council of World Affairs, New Delhi. He took the high road to speak of the "joint pursuit of a dream of National Renewal" where he referred to the connections between ancient China and India. He spoke of their potential partnership and the need to tap their "complementary advantages" and the need for China's westward opening up linking with India's Act East policy. Given the context, observers drew significance from his reference to China as always having been a peaceful nation and going by its ancient belief that "a warlike state, however big it may be, will eventually perish." The boundary issue, he said, was left over from history, a standard Chinese formulation. Both countries were seeking a "fair, reasonable and mutually acceptable solution at an early date through peaceful and friendly consultation."[14] Clearly the sense of urgency evident in Modi's remarks at the joint press conference earlier was absent here.

His words were echoed by the Ministry of Defence spokesman in Beijing on 22 September. In the first comments since the issue cropped up, he said that this problem was left over from history, and the two sides had differing perceptions of the LAC. But, he insisted, Chinese troops had "always strictly observed the relevant agreements signed by the two countries" and the issue could be resolved through dialogue and consultation.

It was only a week after Xi had returned to Beijing on 25 September, that the two sides agreed to pull back their forces from the face-off point in Chumar and go back to the positions they held as of 10 September, and both sides agreed to not carry out any construction in the disputed area. The withdrawal would take place in four phases. A decision was also taken not to patrol that area for some time. Echoes of this agreement were to be heard in 2020 as well.

A large part of the above is the Indian narrative of the Xi visit, seen through the eyes of the Indian and international media. But a look at Xinhua's round up of the Xi tour brings an alternative context. First, the visit was seen as part of a larger set of visits to South and Central Asia, where India was a major stop, but there were also important stops in Sri Lanka, the Maldives and Tajikistan. There was a tone in the report which suggested that the visit was not about India, but China's larger Asian policy.

Second, the visit was also to be viewed through the new lenses of the Belt and Road Initiative (BRI) that Xi had inaugurated during a visit to Kazakhstan, a year earlier. At the time, India's opposition to BRI had not shaped up, and so Chinese Foreign Minister Wang Yi who briefed the media on the tour had no hesitation in stating that all four countries were "pivot points." Third, the visit was seen as part of the commitment to the Shanghai Cooperation Organisation (SCO) whose summit Xi had attended in Tajikistan. It was at this summit that the proposal for enlarging the SCO by including India and Pakistan was first mooted.

The report on the Indian leg of the visit was more than upbeat. Wang said the visit had propelled the development of ties "into a new historic phase." India clearly understood the importance of the relationship with China for its own development. As for the border, the two sides had reaffirmed the need to properly manage and control the border disputes "and find a [permanent solution] at an early date."[15]

India and China had in the meanwhile quietly agreed on a mutual pull-back in Chumar on September 25. Speaking to Indian media personnel in Beijing, Senior Colonel Geng Yangsheng, the spokesman for the Ministry of Defence, said that things had been brought under control and "the Sino–Indian border has regained peace." He repeated the stock phrase of the problem being left over from history and said since the border was undemarcated, it was "only natural that sometimes the two countries run into some problems."

We may wonder about just why the Chinese side did what it did. Why seemingly undermine its own president's visit to another country? But a former intelligence analyst, D. S. Rajan, has pointed out that intrusions/transgressions have been associated with previous visits of Chinese and Indian leaders to each other's countries. Thus, there was a 6-km incursion into Himachal Pradesh two months after Jiang

Zemin's visit in December 1997. When Prime Minister Vajpayee was in Beijing, a Chinese patrol came in to the Asaphi La area in the upper Subansiri district of Arunachal, one of the eight areas where its LAC and that of India overlap in the eastern sector. This area was again visited by Chinese forces just after Wen Jiabao's visit to New Delhi in April 2005. And, of course, there was the incursion which we described above in Depsang, just before the Chinese premier's May 2013 visit. Rajan's explanation was that the Chinese wanted to apply pressure in relation to the boundary issues, as well as signal that China would remain uncompromising when it comes to its core issue of territorial sovereignty.[16]

On the other hand, surveying the issue from the Chinese point of view, Senior Colonel Zhou Bo, an officer at the Academy of Military Sciences, actually saw in the Sino–Indian experience a guide as to how Japan could resolve the Senkaku/Diayou issue with China. According to the senior colonel, that India and China had problems on the LAC was not unexpected since it had no clear alignment. What was important was that despite a few stand offs, there had been no bullets fired across the border. This he said was on account of the agreement between the two countries "that the border issue is not the be all and end all of bilateral relationship." The Chinese and Indian experience was that "territorial dispute is a political issue that needs to be discussed at the top political level."

Second, political guidelines required "confidence building measures to back up," like the 1993 BPTA and other agreements that the two countries had signed. Third, dealing with territorial disputes required "patience and perseverance." He concluded that the best way was that of the ASEAN where differences were resolved "through consensus and patience."[17] There seemed to be an almost hubristic belief that given the succession of border management agreements, China could somehow avoid substantive decisions on the Line of Actual Control, such as indefinitely putting off efforts to clarify its location, without having to pay a price.

Though one part of the standoff related to the disputed border, there was also an emerging and larger geopolitical dynamic shaping up. This was manifested by Prime Minister Modi's signalling in choosing to make his first extra-regional tour to Japan, some weeks before Xi coming to Delhi. He was feted by Shinzo Abe who committed Japan to even greater efforts in providing India with public and private funding for development. Japan lifted a ban that had been in place on exports to six Indian entities after the 1998 nuclear tests. In a move aimed at derailing Chinese expectations, the two sides also agreed on a project to build a Japanese Shinkansen bullet train corridor to link Gujarat's premier city Ahmedabad with Mumbai. Later, in October, Japanese Foreign Minister Fumio Kishida created a minor stir when in New Delhi he termed Arunachal as "an Indian territory which is disputed by China." The Japanese minister backed off somewhat in the face of Chinese protests.[18]

Another signal had come earlier, at the time of Modi's inaugural as the prime minister at the end of May 2014. This was the invitation to Lobsang Sangay, the head of the Central Tibetan Administration, popularly known as the Tibetan-government-in-exile, which operated from the Himalayan town of Dharamshala, where the Dalai Lama also resided. This invitation could not but have rankled Beijing.

Then, days before Xi was to land in India, the Indian president made an official visit to Vietnam. Though the itinerary for the visit had been firmed up well before the Xi visit was scheduled, media commentary made much of the visit. Vietnam, which has problems with China in the South China Sea, was increasingly seen in New Delhi as part of a regional coalition that could help balance China.

Despite all this, the trendline of Sino–Indian relations remained positive. In February, External Affairs Minister Sushma Swaraj was in Beijing to participate in the trilateral Russia-India–China summit. But she also had occasion to call on Xi Jinping and have a bilateral meeting with her counterpart Wang Yi. She told reporters that one of her tasks was to set the stage for the first official visit of Prime Minister Narendra Modi in May 2015. In a statement there she explicitly declared that "my government is committed to exploring an early settlement [of the border issue]. She pointed out that both countries now "have strong leaders. They are also keen on an out-of-the-box solution."[19]

Modi goes to China

Modi certainly took an "out-of-the-box" approach when he met Xi in Xian at the opening leg of his first visit to China as prime minister in

May 2015. This was meant to be the ceremonial entry, much like the way Xi had visited Ahmedabad before the working leg in New Delhi in 2014. According to knowledgeable sources, Modi decided that he would confront the Chinese head on on the border issue and lectured the Chinese leader on the various obstacles to better Sino–Indian relations, principally the lack of clarity at certain points along the Line of Actual Control that marked their border. He picked up the theme which he had first explicated when Xi was in Ahmedabad and New Delhi. This was that the two countries should move fast to clarify the LAC so as to prevent the repeated incidents that had been taking place. The Chinese were livid and thought Modi was being presumptuous by bringing in this item that was not in the agenda in Xian. So Xi refused to respond substantially to Modi's vociferous arguments about the need to fix the border issue.[20]

More important, Modi and his advisers misread the Chinese on the issue. As we have indicated earlier, Beijing was not really interested in a well defined LAC. Its interests are better served by a situation where they could periodically stir up things at the LAC on account of the differing perceptions in some places, in keeping with its larger policy of dealing with India, which included the strategic support to Pakistan.

In Beijing, formal talks were held between Modi and Premier Li Keqiang and their delegations. In these talks, reportedly, Li threw cold water on the notion of clarifying the Line of Actual Control saying that this would complicate matters, rather than resolve them. But he, like most Chinese interlocutors, did not specify as to how exactly clarification of the LAC would "complicate" things. But Modi was not about to be fobbed off. He took the occasion of his public speech at Tsinghua University to return to the subject. After speaking about the range of past and future issues that bound China and India together, he brought upfront the subject that he said led to "hesitation and doubts, and even distrust, in our relationship." This was the issue of the boundary, which "we must try and settle…quickly." He said the two countries had been remarkably successful in maintaining peace and tranquillity through agreements and mechanisms. "But, a shadow of uncertainty always hangs over the sensitive areas of the border region." This was because "neither side knows where the Line of Actual Control is in these areas." For this reason, he said, "I have proposed the process of clarifying it."

The Chinese were not amused. Three weeks after the visit they trotted out a relatively junior official, Huang Xilian, the Deputy Director General in the Asia Department and the man responsible for India in the foreign ministry, to say that Beijing was opposed to restarting the clarification process. This, he told a group of visiting academics, would be "a stumbling block" in the resolution of the boundary question itself and would actually aggravate the situation, rather than narrow the differences between the two sides. He said the two sides had tried some years back to do so but "encountered some difficulties which led to an even more complex situation." Asked what those difficulties were, he sidestepped to say: "Those details are beyond my remit."[21]

Huang, instead, put forward the other proposal that Beijing had been advocating after the BDCA of 2013. This was for a Code of Conduct which would not be simply "one measure to control and manage the border" but a comprehensive set of them.

Considering that the two countries had multiple agreements—1993, 1996, 2005 and 2013—which catered for a range of issues relating to the Line of Actual Control, it was not clear as to what the Chinese were advocating. But it had been evident, even at the time the BDCA was being discussed, that what the Chinese really wanted was a halt on India's border construction which would, in turn, freeze China's dominance of the Sino–Indian border. However, the reality was that the Indian efforts had, if anything, intensified, as projects conceived in the mid-2000s began coming on stream and the Modi government began to step on the gas in relation to border construction.

* * *

In 2016, India took significant steps to build up its forces along the LAC. In places, with additional manpower available, it bulked up its border posts from platoons (some 30 personnel) to companies (120 or so personnel). In Ladakh, a regiment of tanks (52 in number) was deployed in 2014, another in late 2015, and a third was sent in mid-2016 constituting an entire brigade. Three regiments of the Indo-Russian Brahmos supersonic cruise missiles with 100 missiles each had been deployed in the eastern sector beginning 2015 and an additional unit was authorized in 2016. This riled the Chinese, who felt that India had "exceeded its own needs for self-defense and poses a serious threat to China's Tibet and Yunnan provinces."[22]

Even so, at the time, there were significant gaps in India's connectivity. It lacked a road to its strategically important outpost at Daulat Beg Oldi, around 10 km short of its northernmost point, the Karakoram Pass. The road from Tawang in Arunachal Pradesh to the Bum La pass to the north, which marks the boundary with China, was a single potholed track where vehicles took 3 hours to cover 30 km where it faced a region serviced by a four-lane highway on the Chinese side.

In 2016, however, the border remained relatively quiet. Sino–Indian issues played out in other theatres—trade, terrorism, diplomacy and geopolitics. A major issue was China's refusal to accept India within the Nuclear Suppliers Group (NSG). As part of the Indo-US nuclear deal, India had got all the privileges of being an NSG member in terms of civil nuclear trade. But it hankered for the status of being a formal member as well, and China blocked every move in that direction. As recounted earlier, Beijing had tried its best to scuttle the waiver that the NSG had given India on the issue that mattered—civil nuclear trade.

A second issue was in placing the Pakistani terrorist Masood Azhar, head of the Jaish-e-Muhammad (JeM) organization, on the list of terrorists under the UN Security Council Resolution 1267. The list' originally aimed at Al Qaeda and the Taliban placed leading terrorists under sanctions. The JeM, as a group, had been sanctioned back in 2002, but India wanted Azhar, whose organization conducted strikes against India, to be named. This was symbolic, because Azhar lived in Pakistan under the protection of its powerful army, just as the other sanctioned terrorist leader Hafiz Muhammad Saeed of the Lashkar-e-Tayyeba did. But China blocked the move and continued to do so till 2019.

In response, as it were, India continued to find ways to irritate the Chinese. In 2016, New Delhi permitted the US ambassador to India, Richard Verma, to visit Tawang monastery. China accused the US of sabotaging "the hard-won peace and tranquillity in the China-India border again."

In January 2017, the Dalai Lama met Indian President Pranab Mukherjee in the Rashtrapati Bhavan (presidential palace). Though the visit was in the context of another function where he had been an invitee, it was obvious that the invitation had been approved by the government.

Then, in April 2017, the government permitted the Dalai Lama to visit the monastery town of Tawang in Arunachal Pradesh again. This was, to resort to the overused cliché, "the red rag to the bull." His visit was seen as a deliberate provocation of China by India. The Chinese foreign ministry said that the visit would "gravely damage peace and stability of the border regions between China and India, and China-Indian relations." Later they added that by permitting the visit, the Indian side had "violated its commitment on Tibet-related issues, and escalated the boundary dispute."

But New Delhi had, on occasion, second thoughts over playing its Tibet card. In 2016, the government of India abruptly withdrew the visa issued in Germany to Uighur leader Dolkun Issa to attend what would have been a conference of China dissidents in Dharamsala, the headquarters of the Tibetan government-in-exile. "I am not [Masood] Azhhar," protested Issa in an interview to *thecitizen.in*, a news website, after being denied the visa. While the conference had been organized by a US-based Chinese dissident organization, a senior ruling party leader was alleged to have been pushing it, with the covert support of the government.

The last visible play of the card was when, in July 2017, while the Doklam crisis was at its height, New Delhi permitted Lobsang Sangay, the head of the Tibetan government-in-exile, to stage a photo-op, with a Tibetan flag at the Pangong Tso lake, two-thirds of which is in Tibet. Initially the Central Tibetan Administration said that he had "unfurled" the flag on the Indian side, but later said that he had merely paid his respects to an already unfurled flag that had been pitched there by a Tibetan settled in the area since 1989.[23]

Despite all this, it later transpired that the Indian side had actually discouraged a meeting of Xi Jinping with the Dalai Lama. Sonia Singh, a TV anchor, quoted the Tibetan spiritual leader in her book, *Defining India Through Their Eyes*, saying that "in 2014, when Chinese President Xi Jinping visited Delhi for talks with Prime Minister Modi, I requested a meeting with him. President Xi Jinping agreed, but the Indian government was cautious about the meeting, so it didn't happen."[24]

The facts were somewhat more complicated. The government formally asked the Chinese side as to whether President Xi wished to meet the Dalai Lama, who said that there were no plans for such a meeting. The Indian side tried to push the envelope a bit by telling the Chinese that they would not need government of India permission to arrange a meet. They could simply invite him over to the embassy.

Truth be told, the Dalai Lama was somewhat eager to meet the Chinese leader since he had had an association with his father, Xi Zhongxun and had even presented him with a gold watch which the senior Xi occasionally flashed around. Also it was known that Xi Jinping's mother had been a devout Buddhist. The Dalai Lama said he had been receiving messages through various intermediaries from Xi saying that the latter wanted to bring about reconciliation that could lead to the Dalai Lama's visit to China and Tibet. The Indian assessment was that these messages had probably been deliberately floated to mute the Tibetan community's criticism of China during Xi's September 2014 visit.

Belt and Road Initiative

Yet, on the surface, things seemed to be on an even keel between the two countries. Xi had announced the huge Belt and Road Initiative(BRI) in 2013 aimed at redesigning overland trade and maritime routes to serve China's longer term geopolitical and geo-economic plans. India soon began to feel the pressure of the BRI in its own South Asia-Indian Ocean Region (SA-IOR). By now, China was already a major commercial player and a significant supplier of military equipment to Pakistan, Sri Lanka, Bangladesh and Myanmar. It had already built Hambantota port in Sri Lanka, Gwadar in Pakistan and it now began stepping up its footprint in SA-IOR, something that India considered its backyard. Beijing boosted its commitment to Pakistan by proposing a sub-set of the BRI called the China-Pakistan Economic Corridor (CPEC) which went through a part of Kashmir claimed by India and held by Pakistan. It began a phase of investment in roads, railways, pipelines, ports, terminals and so on in Sri Lanka, Nepal, Bangladesh, Myanmar and Maldives in South Asia, as well as the Middle East and East Africa.

There was no way that India could match the kind of resources that the Chinese were putting into their foreign economic policy. Not surprisingly, then, New Delhi became an early critic of BRI. The Indian view was put across by then Foreign Secretary S. Jaishankar at the Raisina Dialogue in New Delhi in March 2016 when he declared: "The key issue is whether we will build our connectivity through consultative processes or more unilateral decisions. ... we cannot be impervious to the reality that others may see connectivity as an exercise in hard-wiring that influences choices."[25]

India had specific concerns about the CPEC and the fact that the Karakoram Highway and many planned investments would take place in what New Delhi says is Pakistan-occupied Kashmir. By 2017, India had sharpened its critique of the BRI and, in rejecting an invitation to the first BRI forum in Beijing, New Delhi said that "connectivity initiatives must be based on universally recognized international norms, good governance, rule of law, openness, transparency and equality." Further, they must follow principles of financial responsibility and not create "unsustainable debt burden for communities."

For many of the smaller South Asian countries, Chinese investment was a no-brainer since they were unlikely to get the kind of money they needed from the multilateral investment banks. An added bonus was that it helped them to balance the Indian salience in the region. China may not be repaid many of the loans, but that is probably taken for granted because many of the investments are meant to achieve its strategic goals.

Just how this works became apparent with the increased Chinese maritime activity in the Indian Ocean Region (IOR). This was a natural outcome of the enormous expansion of the Chinese economy and the growth of its interests in the Indian Ocean littoral. But equally naturally, the flag started following the trade, and soon an increased number of PLA Navy (PLAN) movements in the Indian Ocean began to create unease in New Delhi.

China had been active in the multinational mission to fight Somali piracy in the north-western Indian Ocean beginning 2008. The PLAN used this as a huge learning exercise and, by the end of 2018, it had sent some 31 escort fleets and 100 ships to the region to help escort over 6,600 Chinese and foreign ships.[26] Piracy has faded away, but as of 2021, the missions continue, providing far seas experience for the PLAN.

More alarming for India was the unfolding of a 2004 hypothesis of a US consulting company which said that the Chinese would establish their naval presence in the IOR by first developing civilian maritime infrastructure. Given the geography, it soon began to appear that this was a "string of pearls" around the Indian peninsula in Myanmar, Sri Lanka, Pakistan, Bangladesh, Maldives, Tanzania and Somalia. Many were seen as potential military bases. The first phase of the Hambantota port at the southern tip of Sri Lanka was completed by 2010, and that of Gwadar, at the head of the strategic Hormuz Straits, even earlier in 2007. But both ports were commercial lemons and, in 2013, a Chinese company was given the contract to run the port at Gwadar. The same thing happened in Hambantota when in 2017 a Chinese company was given a 99-year lease to run the port because the Sri Lankan government was unable to service the debt it had built up in building the port. Despite having a "friendly" government in Colombo, New Delhi was unable to influence the decision.[27]

New Delhi woke up to the maritime dimension of the problem when in March 2014 a Type 093 Shang class Chinese nuclear submarine conducted a patrol across the Indian Ocean to the seas of Somalia, allegedly on an anti-piracy mission. "Allegedly" because submarines are not the best vessels to counter pirates with. In November that year, a Chinese submarine docked in Colombo port, seven weeks after another submarine had called on the same port, a little ahead of Xi Jinping's visit to Sri Lanka in the tour that had also brought him to India.

The submarines stopped calling after the 2015 election of Maithripala Sirisena as President of Sri Lanka. Reportedly, India played a significant role in getting him to defect from the ruling party to lead the Opposition alliance against the Rajapakse's United People's Freedom Alliance Party.

What happened next in 2017 was, perhaps, linked to China's continuing efforts to make inroads into India's traditional backyard in South Asia. Of all India's neighbours, it was closest to Bhutan, whose eastern and western flanks are vital for Indian security. This was also a country where the Chinese had little presence and leverage. It was in the extremely sensitive western side of the country that trouble broke out in mid-2017. The Sino–Indian border dispute had effectively spilled over to tiny Bhutan.

8

DOKLAM

In the long history of border face-offs between India and China, the one that occurred in Doklam, in the western trijunction of the China–India–Bhutan border stands out. This is because the border disputed was not between India and China, but between Bhutan and China. Why India got involved had to do with Indian security concerns, as well as its relationship with Bhutan, which is amongst the closest it has with any country.

As the crisis unfolded what became apparent soon enough is that the issue of determining Bhutan's boundary with China, remains inextricably linked to that of the Sino–Indian boundary dispute though New Delhi may exercise lesser agency with Thimphu than could be expected. In retrospect, the Doklam incident appeared to be an effort to shake Bhutan loose from its close embrace of India, something that has been determined more by geography than anything else.

The Doklam issue came up suddenly in June 2017 without much of a preamble. The public would only get a hint of the crisis on 23 June, when newspapers reported that China had abruptly closed the Nathu La pass, the traditional route between India and Tibet and which was now also being used by Hindu pilgrims travelling to the sacred sites of Kailash and Manasarovar. According to the reports, Chinese officials had claimed that there were landslides in the mountain areas on their side. The reports cited the Indian official spokesperson confirming this development, saying that "the matter is being discussed with the Chinese side." (See Map 8)

This was a surprising development. Between 7 and 10 June 2017 the Shanghai Cooperation Organisation (SCO) had its seventeenth annual summit in Astana, Kazakhstan. On the agenda was the acceptance of India and Pakistan, who had been observers till now, as full members of this Beijing-helmed organization. In his briefing on the Xi–Modi meetings at the sidelines of the summit on 9 June, Indian Foreign Secretary S. Jaishankar said that the basic thrust of the meeting was that "at the time of global uncertainty, India–China relations are a factor of stability and as the world becomes more multipolar it was important for India and China to work together more closely." Further, Jaishankar used a phrase that has been heard often since, that the two countries had an understanding that their "differences should not become disputes," and indeed, if they were handled well they "could even be opportunities."

But a week later this narrative came apart. The real story of the closure of the Nathu La route became apparent soon enough when the Chinese official spokesperson Geng Shuang acknowledged on 26 June that the yatra (pilgrimage) was indeed barred from the Nathu La route due to "security concerns." The official said: "Recently, the Indian border troops crossed the China-India boundary at the Sikkim section and entered the Chinese territory, obstructing Chinese border troops' normal activities in Doklam. The Chinese side has taken proportionate measures in response." He pointed out that there was no dispute with India on the Sikkim part of the Sino–Indian boundary which had been defined by the Anglo-Chinese Convention of 1890 and which had been "repeatedly" confirmed by India.[1]

Soon, the real story emerged. Some time on 16 June, a PLA construction party of around 80 people, and ten or twelve bulldozers, arrived at an area adjacent to the Indian military post in Doka La pass overlooking the Doklam plateau which is disputed between Bhutan and China. New Delhi, of course, recognized the territory as belonging to Bhutan. This party began constructing a road moving towards a Royal Bhutan Army (RBA) post 4–5 km away, on the edge of the Doklam plateau, which is marked by the Zompelri (Jampheri) ridge. The RBA personnel made a futile effort to stop them on the basis of a 1998 Chinese commitment to Bhutan to maintain the *status quo* in disputed areas.

It is not known whether the Bhutanese communicated with the Indians, but two days later Indian Army personnel stationed at Doka La pass descended on the site with their own bulldozers, and blocked the Chinese team from moving forward. The Chinese say they were surprised since they had informed the Indian military that they would be upgrading their jeepable road that ran from the Chumbi valley, over the Sinche La pass, to the foot of the Doka La pass in Doklam. (See Map 7)

Subsequently, the matter was taken up at the diplomatic level and also discussed at a Border Personnel Meeting at Nathu La on 20 June. And so began one of the more serious crises between India and China on their border.

India has no claim on the territory south of Batang La, though it believes that the trijunction of the Tibet–Sikkim–Bhutan border is located next to it. And leading from that it believes that the boundary goes along the watershed to Merug La, Sinche La and then down to the Amo Chu or Mochu river. Therefore it believes that the territory to the south of that line, which is the Doklam plateau, belongs to Bhutan. But China has insistently contested the Bhutanese claim because they put the trijunction several kilometres south at Gyemochen/Mount Gipmochi; as far back as 2005, they moved across the Sinche La pass and built a jeepable road into Doklam, which terminated at a point below Doka La pass where the Indians had a strong entrenchment along the ridge. This was the "turning point" where Chinese vehicles would come across the Sinche La and turn back after sending foot patrols to the Zompelri ridge, just 3 or 4 km ahead on foot.

Why did India act as it did? As we will see, the Bhutanese position on the area called Doklam evolved somewhat slowly and tentatively. But, by this time, they had a full-fledged claim over the area, including a post on the Zompelri ridge, at the southern edge of the plateau facing India. However, they lacked the capacity to patrol the area and maintained just that one post there. The ridge is like a high shelf looking down on the Indian plains. There was roughly 30 more km (measured as a crow flies) of Bhutanese territory and thereafter is a narrow neck of land in the plains, wedged between Bangladesh, Nepal Bhutan and India, called the Siliguri Corridor. (See Map 8)

This is between 40 and 60 km wide and runs for some 100 km and provides the overland connection between mainland India and its seven north-eastern states. It also has the only road which connects India to China, via the Nathu La pass in Sikkim. Given its location, it could enable Chinese forces coming through Sikkim or Bhutan to block India from its north-eastern states, including Arunachal Pradesh, which is claimed in its entirety by China.

So sensitive is the Zompelri ridge in Indian calculations, that Indian Army war plans envisaged occupying the ridge, were any hostilities between India and China to become imminent. Fortunately for the Indians, they had a dominating position on the ridge flanking the Chinese. All they had to do was to descend just 100 metres or so down the ridge from Doka La and block their path, which they had done, touching off the crisis.

Till this time, the word "Doklam" or "Donglong", as the Chinese termed it, had not had currency in the Sino–Indian discourse. But soon everyone was talking about it. There was confusion as to where it was. Some maps showed it at the western edge of central Bhutan; only later was it confirmed that it was this small area south of the the trijunction of India–China and Bhutan which was disputed by Bhutan and China.

Since the clashes between the Indian Army and the PLA at Nathu La and Cho La in Sikkim in 1967, this border had been relatively quiet. The alignment of the Sino–Indian border in Sikkim had, to a large extent, been accepted by both sides, as per the Anglo-Chinese Convention of 1890 which described the border as running along the "crest of the mountain range separating the waters flowing into the Sikkim Teesta and its affluents from the waters flowing into the Tibetan Mochu and northwards into other rivers of Tibet." Then came the point that the line commenced at Mount Gipmochi, and went north "to the point where it meets Nipal (*sic*) territory." The Chinese spokesperson noted on 5 July: "the 1890 convention stipulates that the Sikkim section of the China-India boundary commences at Mount Gipmochi."[2] As we will see, things were not as simple as that.

The 2017 Doklam crisis unfolds

On 20 June, Bhutan lodged a protest with China through their mission in New Delhi since Beijing does not have an embassy in Thimphu. Six days later on 26 June through coordinated statements by the Foreign and Defence ministries, Beijing confirmed some of what was happening. The first public Bhutanese response came through a 28 June interview of their ambassador in New Delhi, Major-General (retired) V. Namgyel, with *The Hindu*, noting that the road construction was in an area which is disputed between China and Bhutan and was in fact moving towards a camp of the Royal Bhutan Army at Zompelri ridge. He said, "Bhutan has conveyed that the road construction by the PLA is not in keeping with the agreements between China and Bhutan. We have asked them to stop and refrain from changing the *status quo*."

On the same day, 28 June, in Beijing, the Chinese foreign ministry spokesman Lu Kang declared that, "Doklam has been a part of China since ancient times. It does not belong to Bhutan, much less India. That is an indisputable fact supported by historical and jurisprudential evidence, and the ground situation. It is utterly unjustifiable if the Indian side wants to make an issue of it."[3]

The Bhutanese government finally issued an official press release on 29 June upholding Namgyel's remarks. It provided the backdrop to the events:

> On 16th June 2017, the Chinese Army started constructing a motorable road from Dokola in the Doklam area towards the Bhutan Army camp at Zompelri... Bhutan has conveyed to the Chinese side, both on the ground and through the diplomatic channel, that the construction of the road inside Bhutanese territory is a direct violation of the agreements [of 1988 and 1998 on maintaining the *status quo* pending a settlement] and affects the process of demarcating the boundary between our two countries. Bhutan hopes that the *status quo* in the Doklam area will be maintained as before 16 June 2017.[4]

On the last day of June, India issued its press statement. This detailed its version of the facts largely on the basis of Bhutan's actions. It said that acting "in coordination" with the Royal Government of Bhutan, Indian personnel who were in Doka La also "approached the Chinese construction party and urged them to desist from changing the *status quo*." The statement made it clear that the events that had transpired were not only about Bhutan, but "would represent a significant change of *status quo* with security implications for India." This was because the Chinese action had implications for the determination of the trijunction point between India, China and Bhutan and the alignment of the Sino–Indian boundary in the Sikkim sector.

The statement also made a startling revelation that, contrary to what the Chinese were asserting, the India–China boundary here was no longer determined by the 1890 Anglo-Chinese Convention. In 2012, the Special Representative process had reached a common understanding that while there was an agreement on the "basis of alignment" of the Sikkim–Tibet border, "further discussions would have to take place to actually finalise the boundary." Revealing another decision germane to the issue, the statement added that the Special Representatives had also agreed that "trijunction boundary points between India, China and third countries will be finalised in consultation with the concerned countries."[5] As of that point in time there was, in fact, not even a mutually accepted trijunction.

The rhetoric on both sides began to notch up. On 29 June Chinese defence ministry spokesman Wu Qian said in response to Army Chief General Bipin Rawat's comment that India could fight a two-front (China and Pakistan) war while also handling internal security issues, that "Such rhetoric is extremely irresponsible. We hope (the) particular person in the Indian Army could learn from historical lessons and stop such clamouring for war." This was a clear allusion to the 1962 war in which China defeated India.[6]

The Chinese were livid. This was the kind of goalpost shifting they were wont to do and now the Indians were at it. On 3 July, the Chinese official spokesman complained: "As to the statement issued by India's Ministry of External Affairs last Friday (i.e., 30 June), we have noted that this statement completely left out the Convention Between Great Britain and China Relating to Sikkim and Tibet (1890), none other than which clearly defined the China-India boundary alignment in areas where the incident happened."[7] In subsequent remarks, the Chinese spokesperson also weighed in on the Indian side's perfidy in equating the general region Doklam with the trijunction. On 7 July, he said, "The illegal trespass took place at the Sikkim section of the China-India boundary over 2000 metres from Mount Gipmochi [the trijunction point according to the Chinese and the 1890 Convention] and has nothing to do with the trijunction." (See Map 7)

A month later on 2 August 2017, China issued a 15-page document, "The Facts and China's Position Concerning the Indian Border Troops' Crossing of the China-India Boundary in the Sikkim Sector into the

Chinese Territory." A translated version was put out by the Chinese embassy in New Delhi. The document recounted the events and restated the point that the Indian side had violated a border that had been settled by the 1890 Convention, accepted by Prime Minister Nehru and reconfirmed by the Indian Special Representative (SR) in 2006. "The incident occurred in an area where there is a clear and delimited boundary," it declared, rejecting India's contention that the Chinese road building had security implications for India. Equating the Indian intervention to an armed attack, it referred to a resolution by the United Nations General Assembly (UNGA), declaring that no consideration whatsoever can justify "the invasion or attack by the armed forces of a State on the territory of another state."[8]

The Chinese note said that the China–Bhutan boundary issue has "nothing to do with India" and that India's intrusion not only violated Chinese territorial sovereignty, "but also challenged Bhutan's sovereignty and independence." The statement ignored India's point on the 2012 agreements between the two SRs on the final settlement of the trijunction, and the contention that all that existed with regard to the 1890 Convention was "a basis for alignment" not a fixed border. Indeed, the use of the term 'delimited' in the 2 August Chinese note suggested that notwithstanding references to demarcation of the Sikkim-Tibet border in Nehru's letters, the border has only been delimited and has yet to be actually demarcated on the ground through joint surveys, boundary pillars and other markers.

For their part, the Chinese revealed their own take of the SR's discussions when they included a phrase from a 2006 Indian non-paper (a diplomatic note that does not bind the author to the stated position, and is used as a point of discussion) given by the Indians which noted, "Both sides agree on the border alignment in the Sikkim sector." This was not inconsistent with the Indian view that, as of now, the two sides did have an agreement on the "basis of alignment," but not the alignment itself.

Another revelation from the SR discussions appeared to confirm the Indian view that things were not as fixed on the Sikkim–Tibet border as Beijing was claiming. The note said that "The Chinese and Indian sides have been in discussion on making the boundary in the Sikkim sector an 'early harvest' in the settlement of the entire boundary question." Adding that "China and India ought to sign a new boundary convention in their own names to replace the 1890 Convention," though, they did say it would not alter the delimited boundary. This was strange, since there are always minor differences in the delimitation of a boundary and its demarcation on the ground.

Unlike the Depsang issue in 2013, the Chinese did not restrain their media. In early August, Xinhua reported an online discussion that the news agency had put out. The video, made in the talk-show format, titled "Why India is wrong in Doklam standoff with China," was placed on Facebook, Twitter and YouTube and argued that the Indians had been in the wrong in "trespassing" into Chinese territory in Doklam. Reporting 400,000 views, the discussion featured nationals from India, Bhutan, Canada, New Zealand and Pakistan. It was also a hit on the Chinese platforms WeChat and Weibo, according to the report.[9]

There was much greater outrage a few days later when the state-run agency put out a video making fun of Indians racially. It showed a bearded man with a turban with an Indian accent and spoke of Indians having a thick skin and compared India to being a "robber who breaks into a house (Doklam) and doesn't leave."

The Indian media, too, gave it back in kind. There were articles by hawkish columnists, but the incendiary stuff was on the TV where nightly shows excoriated China and had India prevailing in any war. This was the kind of psywar that Beijing has traditionally employed to subdue adversaries without fighting. A former foreign secretary Kanwal Sibal was quoted as saying that China "barks a lot but is careful about who to bite." He discounted Chinese threats, saying that the Chinese will be taking a huge risk in taking military action because it cannot repeat 1962.

In mid-August, the tensions spilled over to the Pangong Tso area where a Chinese patrol, which may have lost its way in the bad weather, was intercepted by the Indian border troops. The two sides began shouting at each other and this escalated to throwing stones that led to injuries to some of the soldiers in the melee. As we have seen, face-offs had been aplenty in the Pangong Tso area along with instances of pushing and shoving; now stones were used for the first time. In this case, after half an hour or so, the two sides broke off.[10]

As for the other main party in the issue, Bhutan, its media was relatively quiet. It provided straightforward reportage. The *Kuensel*, the

Bhutanese state-owned newspaper, had reported the Bhutanese foreign ministry statement of 29 June.[11] The next day it also reported the Indian official statement and pointed out that Doklam was one of four disputed areas between China and Bhutan in the western region of Haa and Paro districts of Bhutan.[12]

Tangled boundary

Bhutan was not party to the Anglo-Chinese Convention of 1890 and cannot really be bound by its wording that the trijunction must be at Mount Gipmochi. Basing themselves on the intent of the treaty, which was to have the border along the watershed, Bhutan and India have placed the trijunction about 7–10 km north at a point near Batang La pass. Till a Sino–Indian or Sino–Bhutanese boundary is settled, the trijunction will be indeterminate. Actual surveys showed that the true water-parting between the Teesta and the Mochu runs from Batang La to Merug La, Sinche La and then down to the Amo Chu or Mochu river which is also known as the Torsa river.[13]

As M. Taylor Fravel has noted, the problem began with the 1890 Convention trying to square the circle. On one hand, it said that the border began at Mount Gipmochi, on the other it also said that the boundary would follow the watershed. But Gipmochi was not the beginning of the watershed and the British themselves printed maps in 1907 and 1913 showing the border beginning from Batang La. Both sides have chosen the starting points of the border as per their interest, but the letter of the treaty, and its intent, has left room for conflict and confusion.[14] The Indians put the trijunction at a point near Batang La while the Chinese put it at Mount Gipmochi, also known as Gymochen, some 7 km to the south. This location of the trijunction course made the key difference in relation to Doklam.

There was much confusion about the location of the points in the 1890 treaty which was not accompanied by any map. There was a problem in even locating Mount Gipmochi to start with. Many old maps showed the beginning of the border from a place called Gyemochen. Indeed, the Bhutanese themselves noted, as revealed in the records of the 82nd session of their National Assembly, that "the Chinese had been going from Gyemochen and Chela to Amo Chhu."

Gyemochen is mentioned in a 1937 Survey of India map and a 1955 US military map. A British map of 1923 mentions the same feature of 14, 518 ft as "Gipmochi." And a 1910 map also mentions a place called Giaomochi, but shows the trijunction around Batang La.[15]

The conclusion could well have been that Gipmochi and Gyemochen are the same place. But that did not originally seem to be the case. An authoritative database on geonames maintained by the US Geospatial Intelligence Agency showed Gipmochi/Gyemochen at two locations 5 km apart. Till mid-July 2020, at least, the website of the US agency showed only one location of Gipmochi/Gyemochen, which was near a feature called Elephant Lake, some 4 km, or so, east of its actual location. Once the crisis developed, those who maintain the website shifted the location to the right place. Now, as of 2021, the entire reference is missing.[16]

What really emerges here is the difficulty of relying on an 1890 convention for modern-day boundaries, based on possibly flawed surveys that may have taken place in the early part of the twentieth century in a mountainous and inhospitable region. And the confusion has been compounded by various maps published, some showing the trijunction at different places.

India and China are agreed on following the watershed principle for delimiting their boundary in this area. But to have done so in Kolkata in 1890, relying on maps alone, was an imperfect process. It has to be done through a joint process that involving ground surveys, delimitation on maps and then surveys and demarcation on the ground. However, all that was here were some cairns in northern Sikkim, which have been the source of friction between India and China.

Himalayan history

The relationship between China and Himalayan states like Nepal, Bhutan, erstwhile Sikkim is a complex one. At various times Chinese writing and commentary has seen these states as being part of China. The reason is that Nepal has once been a tributary of China, and Sikkim and Bhutan have been under the sway of Tibetan Buddhism. Indeed, Nirupama Rao has recounted an instance when as a prelude to their discussions over the 1954 Agreement, the Chinese authorities demanded that the Tibetans detail any engagement they may have had with the British Indian government. They were presented with the original copy of the map of the McMahon Line initialled by the Lonchen Shatra and Sir Henry McMahon, as well as another Tibetan map which was a hand-drawn one depicting the mountains and rivers but no coordinates. The map claimed all territories north of the Ganga river as Tibetan![17]

With China declaring its intention of annexing Tibet in 1950, a recently independent India moved to assume the role of a successor state to the British and signed treaties with Bhutan in 1949, Nepal and Sikkim in 1950. In Sikkim, India inherited arrangements through which it dealt with Sikkim's external affairs, defence, diplomacy and communications. From the Chinese point of view, the border with Sikkim was settled. So there were no operations there in 1962. But the state had a significant presence of the Indian Army.

Eventually, India annexed Sikkim in 1974. This was an outcome of several factors: the incompetence of its ruling king, Palden Thondup Namgyal, fears relating to the activities of his American wife Hope Cooke, and domestic political dissensions connected to the relationship between the Nepali majority and the native Lepcha people of the state. An Indian covert operation eventually tipped the balance and ensured that not only was the monarchy overthrown, but a proposal for the merger of the kingdom with India was won by an overwhelming majority. Sikkim's location makes it obvious as to why this happened. It is bordered by Nepal, China/Tibet and Bhutan and separated from Bangladesh by a narrow neck of land, the Siliguri Corridor.[18] (See Map 8)

In the case of Bhutan, under the 1949 treaty India agreed not to interfere with its internal affairs, while it would continue to "guide" it on matters of foreign policy. Incidentally, at this time, one of the easiest ways of reaching Bhutan's capital, Thimphu, was through Sikkim and Tibet. When Jawaharlal Nehru visited the country in 1958, he took the route from Nathu La pass in Sikkim, through Yatung or Yadong, in the Chumbi valley and received full protocol as a foreign prime minister from Chinese officials seeing him off at the posts in the flanks of the valley.

Like the Sino–Indian border, the entire Bhutan—China border is also disputed. Significant Chinese claims vary from several points in western Bhutan, to some regions of the north, and, a more recently asserted claim to a large chunk of eastern Bhutan. (See Map 9)The problem for the tiny Himalayan kingdom is that, unlike its neighbourhood, it is not very populous with just some 750,000 people in an area of 38,394 sq. km—a little smaller than Denmark but with one-seventh of its population. The result is that its state capacity to police its disputed borders is limited, as has been evident over the years when it has dealt with China.

Bhutan as buffer: A brief history

The Sikkim-Tibet border, as we noted, was defined through the Anglo-Chinese Convention that was signed in Kolkata in March 1890. Bhutan was not party to this agreement, nor was Sikkim or Tibet; the agreement was solely between two empires—the British and the Qing. The Tibetans refused to implement the convention and for this they were punished when Sir Francis Younghusband, using the Jelep La route in southern Sikkim, went through the Chumbi valley to storm Lhasa in his 1903–1904 expedition.

The hapless Dalai Lama sought the aid of the Chinese emperor and later, another convention was signed between Great Britain and China in Peking in 1906, to confirm China's "suzerainty" over Tibet, in exchange for a number of rights for the British in Tibet. Many have accused the British of selling out Tibet to the Chinese out of their desire to prop up the already tottering Qing, with a view of blocking the Russians.

In the wake of this development, in 1907 the British encouraged the emergence of the Kingdom of Bhutan under a hereditary king and recognized it through a 1910 treaty, and brought it under its own "suzerainty." Bhutan was shaped to be a buffer between India and Chinese-controlled Tibet. It was in 1954 that China first published a map claiming large areas of Bhutan. Following the Tibetan revolt of 1959, China seized a number of enclaves held by Bhutan in western Tibet, near Lake Manasarovar.

In 2007, the 1949 India–Bhutan treaty was upgraded and the new treaty replaced the provision requiring Bhutan to take India's guidance on foreign policy by a broader phrase saying that they "shall cooperate closely with each other on issues relating to their national interests." Further, that "neither government shall allow the use of its territory for activities harmful to the national security and interest of the other." This was the clause that was invoked for India's actions in 2017.

Bhutan, as noted earlier, was not party to the 1890 convention and has not ratified it in any form. In fact, the original survey of the Bhutan boundary and the first official map of Bhutan was made only in 1961–1963 with the help of the Survey of India.

The Bhutanese monarchy has been sensitive to Indian security concerns and went out of its way in undertaking military action to root out a clutch of Assamese separatist groups who had made their base in its southern jungles in December 2003. As Bhutan slowly opened up to the world and democratized, India has kept a wary eye on it. This was evident in 2013, when New Delhi created conditions that led to the defeat of the incumbent prime minister, Jigme Thinley, because he was seen as cosying up to China.

An official map of Bhutan was drawn up through their own surveys in the mid-1980s that was approved by the sixty-eighth session of the National Assembly in 1989. Simultaneously, they engaged India and China in border talks to resolve outstanding issues. The Bhutan–India boundary was delineated in 1963, and by 1971 the demarcation was done with the boundary pillars established. Of the mosaic of 62 maps (minus the two trijunctions), 47 maps were signed immediately, but it took further discussion for the remaining 15 maps to be approved in 2005–2006.[19] However, the resolution of the China–Bhutan boundary has turned out to be more complex.

The Bhutanese decided to hold boundary talks with China in 1980 and in preparation, began gathering material from their own archives, as well as those available in India and the UK. Data on the Royal Bhutan Army patrolling limits, administrative limits and local practices were also ascertained. It was only after this process that the Bhutanese established their claim lines that were plotted on the map that was approved by the members of the sixty-eighth session of the National Assembly in 1989. In the process, Bhutan voluntarily shed territory, though its details were not immediately disclosed. For example, older maps showed Kula Kangri mountain and its surrounding areas in the north within Bhutan, but the new one showed them clearly in Tibetan/Chinese territory.

As Medha Bisht has noted, boundary negotiations between Bhutan and China over their 470-km border took place in three phases—the first, started in 1984, was the "engagement phase"; the second (1996) was the "redistribution phase" in which China offered a package to Bhutan; and the third (2000) was the "normalisation phase" in which Bhutan also advanced its claims.[20] The first five rounds were spent on finalizing the guiding principles and the two sides signed the Guiding Principles on the Settlement of the Boundary issues in 1988. Substantive talks only began in the sixth round in Beijing in 1989 when Bhutan presented its official map to China.

In the seventh round of talks in 1990, the Chinese had offered the Bhutanese a "package proposal" for the Pasamlung and Jakarlung valleys, with a total area of 495 sq. km in the north, if Bhutan conceded the 269 sq. km of their western claims. (See Map 9) This proposal was rejected by the National Assembly, and subsequent sessions of the assembly, too, indicated opposition for any kind of an exchange.[21]

There were two reasons for the Chinese to make this offer. The first was that it would secure the strategic Chumbi valley by widening it. But more important was the fact that it would give them a crucial observation platform to overlook one of the most sensitive parts of India.

There are, however, indications that in the tenth round of talks in 1995, the Bhutanese were ready to strike a deal with the Chinese. This can be gleaned from the king's statement to the seventy-third session of the National Assembly in August–September 1995, which said among other things that the differences in claims have to be negotiated in four areas only—the 89 sq. km of Doklam, 42 in Sinchulung, and 138 in Dramana-Shakhatoe, all totalling 269 sq. km in the west. At the same time, "the northern boundary will be successfully demarcated through the process of friendly dialogue."[22] It needs to be kept in mind that at the time Bhutan was an absolute monarchy and the National Assembly's role was purely advisory.

When the two sides met for the eleventh round of talks in November 1996 there were expectations that an agreement would be signed but "to China's surprise, Bhutan revised its claims in the south and asserted a claim to larger territory than before, leading the talks to break down." There is no doubt that China saw an Indian hand in this development and so Beijing reverted to its earlier stance of calling for an exchange of claims.[23]

It was not just the Indian hand; a National Assembly session report suggests that the deal would not have been popular within Bhutan. As one of the ministers pointed out during the session, the Chinese were offering to conduct the exchange with what were essentially Bhutanese lands. In 1997, the king told the seventy-fifth session of the assembly that the two sides were back to discussing the exchange of the 495 sq. km of the Pasamlung and Jakarlung valleys in the north, with the western claims, that included the 89 sq. km of Doklam.[24]

China and Bhutan now tried to stabilize the situation through an agreement on the "Maintenance of Peace and Tranquillity on the Bhutan—China border," signed in December 1998. Clause 3 of the document specifically noted, "Both sides agreed that prior to the ultimate solution of the boundary issues, peace and tranquillity along the border should be maintained and the *status quo of the boundary prior to March 1959 be upheld*, and not resort to unilateral action to alter the status quo of the border" (emphasis added). This is why in 2017 Bhutan accused China of violating the agreement not to alter the *status quo* on the Sino—Bhutanese border, including Doklam.

After Bhutan reverted to its 1989 claim line at the fourteenth round of talks in November 2000, it also extended "its claim line beyond what the Chinese had offered so far." This was in the Doklam, Sinchulumpa (sometimes written as Sinchulung) and Dramana area. This was a decision taken by the council of ministers who felt "that the earlier agreement was not acceptable to Bhutan and felt that some changes had to be made in the claims."[25]

The proceedings of the National Assembly did not always catch the nuances of the debates within Bhutan and the border talks. As Thierry Mathou wrote, citing the Bhutanese newspaper *Kuensel*, that despite the kerfuffle over Bhutan's shift in the previous round, in the fifteenth round held in Thimphu in December 2001, Chinese Vice Foreign Minister Wang Yi had said at the time that "the boundary issue had, by and large, been resolved."

The following year, however, Foreign Minister Jigme Thinley told the National Assembly that the Chinese had produced new "documentary evidence on the ownership of the disputed tracts of land." The report also said that the Chinese had asked the Bhutanese as to why they were raising new issues after many years of talks. Clearly, the new issues had to do with Doklam.[26] India's response to these developments is not known.

In the fourth session of the new parliament of Bhutan on 4 December 2009, a report on the China–Bhutan border negotiations was presented to the house by Dasho Pema Wangchuk who, for a long time, was the Secretary for International Boundaries. In the question and answer session, there were complaints that had echoed over the years of the activities of the PLA, the Tibetan grazers and medicinal herb collectors who were looking for the highly priced cordyceps, a parasitic fungi which is supposed to have medicinal properties.

Dasho Pema said that the Chinese had on various occasions offered concessions from their own claim line, but, he noted somewhat disarmingly, "We do not know where the line will fall as the Chinese maps and our maps are different in scale, names of places, rivers, passes and ridges are also different." He explained that the Bhutanese government had protested twice in 2008 and five times in 2009 about the road constructions, in addition to protests over 21 PLA incursions in 2008 and 17 in 2009. In any case, Dasho Pema said, parliament decided that the border talks should continue to be held on the basis of the 1989 claim line.

It was in the same meeting that Dasho Pema also disclosed, in response to a question about Kula Kangri mountain in the north being shown as part of Tibet, that "due to cartographic mistakes of the map in the olden days" the mountain was shown in Bhutan whereas it was actually "well inside Tibetan territory." This had deducted a significant chunk of the original Bhutanese claim.[27] (See Map 9)

The last major information about the Sino—Bhutanese negotiations came from the sixth session of the first parliament held in November 2010. There Dasho Pema told legislators that talks in Thimphu in January 2010 and the 2nd Expert Group meeting in Beijing in July 2010 had failed to yield results since there were "differences of views and positions on our border such as Doklam, Charithang, Sinchulumpa and Dramana, all in the western border." The two sides agreed to set up Joint Technical Field Survey teams and exchange 1: 100,000 scale maps.[28]

Boundary talks have continued alternately in Bhutan and China, along with the expert group meetings. The twenty-fourth round of boundary talks took place in 2016 and the ninth round of the expert group talks were held in 2017 just before the Doklam crisis. Then, after a gap of five years, the two sides resumed with the tenth round of their expert group meeting which was held in Kunming in April 2021. A joint press note said that it was held in "a warm and friendly atmosphere" and that they hoped to hold the next round of the expert group meeting as well as the twenty-fifth round of boundary talks "as soon as possible." The Bhutanese embassy in Delhi said, after the expert group talks, that when the boundary talks resume, "all disputed areas" would be discussed.[29]

Beijing break

Even as the war of words between India and China over Doklam continued in the summer of 2017, I was part of a team of four journalists that visited China in the midst of the crisis at the invitation of the All-China Journalists Association, a government front, for a visit to military facilities in the country.

The carefully constructed visit between 7 and 12 August joined by several members of the Indian journalists' community in Beijing, was aimed at signalling that the PLA was a strong and determined force. It had clearly been organized after the outbreak of the Doklam crisis and all the meetings and official briefings featured the issue directly or indirectly.

The first stop was the 3 Garrison Division, located near Huairou, on the outskirts of Beijing, towards the Myitun section of the Great Wall. At the site, the host was Senior Colonel Li Li, whose soldiers gave us a demonstration of marksmanship and counter terrorist tactics. Asked about Doklam, Li declared: "I am a soldier, I will try my best to protect territorial integrity. We have the resolve and determination."

The division is actually the 3rd Guards Division of the PLA, with a history going back to 1940. It had fought in Korea and has been in the Beijing area since 1955. After many permutations and combinations it has evolved as a Garrison Division with an armoured regiment, an air defence regiment, and an artillery regiment. One regiment is used for displays and showcasing the PLA.

Its major duty is the defence of Beijing and in recent times this has meant a specialization on special security including counter-terrorism (CT). It has a mix of armaments, including 35 mm and 25 mm air defence guns, Type 95 tanks, and 152 mm and 122 mm howitzers. Its personnel component comprises 1,362 officers, 3,615 NCOs who serve for 30 years, and 6,023 draftees who serve for 2 years. The forces are of four categories—military, political, logistical and technicians. All this information had been laid out for us.

The next meeting was with the official spokesman of the Ministry of Defence, Senior Colonel Ren Guoqing. Colonel Ren was well known to the Beijing journalists community, was accompanied by a team, comprising among others area specialists like Captain Zhang Heng. Ren's points repeated the 2 August document of the Ministry of Foreign Affairs—that the Doklam area was "indisputably" Chinese, that there was a delimited boundary there and hence the Indian actions were unprecedented. He said India had been notified twice in May and in early June of the Chinese plan, yet some 400 Indian troops had intruded 180 metres into Chinese territory. The Indian action had violated the territorial integrity of China, the 1890 Convention and the UN Charter, and that this would have a severe impact on Sino–Indian relations.

He also, somewhat quaintly, cited a saying of Prime Minister Modi, that China and India were two bodies with one soul and that the Indian action was not a good manifestation of that saying. So, he demanded a withdrawal of Indian troops, followed by an investigation as to how this had happened. "The Chinese military can't understand why this has happened and wonder whether our issues are being understood in New Delhi."

The message at the meeting with Wang Wenli, the sharp, articulate and composed foreign ministry specialist on the border was the same: "Even if there is one Indian soldier, even for a day, it is still a violation of our sovereignty and territorial integrity." She said that it was "impossible to have a dialogue at this time, our people will think our government is incompetent." Adding that it would be tantamount to coercion to "force China into a dialogue." She alluded to the nineteenth-century situation when eight western armies arrived at the gates of Beijing and forced the Qing emperor to negotiate, declaring: "We will not accept any solution of simultaneous withdrawal."

She threw a different light on the actions of the Royal Bhutan Army picket in Doklam, saying that they had asked the Chinese soldiers what they were doing and, on getting the answer, they went back and did not return. "According to our information," she said, "they didn't invite the Indians." She said that the RBA personnel had been unaware of the 16 June incident and had told the Chinese that "Doka La is not a Bhutanese area and they are surprised at the Indian action."

On the Bhutan—China border negotiations, she said that there was "consensus on the alignment of the boundary" and Bhutan had shown no evidence that it has a valid claim on Doklam, and had agreed since the mid-1990s that the area belongs to China. She claimed that in the 1960s the Bhutanese in the area used to pay grass tax to the Chinese, who have the relevant receipts of the period. "On the ground we have full jurisdiction over the area and the Bhutanese have confirmed this through diplomatic channels and in our many rounds of border talks [with them]."

Commenting on the issue of trijunctions, she said that India had trijunctions involving China with other countries as well and "we can raise issue in Kalapani (Nepal) and Jammu and Kashmir." Therefore, using the excuse of unsettled trijunctions does not hold water and will only cause more trouble. Actually, she noted, the trijunction could only be decided after the China—Bhutan border has been delimited.

On 10 August the All-China Journalists Association organized a discussion between three PLA officers and the visiting journalists at its premises. The officers were well known on the international circuit as articulate spokesmen of the PLA in seminars and newspapers. I had met them at the Shangri-La Dialogue in Singapore, where they had come in a phalanx to advocate China's point of view.

The meeting was moderated by an officer I had met at the Shangri-La Dialogue and earlier at the conference venue, Ditchley Hall in UK. Senior Colonel Zhou Bo, who was at the time Director of the Center for Security Cooperation in the Academy of Military Science has also been a prolific commentator in the media. His smooth and articulate English was said to be a result of being educated in the UK.

The Senior Colonel claimed he was familiar with the Sino—Indian border, having served in the South Asia desk of the Ministry of Defence, and was therefore certain that Doklam was not Indian territory. He said it was not a good idea to reopen the Sikkim border to negotiations and that the Indian press release of 30 June was cleverly drafted to speak of "coordination" with the Government of Bhutan, with a view to concealing the fact that "you [India] were not invited."

As an aside he added that India was probably overestimating the military value of claiming Batang La as the trijunction.

Senior Colonel Zhao Xiaozhuo, another well-known international face of the PLA, bluntly remarked that "Your soldiers are in Chinese territory which is an armed attack as per the United Nations. From my point of view it is an armed invasion." When it was pointed out that there had been no demarcation of the 1890 treaty, Zhao, who was then at the Research Centre for China-US Defence Relations, said that he had served in the area and been to Batang La and Doka La and, in any case, there was very little difference between delimitation and demarcation since the soldiers knew where they were on the ground. He said, "I know you are concerned about the so-called Chicken's Neck [Siliguri Corridor]. China was doing road building on its side of the border. You [India] had built so many roads in Arunachal Pradesh, and China hasn't complained." What was striking was the harshness of his tone. Senior Colonel Zhao concluded the discussion declaring: "If you want peaceful resolution, please pull back, else it will be resolved by force."

Struck by the tone I felt compelled to respond. China was a big and powerful country, and would probably prevail in a war against India, I told them, but "I can assure you, Senior Colonel, when we go down, we will take you with us." There was a moment of silence and I was told that the interpreter had simply ignored my remark. Though our three PLA interlocutors would have understood, the Chinese media present there would have been none the wiser.

De-escalation

By the time we came away, back to New Delhi, a de-escalation process had already begun through some quiet background diplomacy. The process had begun following a conversation between Prime Minister Modi and President Xi at the sidelines of the G20 summit in Hamburg on 7 July. This initiated an intense diplomatic dialogue of some thirteen rounds between the Indian ambassador in Beijing and Chinese officials.

As in the case of Depsang, the Chinese were in an uncomfortable position and needed to close the issue as early as possible. Beijing was hosting the Brazil, Russia, India, China and South Africa (BRICS) summit in Xiamen in September which Modi was expected to attend. And, perhaps more important, in the following month in October, was the five-yearly Congress of the Communist Party of China (CPC), the biggest political event in China. Any action against India that backfired would cast Xi Jinping in a bad light.

But, in a sense, the die had already been cast at the outset. The PLA were in tactically inferior positions, facing Indians perched on a ridge overlooking them. A local response would not be easy considering their logistics from their main base in Yadong.

On 27–28 July, Indian Special Representative Ajit Doval was scheduled to visit Beijing to participate in a security forum under the auspices of BRICS. On the eve of the visit, the Chinese launched an information blitz aimed at pressuring New Delhi. Their line was that India must leave Chinese territory unconditionally, unilaterally and without delay. This, the official Ministry of Foreign Affairs spokesman, Lu Kang said was the "prerequisite and basis" for any meaningful dialogue.

The media commentary was tough, with *China Daily* titling an editorial "It's never too late for India to mend its ways." But the *Global Times* was forthright and rejected any notion of talking till Indian troops were withdrawn. "As Doval is believed to be one of the main schemers behind the current order standoff... the Indian media is pinning high hopes on the trip to settle the ongoing dispute," it charged.

The Indian position had been laid out by the Indian External Affairs Minister, Sushma Swaraj just as Doval landed in Beijing. In response to a question in the Rajya Sabha (upper house of parliament) she had said that "If China unilaterally changes the status quo of the trijunction point, then that is a direct challenge to our security. Their demand is that we should withdraw our troops from there. We want that, if we are having a conversation, if we want to have talks, then both should withdraw their armies." This was the first time that the Indian side had publicly articulated its view on the de-escalation of the situation.

A hint that things were moving came across when Doval confirmed to the Chinese that Prime Minister Modi would participate in the Xiamen summit of BRICS nations in September. Such a meeting would have been highly unlikely if the two countries had remained locked in a major military standoff.

Meanwhile there were reports that both sides had thinned their forces at the standoff point. This means that notwithstanding rhetoric, the Chinese had agreed to a mutual withdrawal. The Chinese 2 August statement was more by way of putting issues on the record. What was significant was that the final paragraph of the document had declared that China valued growth of good-neighbourly and friendly ties with India and was committed to maintaining peace and tranquillity on the border. Resolving the crisis "would serve the fundamental interests of both countries…"

Yet, there was no let up in the tough rhetoric from China condemning India and threatening war. As we had seen in our visit to Beijing, neither the threats nor the war rhetoric had come down. On 15 August, even as India celebrated its seventieth anniversary, the *Global Times* cited Hu Ziyong, a prominent Chinese academic, who said in the context of Modi's tough speech on the occasion, that he, Modi, had not been effective in handling domestic issues, and so "He might consider that making problems with China will minimise the domestic impact on his administration."

Another well-known scholar, Ye Hailin, said that the Doklam incident had successfully changed China's view of India from a friend to a rival. In the circumstances Chinese policy would have to adjust to this new reality. He said that the Indian trespass in Doklam was "blackmail" and despite some calling for patience, he believed that "tolerance towards blackmail only reinforces the feeling that it would work again."

Then, on 28 August, there were simultaneous announcements in New Delhi and Beijing announcing that both sides had agreed to withdraw. In a four-line press statement, India said that the two countries had been maintaining diplomatic communications throughout the Doklam incident. "On this basis, expeditious disengagement of border personnel at the face-off site at Doklam has been agreed to and is ongoing." On the Chinese side, the Ministry of Foreign Affairs spokeswoman Hua Chunying said, in response to a question, that the Indian side had "illegally crossed the well-delimited China-India border," and the Chinese had made several representations on the issue demanding "India to immediately pull back its border troops." Now, on the afternoon of 28 August, the Indian side "withdrew all border personnel and equipment" that were on the Chinese side. Pressed as to whether the Chinese were also withdrawing, Hua said that "Chinese border troops continue with their patrols and stationing in the Dong Lang (Doklam) area." However, in an elliptical manner she acknowledged the Chinese action. "In the light of the changing landscape on the ground, China will make necessary adjustments and deployments as it sees fit."[30]

Lost victory

The disengagement was hailed in the Indian media as a great victory for the Modi government. A Bharatiya Janata Party spokesman declared that "China had submitted to India's will" and that the withdrawal was "a major strategic victory for India." The right-wing magazine *Swarajya* declared that Prime Minister Modi and his security adviser Ajit Doval "have secured a massive diplomatic and psychological victory." Even sober commentary such as that of former foreign secretary, Kanwal Sibal, claimed victory indirectly when he spoke of the importance of not humiliating China after this "diplomatic success."[31]

But seasoned observers like M. Taylor Fravel questioned the "emerging consensus that India 'won' and China 'lost'." He noted that the Indians had withdrawn first and that the Chinese would continue to be in Doklam, so claims of victory were premature.[32]

Fravel was right. The Chinese soon decided to ignore the Indians and present Bhutan with a *fait accompli*. Credible reports based on satellite imagery had revealed that shortly after the agreement with India on a pull-back in Doklam, the Chinese went into overdrive to militarily entrench themselves in northern Doklam.[33]

Having consolidated themselves in the northern half of the plateau, and been foiled from going to the south along the Indian border, the Chinese took recourse to a longer strategy. In November 2020 NDTV revealed that the Chinese had been constructing a model village named Pangda in Bhutanese territory on the banks of the Mochu/Torsa river, as well as a road going downriver towards India.[34] They also began constructing roads on the eastern side of Doklam down to the the Torsa Nala (See Map 7), a stream that divides the Doklam plateau. The road, some way from the point of confrontation with the Indians, will most likely in future bridge the Nala and then snake up towards the Zompelri (Jampheri) ridge. A year later, NDTV, citing tweets by imagery analyst @detresfa of the Intel Lab, said that the Chinese were also encroaching into its other western claims with Bhutan and had constructed "multiple new villages" in a 100 sq. km area near Doklam.[35]

Early in 2022, Reuters reported on the basis of satellite imagery that China had accelerated settlement building along Bhutan's disputed western border with Tibet, where more than 200 structures, including double-storeyed buildings, had come up in six different locations, including Doklam.[36]

The news got progressively worse. In May 2021, Robert Barnett, a leading scholar of Tibet, revealed that the Chinese had built a model village, Gyalaphug, in the area of northern Bhutan, which it has long claimed. Two other villages had already been occupied and one more was under construction, as well as a network of roads and even a hydropower facility. Part of this area, Beyul, has great spiritual significance for the Bhutanese. Barnett's report provided a detailed analysis of the manner in which the Chinese have used Tibetan herders to encroach on Bhutanese territory.[37]

As for the hapless Bhutanese, they are unable to do anything when confronted with this juggernaut. When asked about Pangda, the Bhutanese ambassador to India, Maj-Gen. (retd) V. Namgyel, declared: "There is no Chinese village inside Bhutan."[38] This could mean that the Bhutanese have, indeed, conceded Doklam *de facto*, if not *de jure*, to the Chinese.

The ultimate slap in Bhutan's face was the 2020 expansion of the Chinese claims over the country by bringing up one that had not figured in any of the previous twenty-four rounds of Bhutan—China border talks. This claim was to a huge area in eastern Bhutan and was signalled by opposing a funding proposal to the Global Environment Facility in June 2020 to develop the Sakteng wildlife sanctuary in eastern Bhutan. The Chinese representative said that the project "is located in the China—Bhutan disputed areas" and went on to wrongly claim that it was part of the agenda of their boundary talks.[39] (See Map 9)

After Bhutan sent a demarche to Beijing on the issue, the official Chinese foreign ministry spokesman said in July 2020 that "the boundary between China and Bhutan is yet to be demarcated, and the middle, *eastern* and western section of the border are disputed" (emphasis added). Significantly, this area is south of the Tawang tract, which China has been saying is the irreducible minimum for any border settlement with India.[40]

The Chinese action in unilaterally making the Mochu river the border and occupying all of Doklam goes against the 1890 Anglo Chinese

Convention that China itself invoked in 2017. This clearly said that the border would be "the crest of the mountain range separating waters flowing into the Sikkim Teesta, from the waters flowing into the Tibetan Mochu." But today, the Chinese are not on the watershed, but on the very banks of Mochu. Further, all this is in violation of their own solemn commitment to Bhutan in 1988 and 1998 that in the period the two sides were trying to work out a border settlement, "the status quo of the boundary prior to March 1959 be upheld."[41]

Instead of the expected twenty-fifth round, on 14 October 2021, it was announced that Bhutanese Foreign Minister Tandi Dorji and the Chinese Assistant Minister of Foreign Affairs Wu Jianghao had met in Thimphu and signed a Memorandum of Understanding on a Three-Step Roadmap "to expedite boundary negotiations."[42] Given all that has transpired, this is likely to be just the window dressing for an agreement on Chinese terms, which in essence means that the Bhutanese accede to all China's claims on the western border and establish full relations with China, which will mean a Chinese embassy in Thimphu.

9

ILLUSORY RESET

The Doklam crisis ended, Prime Minister Modi attended the Xiamen summit of BRICS in early September 2017, where the Chinese flattered him by naming Pakistan-based terrorist groups for the first time in the joint post-meeting statement. This Xiamen declaration also backed another item with which India had a quarrel with Beijing—support for India to accede to the Nuclear Suppliers' Group (NSG) arrangement. Though the Indians declared it a diplomatic victory, this meant little in practical terms: Beijing continued to oppose India's NSG entry and the naming of Masood Azhar in the UN's Al Qaeda and Taliban sanctions list.

On 18–24 October, 2017, the Communist Party of China conducted its nineteenth Party Congress, whose decisions were momentous. The most notable of these was restructuring the party and government rules to enable Xi Jinping to go beyond the usual two terms as president.

Delivering his Work Report to the 19th Communist Party of China Congress, Xi Jinping declared that China would aim at transforming the PLA into a "world class military by the mid-21st century." He outlined the steps to that goal as: achieving mechanization by 2020, significant advances in the application of information technology and an enhancement of the country's strategic capabilities. The modernization would be substantially completed by 2035.

These developments will have consequences for India, some direct and others indirect. One reason for the termination of the Doklam standoff in the way that it did could be the fact that, the PLA simply lacked the military ability to push the Indians out at that point. Some support for this thesis comes from the fact that after the Doklam crisis, the Chinese decided to strengthen their forces all along the Sino–Indian border, not just by increasing their numbers, but by making them much more capable, enhancing their mobility, their ability to fight in an IT environment and increasing their firepower.[1]

At the time of Doklam, China had only six border regiments and three brigades (just about 1½ divisions) in Tibet, according to Ravi Rikhye, who specializes in orders of battle of the rival forces.[2] By contrast, India had two divisions in Ladakh, Himachal Pradesh and Uttarakhand, four divisions in the east and another four brigades associated with a new strike corps which was being established. India was also raising two new independent armoured brigades for use in the mountains and seeking to develop capabilities for offensive operations.[3] Because the effective use of these forces depended on roads and transportation infrastructure, India, unlike China, kept its forces as close to the LAC as it could.

The reason for the low Chinese numbers is that they had the capacity to build up forces fast in Tibet. According to one estimate, they could move in more than 30 divisions to the border, including its 15th Airborne Corps in thirty to forty days.[4] These forces could easily outnumber the Indian deployment in a drawn-out conflict, which would give them time to acclimatize. However, given that both countries have nuclear weapons, the possibility of a protracted all-out India–China war remains remote. For this reason, the Chinese began to create facilities all along the LAC to house their forces closer to the border.

Things began changing faster than expected. In Doklam, as per their agreement with the Indians, the Chinese stopped work on their road from below Doka La to the Zompelri ridge that had been blocked by Indian soldiers. But almost immediately, they began a systematic build up in northern Doklam to consolidate their position on the disputed plateau. This became apparent within weeks of the Sino–Indian agreement in August 2017 itself. Satellite imagery revealed a hectic pace of construction in the area from Sinche La, over which the Chinese road from Chumbi valley runs down to Doka La, to the point where the Chinese had halted their road construction.

A retired Indian military satellite imagery analyst, Colonel Vinayak Bhatt, noted that as of December 2017 itself, far from thinning down, as claimed by Indian government officials, the PLA had fortified its position in northern Doklam there by creating shelters, as many as 7 helipads, munition storage sites, missile dumps, a radar station, had stationed armoured vehicles and had laid fibre optic cables for communications. In short, they had occupied all northern Doklam.[5]

In early 2018, just four months after the withdrawal agreement, Senior Colonel Zhou Bo also weighed in and said that the Doklam outcome "was not even a tactical victory for India" because the Chinese continued to remain on the plateau and soon resumed road construction activity. But perhaps the most revealing part of Zhou's article was his declaration that India was going to be the net loser now because "the disputed Sino–Indian border had not been on China's strategic radar" but now, the Doklam standoff had "provided China with a lesson on reconsidering its security concerns." As a result Beijing would enhance its infrastructure construction, impliedly along the entire Line of Actual control with India.[6]

While the Indian media had declared the Doklam agreement as a famous victory for India, at the official level the approach was different. In essence it was simply to wash India's hands of the Doklam affair. Having blocked the Chinese road construction, New Delhi became oblivious to developments in other parts of the plateau. But, as Foreign Secretary Jaishankar and his successor Vijay Gokhale told the Indian Parliament's Standing Committee on External Affairs in 2018, "we had only a limited objective. Beyond that if there is a buildup, if they (the Chinese) are doing some activity, that is a matter for China and Bhutan to sort out." The officials took the extraordinary position that what mattered was what the Indians could see "line of sight," presumably from their positions in Doka La, and they were not concerned with other activities which were a matter Bhutan ought to be concerned with.[7]

Wuhan reset

The culmination of sorts of the Doklam crisis was the decision by the two countries to institute a system of informal annual summits where their leaders could interact with each other without an agenda. Although billed as "informal," the Wuhan summit of 27–28 April 2018 was a carefully prepared event. The interactions in Xiamen and the BRICS declaration on terrorism seemed to be a Chinese signal that it was not entirely deaf to India's concerns.

It was also at Xiamen that the two leaders, aware of the dangerous confrontation in Doklam, gave their ministers and officials instructions to enhance "strategic communications" between the two sides. This essentially meant more frequent contact through meetings or the telephone.

The first step in this direction was the decision to hold the twentieth round of talks between the Special Representatives in Delhi after a gap of twenty months. At this meeting in December 2018, India's National Security Adviser and Special Representative Ajit Doval met his counterpart, State Councillor and Politburo member Yang Jichei. As usual, little was revealed about the content of the meeting, but the Indian press release did note that the two officials spoke of the need to emphasize their convergences and to find "mutually acceptable resolutions of their differences with due respect to each other's sensitivities, concerns and aspirations."[8]

Subsequently, Foreign Secretary Gokhale—who had been the Indian ambassador to China till October—made an official visit to Beijing on 23 February. It was on the eve of this visit that he sent a letter to his colleague, the Cabinet Secretary, asking him to advise leaders and government functionaries to stay away from events marking sixty years of the Dalai Lama's arrival in India. Two events to commemorate the event in New Delhi were cancelled. The Central Tibetan Administration head, Lobsang Sangay, said that his government-in-exile "doesn't want to cause inconvenience to host India." After playing the Tibet card all these years, the Modi government was withdrawing it, or to use a cruder metaphor, they were throwing the Dalai Lama under the bus.[9]

On 20 March, Modi spoke directly with Xi to congratulate him on his re-election as president after the 2018 National People's Congress, China's annual parliament. It was during this conversation that the Wuhan visit was finalized. In mid-April NSA Ajit Doval again visited China and met Yang Jichei—now secretary of the Central Foreign

Affairs Commission, the body that really makes Chinese foreign policy—and the new Chinese Special Representative Foreign Minister Wang Yi. Ostensibly the visit was to prepare the ground for the Shanghai Cooperation Organisation (SCO) summit in June, which was to be attended by Prime Minister Modi as well. But in reality, it was to prepare for the informal summit.

On 20 April, after talks with visiting Indian External Affairs Minister Sushma Swaraj, Wang Yi announced that the meeting would take place in Wuhan between 27 and 28 April. He said that both sides had reached a "broad based consensus on high level interactions and cooperation between China and India" and that the two leaders would have discussions "of a strategic nature concerning the once-in-a-century shifts going on in the world… [and] also exchange views on overarching strategic matters concerning the future of China-India relations." Sino–Indian ties appeared to be soaring high after having hit a low point the year before.

The outcome of the Wuhan summit could be interpreted in multiple ways. A press release from the Indian government on 28 April noted, "It will be a positive factor for stability amidst current global uncertainties." It would also be conducive "for the development and prosperity of the region and will create the conditions for an Asian Century."[10] Press releases from the Chinese and the Indian governments emphasized that they had "the maturity and wisdom to handle the differences through peaceful discussion."

The meeting put "strategic communications," or the high-level interaction between the two countries, on a new track. While meetings between officials of the two countries were held regularly, the Wuhan summit sought to take the process to the ministerial level as well. The Chinese and Indian leaders decided that there was a need for them to meet more frequently and engage in a way that was free from the constraints of protocol. In the international domain, the summit sought to establish the idea that while China and India may have troubled relations, their leaders had the political will to deal with difficult situations through dialogue and negotiation.

In practical terms, the Wuhan meet also indicated that the two countries did not want any clash due to miscalculations in their political moves. They would, as the press releases observed, like to retain their respective strategic and decisional autonomy in dealing with their regional and global issues. In recent times, as India moved closer to the US, this had been de-emphasized. A restatement of "strategic autonomy" in this form was a useful signalling exercise in so far as ties with China were concerned.

The Indian press release mentioned the issue of maintaining peace and tranquillity on the border in some detail. The press release noted the two leaders had issued "a strategic guidance to their respective militaries" to enhance communications and implement various Confidence Building Measures (CBMs) and effective border management. The Chinese statement was pithy, noting merely that the two sides would strengthen CBMs and enhance communication and cooperation to uphold peace and tranquillity.

Wuhan fallout

The Indian media observed two immediate practical measures arising from the Wuhan summit. The first was the decision to set up an India–China hotline at the level of Director-General of Military Operations (though that is something that has yet to be activated as of 2021). The second was the set of instructions sent out to the Indian Army to maintain peace at the border, avoiding aggressive patrolling tactics, and to strictly adhere to the 2005 protocol in dealing with the PLA on the border.[11] Presumably, the PLA had also been issued similar instructions.

An immediate consequence of this new bonhomie was visible when Prime Minister Modi attended the Shangri-La Dialogue in Singapore to deliver its keynote address. The Dialogue, which features leaders and officials of various countries, is organized by the Institute of Strategic Studies, London with the blessings of the Singapore government. It has been a premier annual event which often has heads of state and government speak on matters of security in Asia.

Since 2007, it has seen an impressive Chinese military delegation not only participate but actively put their point of view across, even while challenging speakers with questions from the floor. Almost always, Senior Colonel Zhou Bo, to whom we referred to earlier, formed part of the delegation. In 2011, though the keynote speaker was the US Secretary of Defense, the event was dominated by China's

Defence Minister Liang Guanglie. This was the first time an official at the level of the minister had shown up from China.

India has not been a major player in Shangri-La, usually sending a low-key delegation which kept its head down, more because India was not a player in Southeast or East Asia to whom the Shangri-La Dialogue is addressed. But in recent years it has become more active. In 2016 India's Defence Minister Manohar Parrikar had delivered a speech at the event. At the time I had noted in an article that the speech was somewhat rambling and confused and the minister had been careful to avoid hitting at China on account of the South China Sea issue.

Given this, there were expectations that Modi would provide a clearer picture of India's Indo—Pacific strategy. But he, too, side-stepped, probably on account of his recent summit with Xi. He declared, first, that India viewed the Indo-Pacific as a geographic, rather than a geopolitical construct, and that it stretched from the "shores of Africa to those of America." The American view, self-consciously geopolitical, does not go west of the Maldives, the limit of responsibility of their erstwhile Pacific Command, since renamed the "US Indo-Pacific Command." In that sense, it leaves out the western half of the Indian Ocean where New Delhi has far greater geopolitical and economic interests.

Second, he implicitly assured China that India did not see the Quadrilateral Grouping aka the Quad, or the Indo—Pacific strategy, "as a club of limited members." Nor was it a grouping that sought domination, or was "directed against any country." He went on to add: "our friendships are not alliances of containment." Then, in a warning against the negative fallout of Asian rivalry, he used a phrase first used by Foreign Secretary S. Jaishankar: "Competition must not turn into conflict and differences must not be allowed to become disputes."[12]

India and China now rapidly resumed normal relations, and, indeed, developed a sense of bonhomie. The two sides held their second maritime affairs dialogue in Beijing in July 2018 after a gap of two years. Military delegations also resumed with the visit of Lt Gen. Liu Xiaowu, Deputy Commander of the Western Theatre Command, to India's Eastern Command. In a return visit, India's Eastern Army Commander Lt Gen. Abhay Krishna visited China in August 2018 with a delegation.

They didn't have to worry about trade and people-to-people inter-action as Indian businessmen and students flooded China, one in search of cheap goods, the other for less expensive degrees in medicine. In 2017, the year of Doklam, two-way trade reached a record of USD 84.44 billion, an increase of nearly 19 per cent over the previous year and, to mitigate Indian concerns over the imbalance favouring China, New Delhi was heartened to see a 40 per cent rise in Indian exports to China.

In August 2018, in the wake of the visit of Chinese Defence Minister Wei Fenghe, the two sides mooted a new Memorandum of Understanding to boost defence exchanges and cooperation and to update the old one of 2006. Both sides agreed to handle future Doklams with "restraint, rationality and maturity." Under the proposed MOU, the two sides sought to expand the engagement between the armed forces with more joint exercises, training and professional interactions.[13] The issue of hotlines between the Indian and Chinese militaries continued to drag on, on the issue as to who would connect to what; the Chinese wanted a link with their Western Theatre Command in Chengdu, while the Indians felt that in the interests of equivalence, it should be the respective army headquarters in Beijing and New Delhi. This last issue was still outstanding in the summer of 2020 when it could have altered the course of the crisis.

Later in 2018, India and China signed an internal security agreement focusing on terrorism, narcotics and human trafficking, intelligence sharing and disaster management. This was a high-level agreement as evidenced by the fact that it was signed in New Delhi by Home Minister Rajnath Singh on the Indian side, and the Chinese Minister for Public Security Zhao Kezhi. Junior Minister for Home Affairs Kiren Rijiju was kept away from the meetings; he is from Arunachal Pradesh. His absence provoked questions from the media and so, at the last minute, he was trotted out during the signing ceremony.

Election year in India

In India, the first half of 2019 was taken up by the general elections that saw the Modi government return with an even greater majority. Not surprisingly, this period was more about electioneering than anything else. This included the Indian decision to bomb Balakot, in Pakistan, on 26 Feburary to avenge a terrorist attack on a paramilitary convoy in Kashmir killing forty soldiers in Pulwama twelve days earlier. The Balakot strike led to a Pakistani riposte and an aerial battle where India lost an aircraft and its pilot was captured, though returned safely the next day. All this fed into the election rhetoric since being tough on Pakistan is very much a core item in Modi's policy agenda.

In the spirit of its post-Wuhan policy, China adopted a neutral stance with its Ministry of Foreign Affairs spokesman Lu Kang calling on "the two sides to exercise restraint and take actions that will help stabilize the situation in the region." Asked about the phone call from the Pakistan Foreign Minister Shah Mehmood Qureshi to his Chinese counterpart Wang Yi, Lu said that his minister had heard out Qureshi, but he had reiterated the message that the two sides needed to work out the situation through dialogue.

The Indian External Affairs Minister Sushma Swaraj had called various countries, including China, and said all of them had shown an understanding for the Indian position. The next day she flew to Beijing to attend a meeting of the Russia—China—India group in Wuzhen. Presumably, she took the opportunity to brief her Russian and Chinese counterparts.

Yet, in March, China had again blocked the designation of Azhar as a terrorist under the Al Qaeda and Taliban Sanctions Committee of the UN, saying that China had all along participated in the discussions "in a responsible manner" and in accordance with the provisions of the committee. It said it was blocking the move for the fourth time because it needed more time to examine the request.

Then, as the election campaign in India was reaching its climax and it was apparent that Modi was likely to sweep the polls, China made another surprise decision—it said it would withdraw its veto in designating Masood Azhar in the UN list. This may have had less to do with Chinese calculations of Modi's victory, than the threat of the US to make a procedural move that would have bypassed Chinese opposition.

Less than a month after being re-elected to office after a massive victory, Prime Minister Modi had his first bilateral meeting with Chinese President Xi Jinping in Bishkek, Kyrgyzstan on 13 June at the sidelines of the nineteenth summit of the Shanghai Cooperation

Organisation. According to officials the outcome of the meeting was to maintain the momentum of Sino–Indian ties after the Wuhan summit. Modi took the opportunity to discuss Pakistan and thank Xi for China's role in having Azhar designated a terrorist in the UN listing. Nevertheless, the Indian foreign secretary Vijay Gokhale told journalists that "The major highlight was that Sino–Indian relations cannot be looked at through the prism of Pakistan."[14]

Within weeks, at the sidelines of the G20 meeting, the two had a second meeting, this time in Osaka on 28 June; the addition of Russia's Vladimir Putin made this a Russia—India—China summit. The emphasis of the three leaders was on multilateral engagement, at a point in time when the US was asserting its "America First" identity.

Wuhan II or the Chennai summit

The news that Modi and Xi would meet in their second informal summit in India was known within a week of the election results being formally declared. Initial speculation was that the meeting would be held in the holy city of Varanasi, which was also Modi's constituency. Soon, however, it was made known that the summit would take place at another temple town, Mamallapuram or Mahabalipuram, near Chennai, in late 2019. This town flourished in the seventh and eighth centuries AD as a port city of the Pallava kingdom. Its numerous temples and monuments are such that it was made a UNESCO World Heritage site. Though in the seventh century the great Chinese pilgrim Xuanzang (Hiuen Tsang) visited nearby Kanchipuram, another religious centre nearby, there is no record of him visiting Mamallapuram.

There were two hiccups (which in retrospect may have been more serious than that) before the summit, which was officially designated as the Chennai summit because Mamallapuram is now virtually a suburb of India's fourth largest city. First, to fulfill its ideological agenda, the Modi government set aside key Article 370 of the Indian Constitution signifying the special status of Jammu & Kashmir. To rub salt into the wounds of the troubled Muslim-majority state, the government also demoted it from a full-fledged state of India, and divided it into two Union Territories, Jammu & Kashmir and Ladakh, to be ruled directly from New Delhi.

It was the creation of Ladakh, part of which, according to India, is occupied by China (the Aksai Chin region), that sparked heated words between the two countries.

China, which was chairing the UN Security Council at that time, canvassed other members about raising the issue of the Modi government's decisions on Jammu & Kashmir. While the UK was willing to support the move, the US and France opposed it and China and Pakistan had to be content with an informal discussion on the issue without any official statement. Even so, this was the first time since 1971 that the UN Security Council had discussed what remains in the books of the UNSC as the "India—Pakistan issue," since the Kashmir issue was first taken to the UN in 1948.

A day after the Indian action on Kashmir, China expressed its "serious concerns" over the development and said that "China always opposed India's inclusion of Chinese territory in the western section of the China-India border under its administrative jurisdiction." This was a reference to Aksai Chin, occupied by China since the 1950s, which India had reorganized into the Union Territory of Ladakh. The statement went on to add that "The recent unilateral revision of domestic laws by the Indian side, continues to undermine China's territorial sovereignty, which is unacceptable and will not have any effect."

Second, in September, a month before the Chennai summit, Indian and Chinese troops clashed in Ladakh again. Chinese troops stopped an Indian patrol party, twelve strong, from proceeding to Finger 8, which marks the Indian LAC claim line on the north bank of Pangong Tso, which later saw a major standoff in 2020. Both sides called for support and additional troops landed up at the spot. Fortunately, the existing Sino–Indian mechanisms worked and by the evening both sides pulled back.

Expectations were not too high from the Chennai summit between Chinese President Xi Jinping and Prime Minister Narendra Modi, held between 10 and 11 October 2019. But all public accounts suggested that it went off well. The two sides had important differences, but they successfully papered over them, a tribute to the fine art of diplomacy.

They also reiterated their "consensus" from the Wuhan summit that "India and China are factors for stability in the current international landscape and that both sides will manage their differences and not allow differences on any issue to become disputes."

On terrorism, the two sides shared the view that they would work together to ensure that "radicalization and terrorism" did not affect the fabric of the "multicultural, multiethnic and multi-religious societies" of their countries. However, the meaning of "terrorism" differs for both sides. For Beijing, Uighur separatism is terrorism, while India believes that China's "all weather friend," Pakistan, is the fountainhead of all terrorism.

Foreign Secretary Gokhale said in his briefing to the Indian media that there had been no discussion on Kashmir. This is interesting because tensions relating to China's position in Kashmir had become a new item in the contentious Sino–Indian agenda. And that had arisen between the Wuhan and the Chennai summits. Essentially, then, what the two sides did was to sweep the inconvenient issue under the carpet. And determined to work along the lines they have always worked on—India doing what it must and China what it can.

If there was an issue where there appeared to be some forward movement, it was on trade. In 2018, total trade was USD 95.4 billion, some 13.34 per cent higher than the figure for 2017 which, we noted earlier, had itself been 19 per cent higher than 2016. Clearly things were booming, though Chinese investment in India remained at a modest USD 8 billion, but it had risen since Modi came to power from USD 1.4 billion. A lot of the investment was in the pharmaceutical and technology sectors, as well as a host of service startups.

The Chinese side was aware of Indian feelings on the trade deficit issue and the need to provide some corrective. President Xi told the Indians that China was ready to take concrete measures to reduce the trade deficit; as a result of this the Chinese did ease some restrictions on the import of rice and some other pharma products. Besides, Xi assured India that China would discuss India's concerns over the Regional Comprehensive Economic Partnership (RCEP) being negotiated at the time.

The two agreed to set up a new mechanism for matters relating to trade, investment and services. The Chinese nominated Vice Premier Hu Chunhua to deal with the new mechanism and the Indian side proposed Finance Minister Nirmala Sitharaman. Hu is an important figure in China, a Politburo member, who was once spoken of as a potential successor to Xi.

According to Foreign Secretary Gokhale's briefing, President Xi also raised the issue of engaging more on the defence and security side. Both sides reviewed ongoing programmes and Xi called for stepping up military-to-military engagement. There was some discussion on international and regional issues and both sides stressed the importance of countries having independent and autonomous foreign policies. Xi could not be unaware of Washington's pull on New Delhi and therefore he emphasized the need for more intense discussions to promote a common Sino–Indian perspective on some of these issues.

In that sense Modi was right when he said later there was considerable value in ensuring such "strategic communication," pointing out that the Wuhan summit of 2018 had seen "increased stability and fresh momentum" in the relations between the two countries. "We had decided we would prudently manage our differences and not let them become disputes, be sensitive to each other's concerns and be a reason for peace and stability in the world."

When the foreign ministers of the two sides met in Beijing to prepare for the informal Chennai summit, there had been another intriguing development in mid-August 2019. It had been revealed by the Chinese side that they had sent some "early harvest" proposals for the boundary settlement with India. The Chennai summit directions to the SRs was to "actively advance the boundary negotiations" by formulating a road map for negotiations "on the settlement framework" and strive for a final settlement.

They were taken up at the twenty-second meeting of the Special Representatives (SR) India's NSA Ajit Doval and Chinese Foreign Minister Wang Yi in New Delhi in mid-December two months after the Chennai summit, but the details of what they were are not known. Recall, that "early harvest" was used for a possible demarcation of the already agreed to Sikkim-Tibet border where the Doklam incident had occurred.

While the Indian press release following the Doval—Wang meeting was fairly anodyne, the Chinese ones were revealing. In his meeting with Indian Vice President Venkaiah Naidu, Wang spoke of the "consensus" that had been reached at the Chennai summit on properly handling differences and sensitive issues, "so as not to allow them to become disputes." More important he said, a consensus had also been reached "on the proper settlement of border issues." Wang went on to add that China had put forward "a practical framework on solving border issues, to which the Indian side has attached importance."[15]

The Chinese press release after the SR's meeting said that the two sides "exchanged views on the early harvest of boundary negotiations and reached a consensus on strengthening confidence building measures." Further, they agreed to work out additional rules for maintaining peace and tranquility on the border as well to "strengthen communication and exchanges between the border forces of the two countries and set up hotlines between the relevant departments of the armed forces."[16] As of now, no one knows what the proposals relating to the boundary and its settlement were.

* * *

As for India and China, by the end of 2019 it appeared that both sides were developing convergence on a fairly significant agenda. Looking at the Chennai summit and the meeting of the Special Representatives, it would have appeared that Sino–Indian relations were consolidating their post-Doklam upswing. Both appeared to have gotten a new wind on the issue of settling their vexed disputed border and their trade was booming.

Just how wrong this assessment was became evident just months later in early 2020. We can always speculate that, had 2020 been a normal year, perhaps the trajectory may not have changed. But, as we know, because of COVID-19 it was not. As in everything else, the world was turned upside down, and along with it had crashed the patiently constructed edifice of Sino–Indian relations.

10

THE FUTURE

WAR, COMPETITIVE CO-EXISTENCE,
OR ANTAGONISTIC COOPERATION?

The Sino–Indian relationship is actually a complex equation where there are some constants like the boundary dispute, the United States and Tibet, and a number of variables at a given time, like the economic condition, domestic political situation, geopolitical orientations and so on. What happened in 2020 was the consequence of a growing disequilibrium that has been developing for a while in that equation. This imbalance had periodically manifested itself in the relations between the two countries, arising from shifts in the relative weight of the constants, and changes in the variables. What mattered at any given point in time was the total balance of the equation, and focusing on this constant or that variable alone did not often explain things.

The two countries had fought a short war in 1962 and now have powerful militaries and nuclear weapons. Though they have not been able to resolve their boundary dispute in this period, they were remarkably successful in managing the border peacefully well into the second decade of the twenty-first century. Through a variety of protocols, mechanisms, as well as border personnel meetings, beginning with the Border Peace and Tranquillity Agreement (BPTA) of 1993, they had a record of not having had a single shot fired in anger across the Line of Actual Control (LAC) that marked their contested 4,000-km border since 1975.

In the 2000–2020 period, as they developed the infrastructure along their mountainous and inhospitable border, the friction between them had begun to increase. In part this began to happen as better infrastructure enabled their patrols to meet more frequently at points along the LAC where their claims overlapped. In some measure it was on account of developments in Tibet that led to a final breakdown of the reconciliation dialogue that had been taking place between the representatives of the Dalai Lama and the Chinese government. The India-US entente, which was manifested markedly in the growth of their military ties, played its own role in the situation.

Incidents along the LAC such as those in Depsang in 2013, Chumar in 2014 and along the Pangong Tso in 2017 and 2019, were managed through standard operating procedures worked out earlier. However, even at the time, it was noticed, first, that though these face-offs happened in the far off border areas where there were no inhabitants, news filtered out and was amplified by the media and social media, bringing pressure to bear on the respective governments. And second, these incidents were tending towards occasional belligerence and scuffles between the soldiers of the two sides.

The second India–China informal summit in Chennai in October 2019 was expected to stabilize relations between the two countries at a strategically enhanced level. There was talk of new CBMs, possibly an agreement on the long discussed Code of Conduct and even the working out of a settlement framework for the boundary—the third and last stage of the process envisaged by the original Special Representatives, Dai Bingguo and Brajesh Mishra in 2004.

Then what happened in four months to change all that in March 2020?

It would be simple, if not simplistic, to attribute the blame to Chinese perfidy. And argue that the informal summits were all an elaborate scheme of deception to lull the Indians into a sense of complacency. But Xi Jinping had also invested substantial time as well as political capital in participating in the somewhat unusual informal summits that had been held in 2018 and 2019. In the process he had arguably spent more time with Modi than any other foreign leader. So why throw it all away?

The reality, however, is that things did not change in four months, but had been doing so for nearly a decade. As Shivshankar Menon put it: "roughly since 2012 the basic understanding on which you maintained your border from 1988 onwards was no longer valid." That was the year Xi Jinping became General Secretary, and "the balance of power had shifted" against India. When the process of detente began in 1988, the economies of the two countries were roughly equal; in 2012, the Chinese GDP was five times larger.[1]

For the Chinese, Indian behaviour on the border, and in general, now became inexplicable. Instead of accepting that it was now irretrievably behind China in almost all aspects of national power, New Delhi insisted on intensifying its efforts to match Chinese capabilities on the Sino–Indian border. Beijing saw this as a somewhat impertinent attempt to destabilize its military posture of dominance along the Line of Actual Control on account of its superior infrastructure.

The Chinese dominance, as has been seen, was not manifested by a forward deployment of its forces. In that respect India was way ahead since because of the terrain it maintained its forces close to the LAC. On the other hand, the Chinese had a thin screen of border-guarding forces but possessed the ability to build up very rapidly because of their excellent road network which connected them to every significant pass on the LAC. But since 2017, they had been modifying their posture and constructing billets, barracks, helipads and ammunition dumps to facilitate a quicker forward deployment of their forces.

Sinologist M. Taylor Fravel has noted that the Chinese have viewed their border dispute with India as a secondary threat that must be "managed," rather than be overwhelmed or eliminated. India, he said, "has never been China's main or primary opponent." While China may, on occasion, have used force in the "secondary direction," it had done so mainly to maintain stability in that secondary area. Going by the past record, Fravel said, "China has sought to prevent the dispute from dominating its relationship with India, in order to pursue other goals linked with economic growth and to expand Chinese influence around the world."[2]

Looking back, it would appear that the incidents on the border—the stand offs in Depsang and Chumar in 2013 and 2014, the clashes in

Pangong Tso and Demchok—were linked to Chinese proposals in the Border Defence Cooperation Agreement (BDCA) and the Code of Conduct on border affairs, to freeze Indian construction in the border areas. But the Indian process, which had only slowly gathered speed since the mid-2000s, began to move at a much faster pace in the last decade. The completion of the Darbuk Shyok-Daulat Beg Oldi (DS-DBO) road in 2019 was an important marker of the Indian determination to maintain some kind of a parity with China.

Another important marker of Indian behaviour was the Doklam episode of 2017 when China was outplayed because its forces found themselves in a militarily disadvantageous position. They were at the end of a long and narrow valley, dominated by strong Indian forces along the ridgeline and escalation was not an easy option.

It was following this incident that the PLA reviewed its entire posture along the Sino–Indian border and began a systematic build up which involved stationing more forces proximate to the LAC, plugging gaps in the air defence system and hardening airfields and helipads. As part of this, the decision was probably taken to iron out the Line of Actual Control wherever possible, especially near the DS-DBO road and other points where the Chinese perceived some vulnerability for their own forces. The scope of the action, involving the movement of two divisions of the PLA to positions adjacent to the Line of Actual Control would have been planned over a year, and would have had the approval at the highest level in the Central Military Commission (CMC), which includes its chairman, Xi Jinping.

But this act of strategic coercion went out of control on the icy banks of the Galwan river. The incident which, was triggered by an unexpected Indian action, led to casualties. The Chinese could not have expected that the whole situation would blow up in the way it did. Note that for its part and for its own reasons, the government of India has tried its best to limit the fallout of the action, even denying any incursion had occurred. Even now they have not given us a clear picture of the more consequential PLA ingresses in places like the Depsang Plains, the Kugrang valley, Gogra—Hot Springs and the Charding Ninglung Nala area, south of Demchok.

But the government of India found it politically impossible to sweep the Galwan issue under the carpet after twenty Indian soldiers died, more than a hundred were injured and a similar number taken prisoner. PLA intransigence in the disengagement negotiations through July and August 2020 compelled them to allow the Indian Army to undertake an operation along the south bank of Pangong Tso that provided India with a lever in the situation. The Chinese options were now stark. They could have escalated the situation, but a favourable outcome was not guaranteed. So they figured it was simply not worth it to do so, especially since India remained, in Fravel's terms, a secondary direction.

But the move of the scale that the Chinese undertook in April–May 2020 cannot be explained by one causative factor alone. Associated with this was the belief that India was adopting this posture, encouraged by its growing military ties with the United States. Chinese scholar Ye Hailin has suggested that the US is the crucial element that is preventing India from accepting its position in the regional hierarchy as a subordinate power. China led India on almost any parameter of national power, yet, "The US's rejection of China is enough to offset China's power advantage over other actors." He went on to lament that "it is difficult to prove who has the higher absolute international status between the sub-power [India] supported by the hegemony [US] and the power [China] suppressed by the hegemony."[3]

Matthieu Duchatel's assessment based on a number of Chinese writings he has studied also "converge[s] on the key importance of US-India relations in explaining tensions". Associated with this are issues relating to India abandoning non-alignment and strategic autonomy.[4]

My friend Liu Zongyi of the Shanghai Institutes for International Studies went a step further when he argued in September 2020 that the Chinese may believe that the main pressure they are facing is from the US and not India: "But the fact is, India and the United States today have become a single entity. In some respects, it is India which is leading the US and is becoming [the] leading anti-China force."[5]

The years 2008 onwards saw a steady development of the US-India military partnership. The US emerged as a major supplier of defence equipment to India, while the latter signed up to a number of US "foundational agreements" to promote inter-operability. This process intensified under the Modi government, marked by the revival of the Quadrilateral Grouping (Quad) in 2017.

Writing in mid-June 2020 in a Chinese military publication, Zhang Jiadong, a professor at the Fudan University in Shanghai noted the growing gap between the level of Sino–Indian relations and their strategic importance. He said India had "continuously strengthened" its relations with the US, Japan and other countries to "check and balance China." At the regional level, too, India was taking steps to compete with China in South Asia and the north Indian Ocean Region. He then laid out the Chinese bottom line. Chinese policy would not change despite India's actions, provided, first, that "India does not join any anti-China alliance system" and second, "India does not undermine the interactive norms and habits formed by the two sides in the border since 1993."[6]

While the US looms large in the Chinese mind as a villain in the Sino–Indian equation, Beijing's ties with Pakistan are completely ignored. From the Indian point of view their background is extraordinary, considering that China gave Pakistan the design of a nuclear weapon, provided them with materials to make it and then tested the device in 1990 in its own testing area. The India—Pakistan rivalry has been a convenient means for China to keep India pinned down in South Asia, even while developing "normal" relations with India post-1993.

India's American embrace

Galwan was not the only breakdown in 2020; there was another, namely in relations between the US and China. In part this was a deliberate move on the part of the Trump administration hawks like Mike Pompeo and Matt Pottinger, who pushed policy to ensure that it would be difficult for any new administration to reverse course. But Chinese actions in Hong Kong and the South China Sea aided the process. In some ways, the two breakdowns fed into each other.

The US has been a factor in Sino–Indian relations since the 1950s. During India's war with China in 1962, the US was the only country to come to India's aid and undertake an emergency supply of weapons and equipment to New Delhi. But American interest in India waned in the mid-1960 and the clash over Bangladesh in 1971 deepened this to an estrangement; and in any case, from 1972 onwards, China became a key player in US global strategic calculations. From this period till the Tiananmen massacre in 1989, the US and China operated as quasi allies.

But as the Chinese economy began to streak ahead in the 1990s and the country began to accrue significant military power, a mutuality of interests developed in New Delhi and Washington in balancing China. Officially, Indian policy has been to maintain "strategic autonomy" and strive for good relations with all the major poles of the international system—the US, the European Union, Russia and China. But as the gap between India's economy and its military capacity and that of China has widened, India has begun to lean harder on the United States. This has been viewed by Beijing as an attempt to contain China, but is, in reality, a defensive move.

Since the 1980s, the US assigned its Pacific Command (PACCOM) to be the node for political—security relations with India. A new phase of cooperation was triggered when the Indian, US and Japanese navies came together to provide humanitarian assistance after the 2004 Indian Ocean tsunami. In 2007, at the suggestion of Japanese Prime Minister Shinzo Abe, they constituted a Quadrilateral Grouping (Quad) involving Japan, the US, India and Australia in Manila. Suspicious China officially protested, making it a point to ask each participant about the objectives of this relationship. Soon after, however, its key driver, Shinzo Abe, resigned and was replaced by the pro-Beijing Yasuo Fukuda. At this point in 2008, Australia, which had a new government headed by Kevin Rudd, terminated its participation.

In 2011, US President Barack Obama announced a shift in US global strategy whose goal was to rebalance or pivot to the Asia-Pacific. It was as part of this that, in 2015, overcoming the "hesitations of history," the new Prime Minister Narendra Modi invited President Barack Obama to New Delhi to be the chief guest at India's Republic Day on 26 January a special honour, because it was offered to an American president for the first time. Heads of state and government from many countries, including China and Pakistan, had featured as chief guests at this premier Indian national function, but never an American.

In this visit India and the US signed up on a "Joint Strategic Vision for the Asia Pacific and the Indian Ocean." In the document the two sides committed to enter into a "partnership for development," and affirmed the "importance of safeguarding maritime security and ensuring the freedom of navigation and overflight throughout the region, especially the South China Sea." This was as explicit as they could be in opposing China's growing power in the region. Subsequently, though, India preferred statements without the reference to the South China Sea.

India had made a decisive shift when in 2008–2009 it began to acquire US military equipment like C-130J and C-17 transport aircraft and P-8I maritime reconnaissance aircraft. In 2015, there was another burst of acquisitions which had a clear orientation to operations in the mountains and the Indian Ocean, such as the CH-47 Chinook heavy lift helicopters, C-17 heavy transport aircraft, M-777 ultralight howitzers and additional P8I maritime reconnaissance aircraft.

A year later, in August 2016, India agreed to sign the Logistics Exchange Memorandum of Understanding (LEMOA) with the US. This gave both countries access to designated military facilities on either side for refuelling and replenishment. This, the second of four "foundational agreements," was signed by India, thirteen years after the first one when, in 2002, the General Security of Military Information Agreement (GSOMIA) had been signed.

The Trump administration that took office in 2017 shifted gears when it moved from a policy of engagement with China into one of confrontation and competition. As part of this, it crafted a new Indo—Pacific policy and challenged Beijing in the western Pacific, especially the South China Sea. The US also made it clear that the new prefix "Indo" had to do with India's pivotal role which was underscored by changing the name of its Pacific Command to the "Indo-Pacific Command." This is a command with which the Indian military had been interacting since the mid-1990s.

There was shift towards yet a higher gear when the Quad of the US, Australia, Japan and India was revived in 2017. India's military-to-military ties with the US began to take qualitative jumps. It was, perhaps, the revival of the Quad in 2017 that would have sent alarm bells ringing in Beijing. That it took place in the year of Doklam was, of course, coincidental.

The Quad resumed as a talking shop of relatively junior officials, with each country choosing to issue its own press release after meetings. Thereafter it picked up speed. In 2018, the Observer Research

Foundation's semi-official Raisina Dialogue in New Delhi featured the navy chiefs of Japan, the US, Australia and India, signalling its serious intent. Simply put, within the Quad lay the seeds of an Asian NATO, and there is little doubt as to who it would be targetting. In 2019, as the US—China relations went south, the Quad was elevated to a higher level following a meeting of the foreign ministers of the member countries in New York at the sidelines of the UN General Assembly session.

Simultaneously, the erstwhile India-US Strategic and Commercial Dialogue became a full-fledged annual "2+2 Strategic Dialogue" (where the foreign and defence ministers of India and the US met each other in a joint format). The inaugural meeting in September 2018 resulted in an expansive joint statement listing the new agenda. New Delhi signed another "foundational agreement," the Communications Compatibility and Security Agreement (COMCASA) that enabled the US and India to share monitoring data gathered through common platforms such as the US-made P8I reconnaissance aircraft that the Indian Navy also operates.

By 2019 then, the military hue in the texture of the Indo—US relationship had deepened with the activation of the Quad, the foundational agreements and the qualitative enhancement of military-to-military cooperation and ongoing Indian acquisitions of US defence equipment. India was already emerging as a key player in managing information on shipping in the Indian Ocean Region (IOR) through its Information Fusion Centre located in Gurgaon. At the end of 2019, the US, UK, France, Japan and Australia had agreed to post their personnel as liaison officers at the centre.

In 2020, as the China-India confrontation in Ladakh unfolded, Sino-American tensions, too, rose alarmingly with developments in Hong Kong and issues relating to Xinjiang and Taiwan. US officials seemed to suggest that the US thought of the Quad as the core of an Asian NATO.[7] Signalling their intent, the four countries actually managed a face-to-face meeting of Quad foreign ministers in Tokyo in October 2020 despite the COVID pandemic. Simultaneously, India signed the last of the four foundational agreements, the Basic Exchange of Cooperation Agreement (BECA) which enabled the sharing of geospatial information.

A January 2021 leaked policy document of the Trump administration said that the goal of its Indo-Pacific policy was to maintain US primacy there.[8] New Delhi has no problem with that because it does not see itself in competition with the US, but with China. And the document also said that the US objective was to "accelerate India's rise and capacity to serve as a net provider of security and Major Defense Partner." As for actions, besides stronger defence cooperation, it called for offering "support to India—through diplomatic, military and intelligence channels—to help address continental challenges such as the border dispute with China...." That, of course, was the American view signifying the importance of India. As for New Delhi it does not necessarily endorse all of it, and would probably not like to be seen as any kind of a player in Washington's containment of China, though internally there has been talk about how deeper ties with India could lead it to find a role in offsetting Chinese pressure on Taiwan.

The US provided important intelligence to India during the Ladakh face-off and later rushed cold weather equipment clothing to India. Admiral Philip Davidson, Commander of the US Indo-Pacific Command, told a US Senate Armed Services Committee meeting in March 2021 that the Ladakh events had opened India's eyes to the issues of cooperation with the US. He said it presented a historic opportunity to deepen bilateral defence ties and solidify the "defining partnership of the 21st century."[9]

Tibet

A seemingly small move by India—the use of Tibetan Special Forces (SF) to deliver its key riposte along the southern bank of the Pangong Tso in August 2020 contained a larger message. After all, India has no dearth of equally well-trained SF units, but choosing a force of Tibetans belonging to its external intelligence service, the Research & Analysis Wing (R&AW) signalled that Tibet remained an important element in Sino–Indian dynamics.[10]

Tibet literally hovers above everything that happens between India and China. This is, of course, a consequence of the fact that the two countries have collided on the roof of the world, because of the People's Republic of China's assertion of Chinese sovereignty over Tibet, in the place of a loosely autonomous control exercised by the Qing empire.

Today, Beijing insists that Tibet has been part of China "since ancient times." Indeed, this phrase was used to claim the Doklam region in 2017. But facts suggest that Tibet was first conquered by the Mongols, who also subjugated China in the thirteenth century, and many Mongol kings viewed Tibetan Lamas as religious preceptors more than vassals. The Ming empire that succeeded the Mongols in the fourteenth century, left Tibet alone, but Tibetan religious leaders were welcomed at the court.

At this time Tibet was dominated by independent Mongol kings who patronized the Dalai Lama; indeed, the fourth Dalai Lama was reincarnated in the family of a powerful Mongol chief Altan Khan. The next Dalai Lama, Ngwang Lobsang Gyatso, the Great Fifth (1617–1682), was both the religious and temporal ruler of the country. Historian Sam van Schaik has noted that though many modern Chinese historians have taken his "visit [to Beijing to meet the emperor] as marking the submission of the Dalai Lama's government to China, such an interpretation is hardly borne out either by the Tibetan or Chinese records of the time."[11]

It is a fact that Tibet came under loose Chinese suzerainty under the Qing empire in the eighteenth century. In practice this meant that while the Qing assumed some control over Tibet's foreign affairs and security, they had none over its internal affairs. Through the nineteenth century, as the Qing themselves came apart, their control over Tibet was mostly only on paper.

The Communist Party of China initially recognized Tibet's different status through the May 1951 Seventeen Point Agreement where they promised not to alter the existing political system of Tibet, or the status of the Dalai Lama. But after the 1959 revolt, they reconstituted the autonomous region of Tibet into the Tibet Autonomous Region (TAR) which was created in 1965. Tibet today is another province of China with its policies dictated by the Communist Party of China. In practice, it probably has lesser autonomy than the other provinces.

Until 1959 there was extensive trade between Tibet and the cis-Himalayan regions of India and people-to-people contact. Among the most sacred sites for Hindus, Mount Kailash and Lake Manasarovar are in Tibet. Indeed, access to the outside world was far easier through India than China, and Kolkata was the closest port to Lhasa. The Tibetan elite tended to look at the outside world through India and in 1959 thousands of Tibetans came to India as refugees and today India hosts the largest Tibetan diaspora in the world, which stands at more than 130,000 people. It also hosts the Central Tibetan Administration which functions like a kind of government in exile for the Tibetan diaspora.

And, of course, it has hosted the fourteenth Dalai Lama since 1959, and more recently the seventeenth Karmapa, the head of the oldest school of Tibetan Buddhism and many other *tulkus* (reincarnate lamas). Since then, India has emerged as a major centre of Tibetan Buddhism, hosting all four major schools of the religion. According to a study by an Indian think tank, there are 225 monasteries and nunneries with over 30,000 monks and nuns in the country. Many of these monasteries are mirrors of institutions that originally flourished in Tibet itself. These have followers, not just in the traditional areas of the Himalayas, but abroad as well, and are often well-endowed.

From the outset, India recognized Tibet as an autonomous region of China, and its current legal position is that the "Tibetan Autonomous Region is a part of the People's Republic of China." Indeed, its policy was shaped by a desire to promote Tibet's autonomy so as to lessen the likelihood of having China as its neighbour. But this did little to lessen Chinese anxieties, and neither did Indian commitments that they would not allow exiled Tibetans to conduct political activities in its territory.

Earlier it was noted how Mao's fears that India wanted to weaken the Chinese hold on Tibet played a major role in the Chinese decision to make war with India in 1962. Garver has pointed out that following the 1959 Tibetan Revolt and the Cultural Revolution in China, the Tibetans were ruled with extreme repression and even cruelty by the Chinese. He noted that Henry Kissinger's assessment was that, in 1971, the Chinese were worried that just as India had dismembered Pakistan, it could, with Soviet help, detach Tibet from China.[12] Clearly these worries have not quite gone away.

Chinese concerns over India's development of its infrastructure along the Himalayas began to heighten those fears, since they were also accompanied by a steady enhancement of Indian military capacity as well. The Indian decision to create a Mountain Strike Corps meant, baldly, India would have the capability of taking any future war into Tibet, the next time around.

With the death of Mao and the collapse of the Cultural Revolution, Chinese leaders like Deng Xiaoping and Hu Yaobang sought to make amends for the decades of repression. They reached out to Gyalo Thondup, the Dalai Lama's elder brother, who met Deng Xiaoping in early 1979, and, in the course of his conversations, the now paramount leader said that China was willing to discuss everything, and that, except for independence, "everything is negotiable."[13]

Negotiations in the 1980s collapsed in part because of Chinese re-thinking and in some measure because the Indian intelligence agency R&AW and possibly some agencies of other countries did not want a reconciliation between the Chinese and the Tibetans. The *coup de grâce* was delivered when the PLA crushed China's movement for democ-racy at Tiananmen Square in June 1989.

Gyalo, a resident of the West Bengal hill town of Kalimpong and who had also been the point man for the CIA's activities in the 1950s and 1960s, continued to have contact with the Chinese. Between 1979 and 2002 there were more than a dozen meetings between the Dalai Lama's representatives and the Chinese. In 2002, he visited Tibet for the first time since he had begun his negotiations with China. But the process foundered on the increasingly tough attitude of the Chinese government.

Between 2003 and 2010 there were another ten meetings between a Tibetan delegation headed by Lodi Gyari, a senior aide of the Dalai Lama, and several Chinese and Tibetan leaders. Despite the extensive Tibetan protests in March 2008, negotiations were resumed later in the year. But in 2010, the last round was stalled because of protests in Tibet. No dialogue has been held since.

The Tibetan position in the dialogue was defined by the Dalai Lama's "Middle Way Approach" which sought genuine autonomy for Tibetans within the framework of the existing Chinese state and constitution.[14] But this did not reassure the Chinese and they released a White Paper on Tibet in 2015 that denounced the Middle Way saying that its inten-tion was to "split China" and that greater autonomy for Tibet was "not up for discussion." The changed status of China after the Global Financial Crisis of 2008, and the new nationalist leadership of Xi Jinping, manifested itself when the White Paper demanded that His Holiness should publicly affirm that Tibet had been part of China "since antiquity," something that was simply not true.[15]

As the Dalai Lama has aged, a new factor has come to the fore: reincarnation. The Dalai Lama detailed his ideas on reincarnation in an essay in 2011. He expressed his worries that the process of reincarnation would be hijacked by politics. On one hand, he wondered whether it was time that he not reincarnate at all. On the other, he expressed an interest in working out clear-cut guidelines to ensure that there "is no room for doubt or deception" in the process.[16]

This was aimed at the Chinese, who will attempt to "capture" any successor, an action that will almost certainly discredit the high office of the Dalai Lama. As he said in his statement, the Chinese communists "who explicitly reject even the idea of past and future lives", leave alone the concept of *tulkus* (reincarnate lamas), should hardly meddle in such areas.

On the other hand, Beijing's nightmare is the re-incarnation of the Dalai Lama somewhere in the Tibetan community in India, possibly even in Tawang, which is not only associated with the Great Fifth, but is also near the birthplace of the sixth Dalai Lama Tsangyang Gyatso, who was a Monpa, not Tibetan by ethnicity. No doubt eventually, the Chinese will appoint their own Dalai Lama, just as they did with the Panchen. But the issue is credibility in the minds of not just the Tibetans, but the international community.

The Chinese believe that the final authority in appointing a high lama is theirs by history and custom. The Qianlong emperor introduced a system of drawing lots from a golden urn to choose the high lamas. The rules had been established after a Qing army helped the seventh Dalai Lama re-establish his authority and also extend Chinese authority over Nepal in 1720. According to the Manchu law, names of candidates for the top lamas, including the Dalai and the Panchen, were put in urns in temples in Lhasa and Beijing and a draw of lots decided the candidate. This practice was only fitfully carried out since there was little Qing influence in Tibet through most of the nineteenth century, and most high lamas, including the current Dalai Lama, were installed without the golden urn process.

Remarkably, the communist government has now sought to reinstitute this practice for the appointment of the lamas, including the Dalai, Karmapa and Panchen. As a Chinese White Paper of 1997 noted, "approval of the reincarnation of the Grand Living Buddhas by the central government is a religious ritual and historical convention of

Tibetan Buddhism, and is the key to safeguarding the normal order of Tibetan Buddhism."[17] In May that year the Chinese authorities had negated the Dalai Lama's selection of six-year old Gedhun Choekyi Nyima as the reincarnation of the tenth Panchen Lama, and installed Gyaincain Norbu in his place. Nyima and his family have not been seen again. In 2007, the State Administration for Religious Affairs in China made it clear through a decree that reincarnations must be approved by the government or they would be deemed invalid.[18]

In the last twenty years despite the enormous investment Beijing has made in Tibet, protests by Tibetans have not died down. Indeed, as we noted earlier, in 2008 they flared up and affected even areas that had been detached from historical Tibet and attached to neighbouring Chinese provinces. After 2009, protests took on an added edge through self-immolations by young monks in China, as well as in India and Nepal. These peaked in 2012, but have been taking place throughout the past decade and have attracted global condemnation of China. The Chinese have always seen the hand of exiled Tibetans based in India behind these events.

Under Xi Jinping, China's policy towards its ethnic minorities has hardened considerably, even as China has doubled down on its Tibet development strategy. The issue of Xinjiang has already become an international *cause célèbre*. As for Tibet, on one side, the Chinese continue to pour in money to promote development there; on the other, steps to Sinicize Tibetan Buddhism have been enhanced. Speaking at the Sixth Tibet Work Forum in August 2015, Xi called for efforts to promote "patriotism among the Tibetan Buddhist circle and effectively manage monasteries in the long run, encouraging interpretations of religious doctrines that are compatible with a socialist society."[19]

In 28–29 August 2020, his speech to the seventh Forum struck a similar theme. These work fora are the highest level policy-making body for Tibet. According to former Foreign Secretary Shyam Saran, an important edict given by Xi spells out China's current policy in the region: "stability, development, ecology and border area consolidation." Xi made it clear that security was a key consideration when he noted: "We must adhere to the strategic thinking that to govern the nation, we must govern our borders; to govern our borders, we must first stabilize Tibet."[20]

The issue of the Sinicization of Tibetan Buddhism was again raised. After extolling the importance of teaching all the ethnic groups the importance of the Chinese nation, culture and the Communist Party of China, there was need to "actively guide" Tibetan Buddhism "to adapt to the socialist society and promote Sinicisation."[21]

In June 2021, Xi became the first Chinese supreme leader in many years to visit Tibet. He visited the south-eastern border region with India and landed at Nyingchi which is some 20 km from the Arunachal border. From there he travelled by the new fast train link to Lhasa where he visited the Dalai Lama's Potala Palace and the Drepung monastery. Here, besides local officials, he also met senior PLA officers.[22]

Over the years, India has also hardened its approach to Tibet. In 2008, when Prime Minister Manmohan Singh visited China, the familiar Indian reiteration that "it recognized the Tibet Autonomous Region as part of the territory of the People's Republic of China" was missing. It has not recurred in joint statements since. In 2009, the Indian government permitted the Dalai Lama to visit Tawang. This was his first visit since 2003 and was the fiftieth anniversary of the time when he had passed through the town on his exile to India.

The Modi government trod on Chinese toes early, when in 2014 Lobsang Sangay, the then Tibetan Sikyong or head of the Central Tibetan Administration (*de facto* government-in-exile), was invited to attend Modi's inauguration. We referred above to the Dalai Lama's visit to Rashtrapati Bhavan (presidential palace) in January 2017 and then his visit to Tawang in 2017. During the Doklam crisis, the government had allowed Sangay to unfurl a Tibetan flag near Pangong Tso. But, as we noted, India had pointedly withdrawn the card on the eve of the first informal summit in Wuhan in 2018.

In April 2021, Sudhi Ranjan Sen reported that, "senior security officials in India, including the prime minister's office have been involved in discussions about how New Delhi can influence the choice of the next Dalai Lama." As part of this, India convened five separate assemblies of senior monks from the different sects of Tibetan Buddhism with a view of shaping the narrative on the legitimacy of any successor of the Dalai Lama.[23] In July 2021, the Dalai Lama turned eighty-six and his aides have, in the past, said that they will begin thinking about his successor when he turns ninety.

Where the Indians are going, the Americans are not too far behind. In December 2020, the US passed a Tibetan Policy and Support Act which says that on the matter of succession, Tibetan Buddhist leaders, including the Dalai Lama, are the final authority. Earlier in November 2020, Lobsang Sangay was invited for an official meeting to the White House, the first time a Tibetan official of his standing has been invited.

Despite all the wars and alarums, the long and inhospitable terrain where the border runs has little of intrinsic value. Cross-border trade, valuable for the residents of the area was, in its heyday in the 1950s, about basic necessities of life, and economic activity was about primal needs such as accessing pastures for sheep, goats and yaks. Even if highways and railway lines are built, this will not change, though peace could possibly bring a tourism bonanza. Right now, the problem for both sides is one of having people populate the border regions. Life is incredibly tough there and economic growth elsewhere acts as a magnet to draw people away. First the able-bodied leave and soon ghost villages are left.[24]

China is now putting in a special effort to ensure that its border areas are not depopulated. Within days of the end of the 19th Communist Party of China(CPC) Congress on 24 October 2017, one of the first news items put out by Xinhua, was about a letter written by two sisters of a Tibetan herder family during the Party Congress, to President Xi, detailing their experiences in the border areas. Xi promptly replied, praising the girls and thanking them for their loyalty and the contribution they were making in safeguarding China's territory.[25]

Subsequently, there has been a sharp increase in the number of model villages that are appearing along the LAC. We have referred earlier to such construction work taking place in areas near the LAC in Arunachal Pradesh and disputed portions of the China—Bhutan border. These Xiaokang (moderately prosperous) villages serve two functions—one is to upgrade the physical quality of life of the border citizens, the other to ensure border security. According to Jayadeva Ranade, plans call for the building of more than 600 such villages along the LAC over the next few years.[26]

The bigger picture

Tibet, Pakistan and America are old constants in the Sino—Indian equation. Their weight may alter, but we must not overstate their importance to the course of Sino–Indian relations. What is key are China's own interests and the goals it seeks in the South Asian subcontinent and the Indian Ocean Region.

In the past thirty years or so, India and China worked along a policy of "4 C's"—conflict, cooperation, competition and containment. The conflict part of it is well known. Cooperation manifests itself in the Indian participation in Chinese-led banks like the Asian Infrastructure Investment Bank (AIIB) and the New Development (BRICS) Bank (NDB), or organizations like the Brazil, Russia, India, China, South Africa (BRICS), the Shanghai Cooperation Organisation (SCO), the Conference on Interaction and Confidence-Building Measures in Asia (CICA) and the Russia—India—China (RIC) grouping and other multilateral forums. It is visible, too, through events like the Wuhan-type summits, official exchanges and meetings. As for competition, it may appear one-sided, but there should be no doubt that it is there, and both New Delhi and Beijing are aware of it. Whether it is South Asia, the Indian Ocean, East Africa or COVID-19 vaccines export, India sees itself very much in the game of competing with China, notwithstanding the asymmetry in their economic and military resources.

Beijing believes that the US-led Indo—Pacific strategy is nothing but an effort to contain China. And no matter what New Delhi and Washington may say, constraining, if not containing China, is their aim. In turn, New Delhi sees Beijing's military and political support to Pakistan, its economic activities in Sri Lanka, Nepal, the Maldives and Bangladesh, as well as its actions on the LAC, as part of a strategy of pinning down India in South Asia and making it too feeble to compete effectively with Beijing in the Indian Ocean Region and elsewhere.

What has happened, and what is happening on the disputed border, is important. But it is not the real fulcrum of the Sino–Indian relationship. It may have begun as a primal contest between two new republics, staking claims to borders that would give shape to their nation. But today the unsettled border is being used for the larger Chinese goal of attaining regional eminence, if not pre-eminence in South Asia.

There are some who believe, in line with Fravel, that India remains a secondary consideration for China. But it still poses a significant challenge to China's longer-term interests in Tibet and for influence in South Asia and the Indian Ocean Region. More significantly, in recent years, India has developed strong military ties with the country which China believes is its primary threat—the United States. China would like to focus on the western Pacific challenge and retain stable ties with India in South Asia. But the very aim of the US-Japan led strategy is to stretch the old Asia-Pacific into the Indian Ocean and lock India into this new construct of the Indo—Pacific. Looking within Asia—Pacific, China looms large, but, in the Indo—Pacific, it looks a bit smaller because of India.

The Chinese scholar Ye Hailin says that "the optimal state" of China-India relations from Beijing's point of view would be one where the border issues are resolved to China's satisfaction, "India accepts China in South Asia," accepts and promotes the BRI, and India and China join hands "to oppose US bullying." All these would help China to expand its strategic space and national interest. But he concedes that it would not be rational to expect this, and hence the continuing problems with India.[27]

As it is, in the case of the events of 2020, China may well have shot itself in the foot. As Yun Sun has put it: "China might have just won the battle [in Ladakh] and lost the war." What it has done is to have deepened suspicion of its behaviour, not just in India but also abroad. This could very well "eliminate any possibility, however thin, for India to accept China's regional ambitions."[28]

* * *

The immediate consequences of the 2020 events are the acceleration in the enhancement of the military capacity of both India and China along the Line of Actual Control. In 2020, as an emergency measure India increased the number of divisions in Ladakh from one to three. But later it has carried out a more systematic enhancement of its capability across north India. Part of this was the decision to shift the focus of its I Strike Corps away from Pakistan towards China and also reorient reserve forces northwards. Additional forces are also being pushed in to cover the somewhat loosely defended central sector involving the states of Himachal Pradesh and Uttarakhand.[29]

But the issue is no longer eastern Ladakh, but the entire LAC. In late August 2021 a large PLA patrol intruded into the Barahoti bowl, a pasturage in the central sector which emerged as one of the first points of dispute between the two countries in 1954. As Sushant Singh has pointed out, there had been a demilitarization agreement here which meant that no uniformed personnel could enter the area.[30]

On 28 September 2021 there was report of an intrusion by some 200 PLA personnel, 12–16 km at Yangtse, east of Bum La in the Tawang sector in the east. But they were immediately checked by the Indian side and detained for some time but released after intervention at the local commander level. Similar ingresses and intrusions have seen a marked increase in other parts of the LAC in the region. None of these activities is new or unique, except that it appears that the Chinese patrols have increased significantly in size.[31]

With its strong deployments, India is not too concerned, but it has adopted a posture of heightened alert across the east as well, from the Chumbi valley, north of Doklam, to the eastern extremity of Kibithu in Arunachal Pradesh. In Indian Army terminology, the forces are on "Op Alert" which does not require additional deployments, but the observance of specially laid down protocols to prevent being caught by surprise, as was the case in eastern Ladakh in the summer of 2020.

India has also markedly stepped up its efforts at infrastructure construction. By next year, it should have a tunnel at the strategic Se La pass that links the plains of Assam to Tawang. Defences in the Tawang tract have been strengthened, especially since the Chinese have never made any bones about wanting to "recover" this area since the mid-1980s. But a build up is also taking place in other areas of Arunachal in response to the heightened infrastructure development activities across the LAC which, as we noted earlier, also include the construction of model villages close to the border.[32]

There is considerable evidence to show that the Chinese, too, have enhanced their posture on the border. Where earlier it was lightly policed by the PLA's Border Defence Regiments, now, regular forces are being housed in newly built facilities closer to the LAC and new capabilities are being added to the PLA's posture in Tibet.[33] Currently air bases in Hotan and Kashghar in Xinjiang near Aksai Chin, Ngari-Gunsa, Lhasa, Changdu-Bangda (Chamdo), Gongkar and Nyingchi are being upgraded with hardened shelters and additional runways, new airbases are under construction in Tingri and Damxung opposite Sikkim and Arunachal, as well as at Tashkorgan in Xinjiang. Analysts say that their aim is to project "increased firepower along the largely disputed borders with India." But the move is also aimed at reducing vulnerability to the capabilities being deployed by the Indian military.[34]

It could well be that the real goal of the Chinese in 2020 was to raise the cost of border management for the Indians to the point where it demands a larger chunk of its defence budget and checks Indian efforts to grow its maritime profile. India's defence budget has been strained for some time now for a variety of factors. One major problem is manpower costs, such as the ones that arise when the army is used to police borders. India today has an army which is larger than that of China and a pension bill which exceeds Pakistan's entire defence budget.[35] As a result of these constraints the Indian Navy has, for the present, abandoned plans for its second indigenously built aircraft carrier, and its long-term fleet goal of 200 warships by 2027 has been reduced to 175. India risks losing the clear advantage it has over China in the Indian Ocean because of the growth of the PLA Navy in the Indian Ocean Region and its pursuit of military facilities there.[36]

* * *

The Chinese view their Indian interaction through the lens of their concept of "comprehensive national power" (CNP). The concept was developed in the early 1980s based on traditional Chinese military philosophy, whose acme was to win wars without fighting. As Colonel Wu Chunqiu of the Academy of Military Sciences argued in 2000, "Victory without war does not mean that there is no war at all. The wars one must fight are political wars, economic wars, science and technology (S&T) wars, diplomatic wars, etc. To sum up in a word, it is a war of Comprehensive National Power (CNP)."[37]

Till 1990, the GDP and technology levels of both countries were roughly equal, though India was better integrated into the world economy. But as of 2021, China's economy is five times larger than India's, it has created an impressive technological base and it is the world's leading trading nation through which most supply chains run. China today probably exceeds India in almost all the elements of national power: the ones that can be measured, economic, S&T and military and even the ones that can't, like national will, social cohesion and the strength of the governance system.

What we have seen, though, is that as the gap in their respective GNP widened, it changed the dynamics of their relationship. For the past decade or more, Beijing has refused to consider India as an equal. New Delhi is not ready to reconcile with this reality and has sought to right the imbalance by drawing closer to the United States and is working for a coalition of like-minded countries in a bid to balance Chinese power, hoping somehow to kickstart a phase of high economic growth that could right the equation.

As M. Taylor Fravel has pointed out, China has to balance between its primary versus secondary direction. But since the mid-2000s there has been talk in China of India taking advantage of a possible Taiwan contingency. In his view China probably acted to signal to India that despite the increased pressure it is facing on its primary front, New Delhi cannot improve its position at China's cost.[38]

As of now, the Indian military will be able to hold its own in both Himalayan and Indian Ocean settings. In a war, the task before the Indians is to hold their line; but for Beijing to come off with anything less than a victory would be a setback. But as China races to compete with the US, the technological asymmetry between Beijing and New Delhi is growing and, in the words of Sushant Singh, "in a few years it is feared that India and China will be fighting two different generations of war."[39]

Beijing's inability to be a regionally dominant actor in the South Asia—Indian Ocean Region would undermine its longer term goal to be a Great Power. In the east it already confronts the US and Japan, and if it is also constrained in the south-west, its room for maneuver will be limited. It cannot ignore the fact that today, there seems to be a growing fusion between its western and southern adversaries.

Can the toothpaste be put back in the tube?

The trajectory of sharpened geopolitical competition between India and China is not an entirely comfortable one for either country. History has shown that there has been no serious conflict between the Chinese and Indian civilizations; indeed there has been a learning process that has benefited both. But we are now in a different era, with Chinese and Indian armies facing off against each other across thousands of kilometres. Indian warships track Chinese movements in the Indian Ocean and diplomats and spies compete in the region.

The trick so far was to manage the relationship in such a way that it did not lead to an armed clash. Even taking into account the Galwan incident, the two have been successful. But the disequilibrium in their relationship is showing, not only along the Line of Actual Control, but the larger region. Unbridled military competition is certainly not in their interests, especially since their ongoing boundary dispute can always provide an occasion for military clashes that could lead to a wider war with unforeseen consequences. So, the big question is, can the relationship between the two revert to a measure of state-to-state civility, or, to put it another way, can the toothpaste be put back into the tube?

As soon as the Chinese side began to understand the extent to which the Galwan clash had altered Indian mainstream attitudes towards China, there were efforts to mitigate the situation. This was just about when Trump administration officials like Secretary of State Mike Pompeo and Deputy National Security Adviser Matt Pottinger stepped up their efforts to attack China, viewing it as an ideal opportunity to pull India closer to an alignment with the US.

While think tank commentators continued to maintain a hard line on India, the official tone was less belligerent. In August 2020, defence ministry spokesman Senior Colonel Wu Qian called on India to continue the dialogue and cool down the tension, adding that New Delhi should "bear in mind the big picture of bilateral ties" and put the border issue "in an appropriate position in this big picture."[40] Some months later this was echoed by the hawkish foreign ministry spokesman Zhao Lijian who said that an important lesson of moving Sino–Indian ties ahead was the need to delink the border issue from bilateral relations.[41]

Chinese officials, including Ambassador Sun Weidong, conducted a series of outreach meetings in August and September 2020 where the message was that China's basic policy towards India had not changed: "China sees India as a partner instead of a rival, and an opportunity instead of a threat." He hoped to use dialogue and consultation to "push bilateral relations back on track at an early date." Where earlier he had aggressively argued China's case on the Galwan issue, he was now oblique in merely stating that "its merit is very clear."[42]

In November 2020, I participated in a dialogue with Sichuan University which had trundled out the venerable Dai Bingguo as its star participant. The basic point he made was the need to go back to the Wuhan and Chennai "consensus" that the two countries "should be partners and should not become rivals of each other." Further, we should be "sensitive to each other's core interest and manage differences." Dai emphasized that "strategic consensus" was extremely important: "If we give it up this will shake the roots of our bilateral relations." He urged India "to stick to the diplomatic cornerstone of strategic autonomy." In his view, and this has been expressed by other Chinese writers, it was not a good idea to club bilateral relations with the boundary question.[43]

The Chinese message was amplified in March 2021 when China's Foreign Minister Wang Yi addressed the customary press conference at the National People's Congress. In his remarks he pointed out that the boundary dispute was "not the whole story" of the relationship between India and China. The two countries were "each other's friends and partners, not threats or rivals." He said it would take efforts by both sides to set things right.[44] In fact, two weeks earlier in a telephonic conversation with his Indian counterpart S. Jaishankar, Wang Yi had complained that "there had been some wavering and back pedalling in India's China's policy" which had affected "practical cooperation."[45]

The Indian side for its part has not been unreceptive to the message. New Delhi has its problems with China, but it would like to maintain the balance of the 4 "C's" and continue to cooperate and trade with China, because it has no immediate alternative. This is despite the various restraints that had been put on Chinese economic activity in India. Whether it is the Indian consumer, or the industry, it cannot do without its links to the Chinese supply chain. This situation will be intensified as the Regional Comprehensive Economic Partnership (RCEP) comes into effect in 2022 drawing in most major economies of the Indo—Pacific into its orbit, except that of India.

As we noted, the government of India had not wanted to go the way it was forced to after the Galwan incident. It has even now provided little detail of the other Chinese transgressions, especially the ones with serious consequences in the Depsang Plains and the Kugrang river valley near Gogra and the Charding Nala near Demchok. More than a year later, in December 2021, the government was still formally denying that there had been any intrusions whatsoever. As the winter session of the 2021 parliament began, Subramanium Swamy (a maverick ruling party member of parliament) complained that the Rajya Sabha (upper house of parliament) had disallowed a question he had posed on whether the Chinese had crossed the LAC in Ladakh. He said that the Rajya Sabha Secretariat had told him that they had done this on the recommendation of the Ministry of Defence because it involved "national interest."[46]

External Affairs Minister Jaishankar has acknowledged that Sino–Indian ties are "under exceptional stress." He has made it clear that the Indian bottom line is that peace and tranquillity on the border is the basis for development of relations in other domains. Even as he has been seeking an explanation for China's changed stance in Ladakh, he has also been calling for the need for the two sides to maintain "mutual respect, mutual sensitivity and mutual interests."[47]

Speaking at the annual Raisina Dialogue in April 2021, Jaishankar rejected the notion that the Quad was any kind of NATO in the making. He said that building coalitions of like-minded countries was to fill the gaps that had arisen in multilateralism. He said that the latest summit had made it clear that it dealt with a wide variety of issues ranging from vaccine collaboration to resilient supply chains and maritime security.[48]

So, the big question is: can Sino–Indian ties return to some semblance of normality? This need not involve any dramatic resolution of their longstanding boundary dispute, or even clarifying the points of difference on the Line of Actual Control. But it would undoubtedly require a new set of rules to manage the LAC. Some elements of this are already visible, such as the creation of "no patrol" zones in Galwan and Pangong Tso. Additional zones could be established where the Chinese have been blocking Indian access, such as in Depsang, Kugrang and the Charding area. They will all fall on the Indian side of the LAC, but even so, if they are observed and neither side patrols them, it will be better than nothing. There is also something which the western border could adopt from the practice in the east, where Indian and Chinese troops patrol contested areas on alternate weeks. All this will be better than the prospect of a military escalation, which can always lead to war.

Something like this has been suggested by Qian Feng, a well-known former journalist who has worked in India, and who is now with the research department of the National Strategy Institute of Tsinghua University. In an article he wrote for an Indian defence magazine *Force* in September 2020, Qian suggested that "the concept of a 'zone of actual control' can replace the concept of 'line of actual control' in some areas."[49]

All this is possibly doable, but it presupposes that the Chinese will not, as an instrument of policy, exploit the fuzziness on the border, which will not go away with the border zones as they have with the LAC so far. As Yun Sun has put it, "Beijing sees the unsettled border as leverage to bog down India in the region and undermine its global potential."[50] She has argued that the timing and nature of the confrontation raised issues of China's "strategic calculations and tactical objectives." Tactically China would like to put an end to the competitive infrastructure development on the LAC, but strategically it is in no hurry to resolve the disputes India's infrastructure develops.

For this reason, the new *modus vivendi* between the two countries will come with a high level of distrust and will require a new learning process which will require us to first abandon the expectations that came with the 1993 and 1996 agreements and the notion of "mutual and equal security," and then putting together some new set of procedures and protocols for border management.

Chinese policy will be driven not by considerations relating to this or that bit of land along the LAC, or the relations between India and the United States, but by China's own goals and interests, which remain opaque given its system. Whether it will succeed, or not, is a another matter.

But as of now there remains a wide gulf in their respective positions. Remarks at a September 2021 meeting between Indian Foreign Minister S. Jaishankar and his Chinese counterpart Wang Yi at the sidelines of the SCO ministerial meeting at Dushanbe, bring this out. Even while maintaining military vigilance on the LAC, the Indian side has patiently sought to use the diplomatic weapon to push the Chinese to restore the status quo on the Ladakh border. In line with this, Jaishankar called for an early resolution of "remaining issues" along the Line of Actual Control and asked the Chinese not to look at their ties with India through the perspective of its relations with third countries (read the United States).[51]

Wang Yi simply ignored the "early resolution" bit and said that he wanted the Indian side to meet the Chinese "halfway" and promote "continued stability of the [border] situation, and gradually shift from emergency response to normalised management." In his view, there was need "to consolidate the results of the disengagement of frontline forces and strictly abide by the agreements and consensus reached between the two countries."[52]

* * *

Is there a danger of war in the Himalaya?

As of the end of 2021, both India and China have handled the situation on the Line of Actual Control with a great deal of discretion. To start with, China's 2020 operation was carefully crafted: it either targeted unheld areas on the LAC, or resorted to blockades to prevent India patrolling the border up to its claimed line. Strong Chinese forces were deployed to back up this operation, but not strong enough to undertake a broad attack on Indian positions.

The Indian response was equally carefully calibrated to keep the temperature down. It mirrored Chinese deployments and did not for its part indicate at any time that it could involve a cross-LAC military operation. The one it did launch, to occupy the strategic heights of the Kailash range overlooking the Spanggur Tso, was restricted to positions that were clearly within the Indian side of the LAC. New Delhi has taken recourse to negotiation and dialogue to persuade China to restore the situation as it existed in April of 2020. In the words of its Army Chief General M.M. Naravane in May 2021, after the pull back in Pangong Tso and Galwan, negotiations were taking place "for resolution of other friction points in a firm but non-escalatory manner." He added that as of that date the Chinese continued to deploy its mechanized forces and troops in the "depth areas" behind the LAC.[53]

Both sides have been presented with situations where they were being pushed to escalate the situation—India at the outset and China when India moved onto the Kailash range—but they forbore. Both have powerful armies and a major war between them would be devastating, and we are not even talking about the total destruction that could accompany a nuclear escalation. Both are sharply aware that war, even a conventional one, would set them back by decades.

Through 2021, even as the Ladakh sector saw some disengagement, the two sides remained frozen in their existing positions. There was some contention in the central and eastern sectors, but they played largely by the ground rules established earlier. Face-offs and near clashes were reported, but were quickly dealt with by existing mechanisms, which seem to be functioning in the other parts of the LAC other than eastern Ladakh.

At the same time, both sides have stepped up their infrastructure construction and the enhancement of the quality of their military deployments on either side of the LAC. The Chinese have upgraded the equipment of their ground forces and have been focusing on the perceived weakness, especially in relation to the Indian Air Force, while the Indian side continues to push the building of roads and tunnels to access the LAC.[54]

There has been a qualitative change in the patterns of deployment of both armies. The Chinese, who normally kept the PLA well away from the LAC, are now building facilities to have them closer in certain areas. The Indian side has, probably permanently, shifted some forces from their orientation towards Pakistan to the northern border. More important, with the creation of two key strike formations, the Indian side has indicated that any future border war will feature offensive action on the part its army in Tibet.

Now, in Ladakh at least, the two sides no longer have the web of confidence-building measures and protocols that prevented face-offs from degenerating into skirmishes that could escalate into war. Indeed, after Galwan, India authorized its forces to use their guns should the need for them arise in any contingency. There are two reasons for this. First, the wounds of Galwan are still raw. And second, the Indian grievance over the continued blockade of certain parts of the LAC in Depsang, the Kugrang river valley and the Charding-Ninglung Nala has yet to be addressed.

So, the enduring threat of war remains high in the Himalaya. Since both India and China are expanding their war-making capacity, it does enhance the risk of conflict. Both sides seem to be caught in a classic security dilemma where the actions of A to increase its security appear to diminish the security of B. But as B reacts to increase its security, it diminishes the security of A.

Given its resources and technological proficiency, China may hope to come out ahead in this contest. But even if India reconciles itself to being the weaker party, it is unlikely to accept Chinese primacy in the South Asia—Indian Ocean Region. It has with it the lesson of Pakistan which has successfully used asymmetrical strategies to contest India's claim to South Asian primacy. India has more options than Pakistan since the Chinese ineptitude has alienated many countries, especially the United States.

Yet, relations between the two countries have reached a certain level of stability. Trade has grown sharply, despite the clash of 2020 and the COVID pandemic. In 2021, India's trade with China grew a substantial 43 per cent, which was in keeping with the increase of Chinese trade with its other major trading partners—the ASEAN, EU and the US. But the Indian increase was the highest. This indicates a level of mutual benefit in the relations between the two countries. Though India has introduced schemes to lessen its dependence on China, it is not clear as to whether they will succeed. Further, the two sides continue to talk to each other, at the ministerial, if not the summit level. At various forums like the SCO, BRICS and the Russia—India—China meetings, India's External Affairs Minister S. Jaishankar has engaged his Chinese counterpart Wang Yi in discussions over their vexed border issue. Other mechanisms such as the military-to-military meetings at the Chushul-Moldo point and elsewhere have continued, as does the Working Mechanism for Consultation and Cooperation (WMCC): and the hotlines in Chushul and DBO continue to buzz.

So, as Shivshankar Menon puts it: "more likely we will see continued efforts to negotiate side by side with jostling for local advantage along the LAC and a continued build-up of infrastructure and capabilities by both sides." In essence what the two Asian giants will see is "antagonistic cooperation in a fragmented world."[55]

NOTES

INTRODUCTION

1. A confidential cable by a US diplomat to his headquarters gives details of the incident which were contested by the two sides. "Sino–Indian border incident" dated 5 November 1975, https://www.wikileaks.org/plusd/cables/1975NEWDE14671_b.html

2. Bharti Jain, "No Chinese intrusion since 2010, only 'transgressions': Govt," *The Times of India*, 20 August 2014, https://timesofindia.indiatimes.com/india/No-Chinese-intrusion-since-2010-only-transgressions-Govt/articleshow/40457901.cms

3. The figure is from Frank Dikötter, *The Tragedy of Liberation: A history of the Chinese revolution, 1945–57* (New York, Bloomsbury, 2013), p. 100.

4. Jagat S. Mehta, *Negotiating for India: Resolving problems through diplomacy* (New Delhi, Manohar, 2006), p. 118.

5. A.G. Noorani, *India–China Boundary Problem 1846–1947: History and diplomacy,* (New Delhi, Oxford University Press, 2011), pp. 188–95.

6. Shyam Saran, *How India Sees the World: From Kautilya to the 21ˢᵗ century* (New Delhi, Juggernaut, 2017), p. 126. Saran, a Mandarin speaker, has specialized in Chinese affairs.

7. Brigadier K. Bag Singh, "The saga of Chushul ALG, 14260 ft. SL," *Vayu Aerospace Review*, 2 December 2020, https://www.vayuaerospace.in/article/576/the-saga-of-chushul-alg-14260-ft-asl

8. Saran, *How India Sees the World*, p. 135.

9. Ye Hailin, "The impact of identity bias on the prospects of Sino–Indian relations," *Indian Ocean Economy Research*, Issue 3, 30 July 2020, http://www.cssn.cn/gjgxx/gj_ytqy/202007/t20200730_5163496.html (machine translation)

10. Yun Sun, "China's strategic assessment of India," *War on the Rocks*, 25 March 2020, https://warontherocks.com/2020/03/chinas-strategic-assessment-of-india/?

1. BREAKDOWN

1. Sushant Singh, Subhajit Roy and Krishn Kaushik, "Delhi prepares for long haul: Military, diplomatic engagements to continue," *Indian Express*, 8 June 2020, https://indianexpress.com/article/india/india-china-ladakh-lac-border-6447884/

2. Rahul Tripathi and Manu Pubby, "Covid 19 delayed Indian exercise, Chinese moved into key positions," *The Economic Times*, 3 June 2020, https://economictimes.indiatimes.com/news/defence/covid-19-delayed-indian-exercise-chinese-moved-into-key-positions/articleshow/76163629.cms?from=mdr

3. Sushant Singh, "First intel on PLA came mid-April, long before Pangong clash," *Indian Express*, 15 July

2020, https://indianexpress.com/article/india/pla-troop-movement-lac-pangong-clash-indian-army-6506134/

4. Dinakar Peri, "Indian, Chinese troops face off in Eastern Ladakh, Sikkim," *The Hindu*, 10 May 2020, https://www.thehindu.com/news/national/indian-chinese-troops-face-off-in-eastern-ladakh-sikkim/article31548893.ece

5. Ibid.; The Wire Staff, "India calls last week's face-offs with Chinese troops regular feature caused by unresolved LAC," *The Wire*, 14 May 2020, https://thewire.in/external-affairs/india-china-border-faceoff-lac

6. Media Center, "Transcript of media briefing by official spokesperson (May 14, 2020)," *Ministry of External Affairs, Government of India*, 15 May 2020, https://mea.gov.in/media-briefings.htm?dtl/32696/Transcript_of_Media_Briefing_by_Official_Spokesperson_May_14_2020

7. Ajay Bannerjee, "India completes vital Ladakh road," *The Tribune*, 22 April 2020, https://www.tribuneindia.com/news/archive/nation/india-completes-vital-ladakh-road-762332

8. "The Indian army crosses the line and enters Galwan Valley area of China to block our army from patrolling on duty," *sina.com*, 18 May 2020, https://mil.news.sina.com.cn/china/2020–05–18/doc-iircuyvi3748861.shtml

9. Henry Boyd and Meia Nouwens, "Understanding the military buildup on the China-India border," *IISS blogs* (International Institute for Strategic Studies, London), 18 June 2020, https://www.iiss.org/blogs/analysis/2020/06/china-india-border

10. Himanshi Dhavan's interview with Shyam Saran, *The Times of India*, 24 May 2020, https://timesofindia.indiatimes.com/india/chinese-reaction-may-be-a-warning-so-that-india-sides-with-it-on-covid-taiwan-says-ex-foreign-secy-shyam-saran/articleshow/75926909.cms?

11. H. S. Panag "China believes India wants Aksai Chin back. PLA likely secured 40–60 sq. km in Ladakh," *The Print*, 28 May 2020, https://theprint.in/opinion/china-believes-india-wants-aksai-chin-back-thats-why-it-has-crossed-lac-in-ladakh/430899/; Yash Mor, "The lesson for RAW, IB from Kargil to Ladakh—fix responsibility," *The Print*, 5 January 2021, https://theprint.in/opinion/the-lesson-for-raw-ib-from-kargil-to-ladakh-fix-responsibility/579262/; "Were aware of Chinese mobilization in Eastern Ladakh but couldn't anticipate intentions, says Army Chief," *News18 India*, 12 January 2021, https://www.news18.com/news/india/were-aware-of-chinese-mobilisation-in-eastern-ladakh-but-couldnt-anticipate-intentions-says-army-chief-3275678.html

12. Press Trust of India, "Chinese soldiers in large numbers along LAC: Rajnath Singh," *India Today*, 2 June 2020, https://www.indiatoday.in/india/story/chinese-soldiers-in-large-numbers-along-lac-rajnath-singh-1684842–2020–06–02

13. Mao Yuelin, "The People's Liberation Army returns to the line of control in 1962, China refuses to border gray areas," *Hong Kong News*, 4 June 2020, https://www.hk01.com/International Analysis/481736/China-India confrontation-the People's Liberation Army returns to the 1962 line of control-China rejects the border gray area (Machine Translation)

14. Media Center, "Text of Raksha Mantri (Defence Minister) Shri Rajnath Singh's statement in Lok Sabha on September 15, regarding the situation on eastern border in Ladakh," *Ministry of External Affairs, Government of India*, https://mea.gov.in/Speeches-Statements.htm?dtl/32971/Text+of+Raksha+Mantri+Shri+Rajnath+Singhs+Statement+in+Lok+Sabha+on+September+15+Regarding+Situation+on+Eastern+Border+in+Ladakh

15. Vijaita Singh, "China controls 1,000 sq. km of area in Ladakh," *The Hindu*, 31 August 2020, https://www.thehindu.com/news/national/china-controls-1000-sq-km-of-area-in-ladakh-say-intelligence-inputs/article32490453.ece

16. Shishir Gupta, "Galwan river bridge that China tried to stop in Ladakh is complete, says official," *Hindustan Times*, 19 June 2020, https://www.hindustantimes.com/india-news/galwan-valley-bridge-that-china-tried-to-stop-in-ladakh-is-complete-official/story-ODJ7CHLEtwr1Wn34kZnEkM.html

17. Press Trust of India, "India,China disengagement has begun north of the Galwan river, says Army

chief Naravane," *The Print*, 13 June 2020, https://theprint.in/defence/everything-under-control-on-borders-with-china-says-army-chief-general-mm-naravane/440920/

18. For a version of the incident see, Barkha Dutt, "Opinion: The inside story of how India and China came to blows in the Himalayas," *The Washington Post*, 22 June 2020, https://www.washingtonpost.com/opinions/2020/06/22/inside-story-how-india-china-came-blows-himalayas/; see also Shiv Aroor, "3 separate brawls, 'outsider' Chinese troops & more: Most detailed account of the brutal June 15 Galwan battle," *India Today*, 22 June 2020, https://www.indiatoday.in/india/story/3-separate-brawls-outsider-chinese-troops-more-most-detailed-account-of-the-brutal-june-15-galwan-battle-1691185-2020-06-21

19. Sushant Singh, "India–China Galwan faceoff: How serious is the situation, what happens next?," *Indian Express*, 19 June 2020, https://indianexpress.com/article/explained/gulwan-faceoff-china-india-border-dispute-explained-6463394/

20. Liu Xin, Guo Yuandan and Zhang Hui, "China unveils details of 4 PLA martyrs at Galwan Valley border clash for first time, reaffirming responsibility falls on India," *Global Times*, 19 February 2021, https://www.globaltimes.cn/page/202102/1215914.shtml

21. Wang Tianyi, "The heroic officers and soldiers approaching the border guarding the country in the new era: The heroes stand tall in Karakorum," *China Military Net*, 19 February 2021, http://www.81.cn/yw/2021-02/19/content_9987403.htm (machine translation)

22. For the pictures of 9 October 2021, see https://twitter.com/aadilbrar/status/1446853465196666889?s=20 and for the video see https://twitter.com/shen_shiwei/status/1448622742853591042; https://twitter.com/Dfllite/status/1446734619349377025

23. https://twitter.com/aadilbrar/status/1364560957205336071/photo/1

24. The figures of those dead correspond to endnotes 20 and 25. As for those taken captive, they are surmised from photos cited in endnote 22.

25. See Happymon Jacob's interview with M. Taylor Fravel, 5 April 2021, https://www.youtube.com/watch?v=fm8u—Fz5MM

26. "Army says 20 Indian soldiers killed in Ladakh clash with Chinese troops, 'Both sides now disengaged,'" *The Wire*, 16 June 2020, https://thewire.in/security/indian-army-officers-killed-china-galwan-valley

27. Steven Lee Myers, Maria Abi-Habib and Jeffrey Gettleman, "In China-India clash, two nationalist leaders with little room to give," *The New York Times*, 17 June 2020, https://www.nytimes.com/2020/06/17/world/asia/china-india-border.html

28. "The military responds to the conflict between China and India border guards: The Indian army deliberately provocative attack," *People's Daily Online Military Channel*, http://military.people.com.cn/n1/2020/0616/c1011-31749029.html (Google translate)

29. Hu Xijin, Twitter 17 June 2020, https://twitter.com/HuXijin_GT/status/1272973497766051840

30. Media Center, "Phone call between External Affairs Minister, Dr S. Jaishankar and Foreign Minister of China, H.E. Mr Wang Yi," *Ministry of External Affairs, Government of India*, 17 June 2020, https://mea.gov.in/press-releases.htm?dtl/32765/phone+call+between+external+affairs+minister+dr+s+jaishankar+and+foreign+minister+of+china+he+mr+wang+yi

31. Press Information Bureau, Government of India, "Prime Minister Narendra Modi's remarks to the All Party meeting June 19, 2020," https://www.pib.gov.in/PressReleaseDetail.aspx?PMO=3&PRID=1632743

32. Press Information Bureau, Government of India, "Prime Minister's Office statement on all Party meeting on 19 June 2020," *Press Information Bureau, Government of India*, 20 June 2020, https://www.pib.gov.in/PressReleaseDetail.aspx?PMO=3&PRID=1632856

33. Embassy of China, New Delhi, "Foreign Ministry spokesperson gave a step by step account of the Galwan Valley incident," *Embassy News*, 20 June 2020, http://in.china-embassy.org/eng/embassy_news/t1790579.htm

34. Interview of Prof. Jin Yinan by *CCB News*, 23 June 2020 (Machine translation), http://m.cnr.cn/mil/20200623/t20200623_525140587.html

35. Embassy news, "Chinese Ambassador to India H.E. Sun Weidong gave interview to Press Trust of India on Galwan Valley Incident," *Embassy of the People's Republic of China in the Republic of India*, 25 June 2020, http://in.china-embassy.org/eng/embassy_news/t1792381.htm

36. Ananth Krishnan, "China has crossed its 1960 claims along the LAC," *The Hindu*, 20 July 2020, https://www.thehindu.com/news/national/china-has-crossed-its-1960-claims-along-the-lac/article32133689.ece

37. Press Trust of India, "India and China hold Major General-level talks," *The Hindustan Times*, 8 August 2020, https://www.hindustantimes.com/india-news/indian-chinese-armies-hold-talks-on-ladakhs-depsang-plains/story-S1GATamAArhn7avZwMLyTM.html

38. "Text of Shreya Dhoundiyal interview of Lt Gen Y.K. Joshi", *News18*, 17 February 2021, https://www.news18.com/news/india/exclusive-india-has-not-ceded-land-china-has-just-earned-a-bad-name-at-least-45-chinese-soldiers-were-killed-3444080.html

39. Lt Gen. (Dr) Rakesh Sharma (retd), "Eastern Ladakh: NTR (Nothing to Report)—'Trust but Verify' Information," *Vivekanand International Foundation*, 26 April 2021, https://www.vifindia.org/article/2021/april/26/eastern-ladakh-ntr-trust-but-verify-information

40. Dinakar Peri, "'Patrol blocking in Depsang by both sides will take time to resolve,'" *The Hindu*, 27 July 2021, https://www.thehindu.com/news/national/patrol-blocking-in-depsang-by-both-sides-will-take-time-to-resolve/article35567904.ece

41. Sushant Singh, "What Rajnath left out: PLA blocks access to 900 sq. km of Indian territory in Depsang," *The Wire*, September 2020 https://thewire.in/diplomacy/depsang-ladakh-india-china-rajnath-singh-parliament

42. Secretary of Defense Lloyd J Austin III Press Conference in New Delhi, 20 March 2021, https://www.defense.gov/Newsroom/Transcripts/Transcript/Article/2544454/secretary-of-defense-lloyd-j-austin-iii-press-conference-in-new-delhi/

43. Media Center, "Joint Press Statement—Meeting of External Affairs Minister and the Foreign Minister of China (September 10, 2020)," *Ministry of External Affairs, Government of India*, 10 September 2020, https://www.mea.gov.in/press-releases.htm?dtl/32962/Joint+Press+Statement++Meeting+of+External+Affairs+Minister+and+the+Foreign+Minister+of+China+September+10+2020

44. Abhishek Bhalla, "India buys winter clothing from US and Europe for Ladakh troops," *India Today*, 16 October 2020, https://www.indiatoday.in/india/story/india-buys-winter-clothing-ladakh-troops-us-europe-1732371-2020-10-16

45. "PLA at China-India border has upgraded logistics to brave winter," *Global Times*, 9 November 2020, https://www.globaltimes.cn/page/202111/1238568.shtml

46. Nitin A Gokhale, "Ladakh standoff: Breakthrough in India–China talks imminent," *Stratnewsglobal*, 11 November 2020, https://stratnewsglobal.com/india/ladakh-standoff-breakthrough-in-india-china-talks-imminent/

47. Guo Yuandan and Liu Xin, "Indian media's reports on detailed border disengagement plan with China 'inaccurate': Sources," *Global Times*, 12 December 2020, https://www.globaltimes.cn/content/1206606.shtml

48. Shiv Aroor, "'Inflexible' China refuses to disengage at Gogra, Hot Springs in eastern Ladakh," *India Today*, 19 April 2021, https://www.indiatoday.in/india/story/india-army-china-pla-ladakh-stand-off-talks-disengagement-gogra-hot-springs-depsang-1789525-2021-04-10

49. "India–China: 'Probability of an Armageddon is Zero': Excerpts of interview of Lt Gen. H. S. Panag," *The Citizen*, https, 12 April 2021, https://www.thecitizen.in/index.php/en/NewsDetail/index/4/20204/India-China-Probability-of-an-Armageddon-is-Zero-

50. Rajat Pandit, "India, China lash out at each other as talks reach bitter deadlock," *The Times of India*,

12 October 2021, https://timesofindia.indiatimes.com/india/lac-row-no-breakthrough-in-13th-round-of-india-china-talks/articleshow/86928076.cms

51. Krishn Kaushik, "No breakthrough in 14th round of India–China military talks, but two sides agree to 'meet soon'," *The Indian Express*, 13 January 2022, https://indianexpress.com/article/india/india-china-release-joint-statement-on-14th-round-of-talks-7721658/

52. Dinakar Peri, "Deal for disengagement at Gogra, Hot Springs in sight at 12ᵗʰ round of Corps Commander-level talks," *The Hindu*, 25 July 2021, https://www.thehindu.com/news/national/deal-for-disengagement-at-gogra-hot-springs-in-sight-at-12th-round-of-corps-commander-level-talks/article35524796.ece?homepage=true

53. Shivshankar Menon, "What China hopes to gain from the present border standoff," *The Wire*, 3 December 2020, Part 2, https://thewire.in/external-affairs/what-changed-india-china-ties-2020-result-rising-tensions

54. Shyam Saran, "Has China bitten off more than it can chew?" *The Hindustan Times*, 10 February 2021, https://www.hindustantimes.com/opinion/has-china-bitten-off-more-than-it-can-chew-101612878357695.html

55. Mathieu Duchatel, "The border clashes with India: In the shadow of the US," *China Trends* (Institut Montaigne), February 2021, https://www.institutmontaigne.org/ressources/pdfs/publications/china-trends-8-EN.pdf#page=7

56. Yun Sun, "China's strategic assessment of the Ladakh clash," *War on the Rocks*, 19 June 2020, https://warontherocks.com/2020/06/chinas-strategic-assessment-of-the-ladakh-clash/

57. M. Taylor Fravel, "Why are China and India skirmishing at their border? Here's four things to know," *The Washington Post*, 2 June 2020, https://www.washingtonpost.com/politics/2020/06/02/why-are-china-india-skirmishing-their-border-heres-4-things-know/

58. Sutirtho Patranobis, "China takes 1959 line on perception of LAC," *Hindustan Times*, 29 September 2020, https://www.hindustantimes.com/india-news/china-takes-1959-line-on-perception-of-lac/story-ciMDJjOeTLuvyvsNy7gJXI.html. According to Patranobis, one previous reference had been made during the Doklam crisis referring to the tussle that had been going on separately in the Pangong Tso area in August 2017.

59. "Official spokesperson's response to queries on the recent media report quoting a Chinese foreign ministry statement regarding China's position on the LAC, September 29, 2020," *Ministry of External Affairs, Government of India*, https://www.mea.gov.in/response-to-queries.htm?dtl/33074/Official_Spokespersons_response_to_queries_on_the_recent_media_report_quoting_a_Chinese_Foreign_Ministry_statement_regarding_Chinas_position_on_the_LA

60. "Foreign Ministry spokesman Wang Wenbin's regular press conference on September 29, 2020," *Ministry of Foreign Affairs of the People's Republic of China* https://www.fmprc.gov.cn/mfa_eng/xwfw_665399/s2510_665401/2511_665403/t1820149.shtml

61. "Foreign Ministry spokesperson Hua Chunying's remarks on the Indian government's announcement of the establishment of the Ladakh Union Territory which involved Chinese territory on August 6, 2019," *Ministry of Foreign Affairs, People's Republic of China*, https://www.fmprc.gov.cn/mfa_eng/xwfw_665399/s2510_665401/2535_665405/t1686549.shtml

62. "Foreign Ministry spokesman Zhao Lijian's regular press conference on October 13, 2020," *Ministry of Foreign Affairs, People's Republic of China*, https://www.fmprc.gov.cn/mfa_eng/xwfw_665399/s2510_665401/2511_665403/t1823606.shtml

63. Sushant Singh's interview with Chris Biggers, *The India Cable*, 21 December 2021, https://www.theindiacable.com/p/from-ladakh-to-eastern-sector-latest

64. M. Taylor Fravel, "A short thread on China's claims and maps in the Galwan Valley," *Twunroll*, https://twunroll.com/article/1275071132844978178

65. Zhang Li "Line of Control as a factor in Sino–Indian boundary issue," *South Asian Studies Quarterly* (Sichuan), Issue 2, 2017 (Google translate).

2. THE SINO–INDIAN BORDER DISPUTE

1. Ranjit Singh Kalha, *India–China Boundary Issues: Quest for a settlement* (New Delhi, Indian Council of World Affairs/Pentagon Press, 2014), pp. 109–14.

2. Steven A. Hoffman, *India and China Crisis* (New Delhi, Oxford University Press, 1990), p. 28.

3. Garver, *Protracted Contest Sino–Indian rivalry in the twentieth century*, (New Delhi, Oxford University Press, 2001), pp. 83–4.

4. Kalha, *India–China Boundary Issues*, p. 64.

5. A.S. Bhasin, *Nehru, Tibet and China* (New Delhi, Penguin/Viking, 2021), pp. 141–3.

6. Ibid., pp. 145–6.

7. Dorothy Woodman, *Himalayan Frontiers: A political review of British, Chinese, Indian and Russian rivalries* (London, Barrie and Rockliff, 1969), p. 225.

8. A. G. Noorani, *India–China Boundary Problem 1846–1947: History and diplomacy*, (New Delhi, Oxford University Press, 2011, p. 221.

9. Bhasin, *Nehru, Tibet and China*, pp. 208 and 216.

10. Nirupama Rao, *The Fractured Himalaya: India, Tibet, China 1949–1962* (New Delhi, Penguin/Viking, 2021), pp. 461–2.

11. "Letter from the Prime Minister of India to the Prime Minister of China, 14 December 1958," *White Paper Vol. 1: 1954–1959* (New Delhi, Ministry of External Affairs, Government of India), pp. 48–51.

12. "Letter from the Prime Minister of China to the Prime Minister of India, 23 January 1959," *White Paper Vol. 1: 1954–1959* (New Delhi, Ministry of External Affairs, Government of India), pp. 52–4.

13. "Letter from the Prime Minister of India to the Prime Minister of China, 22 March 1959," *White Paper vol 1: 1954–1959* (New Delhi Ministry of External Affairs, Government of India), pp. 55–7.

14. Kenneth Conboy and James Morrison, *The CIA's Secret War in Tibet* (Lawrence (KA), University Press Kansas, 2002), pp. 59–63; John Kenneth Knaus, *Orphans of the Cold War: America and the Tibetan struggle for survival* (New York, Public Affairs, 1999), pp. 153–5.

15. Bruce Riedel, *JFK's Forgotten Crisis: Tibet, the CIA and the Sino–Indian war* (New Delhi, Harper Collins, 2016), p. 61.

16. Editorial Department, "Renmin Ribao"(People's Daily), "The Revolution in Tibet and Nehru's Philosophy, May 6, 1959," in *Concerning the Question of Tibet* (Peking, Foreign Languages Press, 1959), p. 268.

17. "Letter from the Prime Minister of China to the Prime Minister of India, 8 September 1959," *White Paper Vol. II: September-November 1959*; and a historical background of the Himalayan frontier of India, p. 27.

18. "Letter from the Prime Minister of China to the Prime Minister of India, 17 December 1959," *White Paper Vol. III: November 1959–March 1960* (New Delhi, Ministry of External Affairs, Government of India).

19. "Letter from the Prime Minister of China to the Prime Minister of India, 7 November 1959," *White Paper Vol. III: November 1959–March 1960* (New Delhi, Ministry of External Affairs, Government of India), pp. 52–7.

20. "Note of the Ministry of Foreign Affairs of the People's Republic of China to the Indian Embassy in China, December 26, 1959," *Documents on the Sino–Indian Boundary Question* (Peking, Foreign Languages Press, 1960), pp. 29–72.

21. "Premier Chou En-lai's Letter to Prime Minister Nehru December 17, 1959," *Documents on the Sino–Indian Border Question*, p. 21.

22. See Library of Congress, *Zhonghua Renmin Gongheguo gua tu*, https://www.loc.gov/resource/g7820. ct004232/?r=-0.105,0.086,0.447,0.353,0

23. Hoffman, *India and China*, p. 82.

24. Kalha, *India–China Boundary Issue*, p. 133.

25. Rao, *Fractured Himalaya*, p. 373.

NOTES pp. [59–66]

26. Kalha, *India-China Boundary Issue*, pp. 167–9.

27. The maps were attached to the Indian and Chinese versions of "Report of the Officials of the Governments of India and the People's Republic of China on the Boundary Question" which was published by the Ministry of External Affairs, Government of India in 1961. This report and the attached maps are most conveniently accessed through their publication in the Selected Works of Jawaharlal Nehru, Second Series Volume 66 Supplement (14 February 1961). See The Internet Archive, https://archive.org/details/selectedworksofj66nehr/page/n5/mode/2up

28. "Report of the Officials of the Governments of India and the People's Republic of China on the Boundary Question", p. 19

29. Jagat S. Mehta, *Negotiating for India: Resolving problems through diplomacy* (seven case studies 1958–1978) (New Delhi, Manohar, 2006), p. 96.

30. Hoffman, *India and China*, p. 89.

31. Ibid., p. 30.

32. Garver, *Protracted Contest*, pp. 82–5.

33. Srinath Raghavan, "Sino–Indian boundary dispute, 1948–1960: A reappraisal," *Economic and Political Weekly* (Mumbai), 9 September 2006, pp. 3882–92.

34. Kang Minjun, "The Chinese government's efforts to peacefully resolve border disputes during the Sino–Indian border war," *Quishi*, 9 October 2013, http://theory.people.com.cn/n/2013/1009/c83867–23139029.html

35. The Henderson-Brooks/Bhagat report, pp. 8–10. The report on the inquiry held by Lt Gen. D. B. Henderson-Brooks and Lt Gen. P. S. Bhagat into the debacle of the Indian Army in 1962 was leaked to journalist Neville Maxwell and formed a basis of his path-breaking *India's China War* (London, Jonathan Cape, 1970). The report was posted on the web by Maxwell himself after half a century in 2014. Archived in the Wayback Machine, http://www.nevillemaxwell.com/TopSecretdocuments.pdf

36. Ibid.

37. S.N. Prasad et al. (eds), *History of the Conflict with China, 1962* (New Delhi, Ministry of Defence History Division, 1992), Chapter III. It needs to be noted that this is a manuscript of the history as readied for publication. It has yet to be actually published.

38. Air Marshal Bharat Kumar, *Unknown and Unsung: Indian Air Force in Sino-Indian War of 1962* (New Delhi, KW Publishers, 2013).

39. Ibid., pp. 318–27.

40. A 14 November 1962 instruction by the Central Military Commission to the PLA is cited in P.J.S. Sandhu, *1962: A view from the other side of the hill* (New Delhi, United Services Institution, 2015), p. 63.

41. Shyam Saran, *How India Sees the World: From Kautilya to the 21st century* (New Delhi, Juggernaut, 2017), pp. 135–6.

42. John W. Garver, "China's decision for war with India in 1962," in Alastair Iain Johnson and Robert S Ross (eds), *New Directions in the Study of China's Foreign Policy* (Stanford, Stanford University Press, 2006), pp. 86–130.

43. Zorawar Daulet Singh, *Power Shift: India–China relations in a multipolar world* (New Delhi, Macmillan, 2020), pp. 60–4.

44. Shivshankar Menon, *Choices: Inside the making of India's foreign policy* (New Delhi, Penguin, 2016), pp. 40–1.

45. "Letter from Premier Chou En-lai to Prime Minister of India, 24 October 1962," *White Paper Part III No. VIII* (Ministry of External Affairs, Government of India), pp. 1–2.

46. "Letter from Prime Minister of India to Premier Chou En-lai, 27 October, 1962," *White Paper Part III No. VIII* pp. 6–7

259

47. "Letter of Premier Chou En-lai to the Prime Minister of India, 4 November 1962," *White Paper Part III no. VIII* pp. 9–10.

48. "Letter from the Prime Minister of India to Premier Chou En-lai, 14 November 1962," *White Paper Part III, No. VIII*, p. 15.

49. "Letter from Premier Chou En-lai to the Prime Minister of India 28 November 1962," *White Paper Part III, No. VIII*, p. 32.

50. "Letter from the Prime Minister of India to Premier Chou En-lai, 1 December 1962," *White Paper Part III, No. VIII*, p. 37.

51. Memorandum given by the Ministry of External Affairs, New Delhi, to the Embassy of China in India, 30 November 1963, *White Paper Part III, No. VIII*, pp. 26–8.

52. Purnendu Kumar Banerjee, *My Peking Memoirs of the Chinese invasion of India* (New Delhi, Clarion Books, 1990), pp. 85–6.

53. Ibid., pp. 99–101.

3. NINETEEN NINETY-THREE

1. Oral history interview of Brajesh Mishra, "The 'Mao Smile' revisited: Sino–Indian relations during an important period," *Indian Foreign Affairs Journal*, vol. 1. no. 4, October–December 2006, pp. 109–18.

2. Shyam Saran, *How India Sees the World: From Kautilya to the 21st century* (New Delhi, Juggernaut, 2017), p. 138.

3. Major General Pradeep K. Batra, "'Operation Falcon': The Chinese intrusion in Wangdung-Sumdorong Chu in 1985–86," *Vayu Aerospace Magazine* (New Delhi), Issue 1, 2020 gives details of the Indian operation.

4. An aide of General Sundarji who was present at the meeting gave me these details. A completely different version comes from Natwar Singh who was junior External Affairs Minister in the Rajiv Gandhi government. According to Singh, this was a Cabinet Political Affairs Committee meeting in Parliament House and he, Singh, was the only one to bluntly question Sundarji's assessment—to which the general had had no response. K. Natwar Singh, *My China Diary: 1956–1988* (New Delhi, Rupa, 2009), p. 115.

5. "Introductory remarks and press conference by Prime Minister Rajiv Gandhi in Beijing on December 21, 1988," in *Prime Minister Rajiv Gandhi visits the People's Republic of China, December 19–23 1988* (Pamphlet produced by Ministry of External Affairs), p. 31.

6. For the course of talks and the discussions, see Ranjit Singh Kalha, *India–China Boundary Issues: Quest for settlement* (New Delhi, Indian Council for World Affairs, 2014), pp. 195–8.

7. Saran, *How India Sees the World*, p. 140.

8. Manoj Joshi, "The Sino–Indian border problem," *Strategic Analysis*, October 1992 (Institute for Defence Studies and Analysis, New Delhi), pp. 683–94.

9. Kalha, *India–China Boundary Issues*, p. 211.

10. Manoj Joshi, "Sino–Indian pact on LAC likely," *The Times of India* (New Delhi), 4 September 1993.

11. Shivshankar Menon, *Choices: Inside the Making of India's Foreign Policy* (New Delhi, Penguin, 2016), p. 25.

12. Shishir Gupta, *The Himalayan Face-off: Chinese assertion and the Indian riposte* (New Delhi, Hachette, 2015), pp. 92–3.

4. THE SEARCH FOR STABILITY

1. Ranjit Singh Kalha *India–China Boundary Issues: Quest for settlement* (New Delhi, Indian Council of World Affairs, 2014), p. 54.

2. Namrata Hasija, "India, China and Nathu La: Yesterday, today and tomorrow," *IPCS Issue Brief* No. 203, January 2013 (Institute of Peace and Conflict Studies, New Delhi), p. 2, http://www.jstor.org/stable/resrep09084

3. Manoj Joshi, "China is the potential threat No. 1, says George Fernandes," *India Today*, 18 May 1998, https://www.indiatoday.in/magazine/cover-story/story/19980518-china-is-the-potential-threat-no.-1-says-george-fernandes-826430-1998-05-18

4. "Nuclear anxiety; Indian's letter to Clinton on the Nuclear Testing," *The New York Times*, 13 May 1998, https://www.nytimes.com/1998/05/13/world/nuclear-anxiety-indian-s-letter-to-clinton-on-the-nuclear-testing.html

5. "Sino-US Joint Statement on South Asia," Beijing 27 June 1998, available on the Chinese embassy website in Washington DC, http://www.china-embassy.org/eng/zmgx/zysj/kldfh/t36228.htm

6. Government of India's response to the US-China "Joint statement on South Asia" 27 June 1998, Embassy of India, Washington DC, https://www.indianembassyusa.gov.in/ArchivesDetails?id=204

7. Strobe Talbott's *Engaging India: Diplomacy, democracy and the bomb* (Washington DC, Brookings, 2004) has detailed the process.

8. Jaswant Singh, *A Call to Honour: In service of emergent India* (New Delhi, Rupa, 2006), pp. 147–50.

9. General V. P. Malik, *Kargil: From surprise to victory* (New Delhi, Harper Collins, 2006), has published the translated version of the conversations in the Appendix. Malik was the Indian Army Chief at the time of the Kargil war.

10. Howard B. Schaffer, *The Limits of Influence: America's role in Kashmir* (New Delhi, Penguin, 2009), p. 162.

11. The details are there in Talbott, *Engaging India*, pp. 160–9.

12. Malik, *Kargil: From surprise to victory*, pp. 297–8.

13. Manoj Joshi, "The Kargil War: The fourth round," in Kanti Bajpai et al. (eds), *Kargil and After: Challenges for Indian policy* (New Delhi, Har Anand, 2001), p. 35.

14. Polly Naik and Michael Krepon, "US crisis management in South Asia's twin peaks crisis," Report 57, Stimson Center, September 2006 (second edn September 2014), https://www.stimson.org/wp-content/files/file-attachments/Twin_Peaks_Crisis.pdf

15. Statement in the Lok Sabha by Minister of Defence George Fernandes in response to unstarred question no. 2958 by Raghunath Jha on December 7, 2000.

16. Statement in the Rajya Sabha by Minister of Defence George Fernandes in response to unstarred question no. 1167 by P. Prabhakar Reddy March 7, 2001

17. Manoj Joshi, "India, China agree to exchange border maps," *The Times of India*, 31 March 2002, https://timesofindia.indiatimes.com/india/India-China-agree-to-exchange-border-maps/articleshow/5408781.cms

18. Kalha, *India–China Boundary Issues*, p. 215.

19. P. Stobdan, "As China intrudes across LAC, India must be alert to a larger shift," *Indian Express*, 26 May 2020, https://indianexpress.com/article/opinion/columns/the-ladakh-warning-india-china-border-dispute-6427131/

5. POLITICAL BARGAIN

1. John W. Garver, "The restoration of Sino–Indian comity following India's nuclear tests," *The China Quarterly*, December 2001, No. 168, https://www.jstor.org/stable/3657362 p. 865.

2. Select Committee of the United States House of Representatives, *US National Security and Military/Commercial Concerns with the People's Republic of China*, (Washington DC GPO, redacted version May 1999), 3 vols. See all-volume overview vol. 1, pp. i-xxvii, https://www.govinfo.gov/content/pkg/GPO-CRPT-105hrpt851/pdf/GPO-CRPT-105hrpt851.pdf

3. "Planning for Innovation: Understanding China's plans for technological, energy, industrial and defense

development," *A report prepared for the US-China Economic and Security Review Commission 28 July 2016*, https://www.uscc.gov/sites/default/files/Research/Planning%20for%20Innovation%20-%20 Understanding%20China's%20Plans%20for%20Tech%20Energy%20Industrial%20and%20 Defense%20Development072816.pdf. The report is authored by Tai Ming Cheung, Thomas Mahnken, Deborah Seligsohn, Kevin Pollpeter, Eric Anderson and Fan Yang

4. Ranjit Singh Kalha, *India–China Boundary Issues Quest for settlement* (New Delhi, Indian Council of World Affairs, 2014), p. 216.

5. Prabhu Chawla, "Historic visit to China by Prime Minister Vajpayee brings Beijing and Delhi closer," *India Today*, 3 July 2003, https://www.indiatoday.in/magazine/neighbours/story/20030707-his-toric-visit-to-china-by-prime-minister-vajpayee-brings-beijing-and-delhi-closer-792525-2003-07-07

6. Gyalo Thondup and Anne F. Thurston provide one account of the discussions the former had with Deng Xiaoping and other officials. See *The Noodle-maker of Kalimpong: The untold story of my struggle for Tibet* (Gurgaon, Random House India, 2015). Thondup is the Dalai Lama's elder brother and was the Tibetan point man for relations with the CIA in the 1950s.

7. Bernard Weinraub, "Peking reaction is worrying India," *The New York Times*, 4 May 1975, https://www.nytimes.com/1975/05/04/archives/peiking-reaction-is-worrying-india-criticism-of-sikkim-seizure-seen.html

8. Dai Bingguo, *Strategic Dialogues: The memoirs of Dai Bingguo* (Beijing, People's Publishing House, 2016) Chapter 8, p. 269. Translated by NB.

9. Manoj Joshi, "Delhi, Beijing close to settling border dispute," *The Hindustan Times*, 25 March 2005, pp. 1, 15.

10. Media Center, "Protocol between the Government of the Republic of India and the Government of the People's Republic of China on Modalities for the Implementation of Confidence Building Measures in the Military Field along the Line of Actual Control in the India–China border areas, 11 April 2005," *Ministry of External Affairs, Government of India*, https://www.mea.gov.in/bilateral-documents. htm?dtl/6539/Protocol+between+the+Government+of+the+Republic+of+India+and+the+Go vernment+of+the+Peoples+Republic+of+China+on+Modalities+for+the+Implementation+of +Confidence+Building+Measures+in+the+Military+Field+Along+the+Line+of+Actual+Contr ol+in+the+IndiaChina+Border+Areas

11. Anil K. Joseph, "Wen to seek resolution of border dispute," *Indian Express*, 15 March 2005, https://indianexpress.com/article/news-archive/wen-to-seek-resolution-of-border-dispute/

6. THE CRACKS BEGIN TO SHOW

1. "Pranab, Yang meet in Hamburg on boundary issue," *Outlook*, 29 May 2007, https://www.outlookin-dia.com/newswire/story/pranab-yang-meet-in-hamburg-on-boundary-issue/476889

2. Diwakar, "Settle the border dispute without displacing people, PM tells Hu," *The Times of India*, 8 June 2007, https://timesofindia.indiatimes.com/world/europe/Settle-border-dispute-without-displacing-people-PM-tells-Hu/articleshow/2107711.cms

3. Zhang Yan, "A perspective on India & China-India ties," *The Hindu*, 1 July 2008, https://www.the-hindu.com/todays-paper/tp-opinion/A-perspective-on-India-amp-China-India-ties/article1525 1822.ece

4. "Figures and facts: Five decades of Tibet's development," *China Daily*, 14 April 2008 https://www.chinadaily.com.cn/china/2008–04/14/content_6614912.htm

5. Karishma Waswani, "Why Asia turned to China during the global financial crisis," *BBC News*, 12 September 2018, https://www.bbc.com/news/business-45493147

6. Jonathan Kirshner, "Geopolitics after the Global Financial Crisis," *ISN/ ETH Zurich*, 3 September 2014, https://www.files.ethz.ch/isn/187867/ISN_183303_en.pdf

7. Indrani Bagchi, "Chinese incursions into Indian territory rose sharply in 2008," *The Times of India*, 9 June

2009, https://timesofindia.indiatimes.com/india/Chinese-incursions-into-Indian-territory-rose-sharply-in-2008/articleshow/4632640.cms

8. Special Correspondent, "Don't sensationalise boundary question, Wen tells media," *The Hindu*, 18 December 2010, http://www.thehindu.com/news/national/dont-sensationalise-boundary-question-wen-tells-media/article959327.ece

9. The back and forth between India and China formed the basis of a US embassy cable detailing the "war of words." This is part of the trove of US State Departments communications put out into the public domain by Wikileaks, https://wikileaks.org/plusd/cables/09NEWDELHI2248_a.html

10. United States Department of State, Bureau of Oceans and International Environmental and Scientific Affairs, *Limits in the Seas No. 143 China: Maritime Claims in the South China Sea*, 5 December 2014, https://2009-2017.state.gov/documents/organization/234936.pdf

11. See the translated version of the Chinese complaint against the Vietnamese deposition to the Limits of the Continental Shelf Commission. To this was attached a map detailing the Nine-Dash Line, https://www.un.org/depts/los/clcs_new/submissions_files/vnm37_09/chn_2009re_vnm.pdf

12. D.S. Rajan, "China: Post-Party Congress scenario: Policy indicators in two speeches of Xi Jinping," *Chennai Centre for China Studies*, 17 February 2013, https://www.c3sindia.org/geopolitics-strategy/china-post-party-congress-scenario-policy-indicators-in-two-speeches-of-xi-jinping/

13. Wikileaks, "PRC: Indian actions on Arunachal Pradesh designed to pressure China, say China scholars," Confidential cable from US Embassy, Beijing 14 July 2009, https://wikileaks.org/plusd/cables/09BEIJING1989_a.html

14. Vikram Seth, *From Heaven Lake: Travels through Sinkiang and Tibet* (New Delhi, Penguin, 1990).

15. "'Go West' campaign to accelerate," *China Daily*, 17 January 2005 http://www.china.org.cn/english/2005/Jan/118055.htm

16. Ananth Krishnan, "China spruces up highway through Aksai Chin," *The Hindu*, 11 July 2012, https://www.thehindu.com/news/international/china-spruces-up-highway-through-aksai-chin/article3628525.ece

17. For the military implications of the Qinghai Tibet Railway, see Shailender Arya, "The train to Lhasa," *Journal of Defence Studies* (IDSA, New Delhi) vol. 2 no. 2, 2008, https://idsa.in/system/files/jds_2_2_sarya.pdf

18. Monika Chansoria, "China's infrastructure in Tibet: Evaluating trendlines," *Manekshaw Paper*, No. 32, 2011 (New Delhi, Centre for Land Warfare Studies), pp. 12–13.

19. Ananth Krishnan, "China plans air and rail network to boost border infrastructure," *The Hindu*, 27 July 2010, https://www.thehindu.com/news/international/China-plans-air-and-rail-network-to-boost-border-infrastructure/article16212220.ece

20. Willy Lam, "Hu's 'New Deal' with Tibet: Chinese characteristics and Tibetan traits?" *ChinaBrief* (The Jamestown Foundation) vol. X, Issue 2, 21 January 2010, https://jamestown.org/program/hus-new-deal-with-tibet-chinese-characteristics-and-tibetan-traits/

21. Standing Committee on Defence (2010–2011), *Eleventh Report* [Action taken by the government on the recommendation/observations contained in the Eighth Report (Fifteenth Lok Sabha) on Construction of Roads in the Border Areas of the Country] New Delhi, Lok Sabha Secretariat, March 2011.

22. Shishir Gupta, *The Himalayan Face-off: Chinese assertion and the Indian riposte* (New Delhi, Hachette, 2015), pp. 232–5.

23. Ibid.

24. Press Trust of India, "China has 58,000 km of road network in TAR: Antony," *The Hindu*, 7 March 2011, https://www.thehindu.com/news/national/China-has-58000-km-of-road-network-in-TAR-Antony/article14938048.ece

25. Lora Saalman pointed out in 2011 that the Sino–Indian security dilemma was a complex affair and could not be viewed "through the prism of the border anymore." Lora Saalman, "Divergence, simi-

larity and symmetry in Sino–Indian threat perceptions," *Journal of International Affairs* (Columbia University New York), vol. 64, no. 2, Spring/Summer 2011, pp. 169–94, https://www.jstor.org/stable/24385541

26. Murray Scot Taner with Kerry B. Dumbaugh and Ian M. Easton, "Distracted antagonists, wary partners: China and India assess their security relations," *CAN Analysis & Solutions* (Alexandria, VA), pp. 31–4, https://app.s.dtic.mil/dtic/tr/fulltext/u2/a552567.pdf

27. Wei Wei, "Five basics to handle our border differences," *The Hindu*, 10 May 2013, https://www.thehindu.com/opinion/op-ed/five-basics-to-handle-our-border-differences/article4699681.ece?

28. Sheela Bhatt's interview of Shivshankar Menon, "By 2012, we brought China boundary row to point of solution," *Rediff.com*, 10 August 2015, https://www.rediff.com/news/interview/exclusive-by-2012-we-brought-china-boundary-row-to-point-of-solution/20150720.htm?print=true

29. Dai Bingguo, *Strategic Dialogues: The memoirs of Dai Bingguo* (Beijing, People's Publishing House, 2016), Chapter 8, pp. 291, 296. Translated by NB.

7. FOUR TENTS, NINE MEN AND A DOG

1. See S.N. Prasad et al. (eds), *History of the Conflict with China, 1962* (New Delhi, Ministry of Defence History Division, 1992), pp. 317–21.

2. Prasad et al. (eds), *History of the Conflict with China*, map "Ladakh to Changchenmo," p. 308.

3. P. J. S. Sandhu, "It is time to accept how badly India misread Chinese intentions in 1962—and 2020," *The Wire*, 21 July 2020, https://thewire.in/security/india-china-xi-jinping-lac-border-modi-1962-war

4. Editorial, "New Delhi bears brunt of border hysteria," *Global Times*, 2 May 2013, http://www.globaltimes.cn/content/778692.shtml#.UYoSE0pOnu4

5. Isabelle Saint-Mézard, "The border incident of Spring 2013: Interpreting China-India relations," in *Herodotus*, Vol. 150, Issue 3, 2013, pp. 132–49, translated from French by JPD systems, https://www.cairn-int.info/journal-herodote-2013-3-page-132.htm#no6

6. Liu Zongyi, "Sino–Indian border dispute and their competitive symbiotic relationship," *Associate Paper*, 28 May 2013, *Future Directions International* (Dalkeith, Australia), https://www.futuredirections.org.au/publication/the-china-india-border-issue-in-2013-point-and-counter-point/

7. Pranab Dhal Samanta, "Freeze troop levels at border, says China in draft pact," *Indian Express Archive*, 24 April 2013, http://archive.indianexpress.com/news/freeze-troop-levels-at-border-says-china-in-draft-pact/1106708/

8. For a text of Defence Minister Antony's statement see NDTV.com, 6 September 2013, https://www.ndtv.com/india-news/read-defence-minister-antonys-statement-on-reports-of-chinese-incursion-533782

9. Bibhudatta Pradhan and Kartikay Mehrotra, "China prepared to settle India border dispute, Wang says," *Bloomberg*, 10 June 2014, https://www.bloomberg.com/news/articles/2014–06–09/china-ready-for-india-border-dispute-final-settlement-wang-says

10. Bharti Jain, "No Chinese intrusion since 2010, only 'transgressions': Govt," *The Times of India*, 20 August 2014, https://timesofindia.indiatimes.com/india/No-Chinese-intrusion-since-2010-only-transgressions-Govt/articleshow/40457901.cms

11. Special Correspondent, "India has transgressed LAC more often than China: V.K. Singh," *The Hindu*, 7 February 2021, https://www.thehindu.com/news/national/tamil-nadu/india-has-transgressed-into-lac-more-times-than-china-says-v-k-singh/article33774108.ece

12. Media Center, "Press statement by Prime Minister during visit of President Xi Jinping of China to India," *Ministry of External Affairs, Government of India*, 18 September 2014, https://www.mea.gov.in/Speeches-Statements.htm?dtl/24014/Press_Statement_by_Prime_Minister_during_the_visit_of_President_Xi_Jinping_of_China_to_India_September_18_2014

13. "Live: As Modi raises border issue, Xi agrees with a Chinese yes," *India Today*, 18 September 2014, https://www.indiatoday.in/india/north/story/chinese-president-xi-jinping-india-narendra-modi-293124-2014-09-18

14. "In Joint Pursuit of a Dream of National Renewal," speech by Xi Jinping at the Indian Council of World Affairs, New Delhi, 18 September 2014, https://www.fmprc.gov.cn/mfa_eng/topics_665678/zjpcxshzzcygyslshdsschybdtjkstmedfsllkydjxgsfw/t1194300.shtml

15. "Revive the Silk Road and jointly build a harmonious neighbourhood: Foreign Minister Wang Yi talks about President Xi Jinping's attendance at the SCO summit in Dushanbe and visits to Tajikistan, Maldives, Sri Lanka and India," *Embassy of the People's Republic of China in India*, 20 September 2014, http://in.china-embassy.org/eng/zt/xjp1/t1193711.htm

16. D. S. Rajan, "The meaning of the latest Chinese transgression in Ladakh, ahead of Chinese President's visit to India," *Chennai Centre for China Studies* C3S Paper no. 2040, 17 September 2014, https://www.c3sindia.org/archives/the-meaning-of-latest-chinese-transgression-in-ladakh-ahead-of-chinese-presidents-visit-to-india-by-d-s-rajan/

17. Zhou Bo, "Lessons of Sino–Indian border management," *China Daily*, 25 November 2014, http://usa.chinadaily.com.cn/opinion/2014-11/25/content_18973871.htm

18. Ananth Krishnan, "Arunachal row: Chinese expert cautions India against Japan's 'tricks'," *India Today*, 28 October 2014, https://www.indiatoday.in/world/asia/story/arunachal-pradesh-border-row-chinese-expert-cautions-india-against-japan-tricks-237015-2014-10-28

19. Saibal Das Gupta "'Out of the box' solution for border problem planned as PM Narendra Modi prepares to visit China; Manasarovar route confirmed," *The Times of India*, 2 February 2015, https://timesofindia.indiatimes.com/india/Out-of-box-solution-for-border-problem-planned-as-PM-Narendra-Modi-prepares-to-visit-China-Mansarovar-route-confirmed/articleshow/46089646.cms

20. This was conveyed to me by a senior official who was part of the prime minister's delegation.

21. Ananth Krishnan, "One step forward, two steps back," *India Today*, 11 June 2015, http://indiatoday.intoday.in/story/china-india-lac-modi-visit-xi-jinping-border-dispute/1/443886.html

22. Ananth Krishnan "China warns India against deploying BrahMos cruise missile in Arunachal," *India Today*, 22 August 2016, https://www.indiatoday.in/mail-today/story/brahmos-china-warns-india-336455-2016-08-22

23. Devirupa Mitra, "Exiled Tibetan leader's photo op with flag at Pangong Tso adds Tibet card to India–China border mix," *The Wire*, 19 July 2017, https://thewire.in/diplomacy/lobsang-sangay-central-tibetan-administration-tibet-flag-india-china

24. Book excerpt from Sonia Singh's *Defining India through Their Eyes*, "Dalai Lama exclusive: Chinese President had agreed to meet me," *Ndtv.com*, 15 May 2019, https://www.ndtv.com/book-excerpts/president-xi-was-to-meet-me-in-delhi-in-2014-but-dalai-lama-exclusive-2037863

25. "Speech by Foreign Secretary at Raisina Dialogue in New Delhi, 2 March 2016," *Ministry of External Affairs, Government of India*, http://www.mea.gov.in/incoming-visit-detail.htm?26433/Speech+by+Foreign+Secretary+at+Raisina+Dialogue+in+New+Delhi+March+2+2015

26. "The China Anti-Piracy Bookshelf: Statistics & implications from ten year's deployment… & counting," *blogpost andrewerickson.com*, 2 January 2019, https://www.andrewerickson.com/2019/01/the-china-anti-piracy-bookshelf-statistics-implications-from-ten-years-deployment-counting/

27. Kai Schultz, "Sri Lanka struggling with debt, hands major port to China," *The New York Times*, 12 December 2017, https://www.nytimes.com/2017/12/12/world/asia/sri-lanka-china-port.html

8. DOKLAM

1. "Foreign Ministry Spokesperson Geng Shuang's Remarks on Indian Border Troops Overstepping China-India Boundary at Sikkim Section," 26 June 2017, *Ministry of Foreign Affairs, People's Republic of*

China, http://www.fmprc.gov.cn/mfa_eng/xwfw_665399/s2510_665401/2535_665405/t147 3280.shtml

2. Foreign Ministry Spokesperson Geng Shuang's regular press conference on 5 July 2017, *Ministry of Foreign Affairs, People's Republic of China*, http://www.fmprc.gov.cn/mfa_eng/xwfw_665399/ s2510_665401/2511_665403/t1475680.shtml

3. Foreign Ministry Spokesperson Lu Kang's regular press conference on 28 June 2017, *Ministry of Foreign Affairs of the People's Republic of China*, https://www.fmprc.gov.cn/mfa_eng/xwfw_665399/ s2510_665401/t1473905.shtml

4. Press release, *Ministry of Foreign Affairs, Royal Government of Bhutan*, 29 June 2017 http://www.mfa. gov.bt/press-releases/press-release-272.html

5. See Press release, "Recent developments in Doklam area, 30 June, 2017," *Ministry of External Affairs, Government of India*, http://mea.gov.in/press-releases.htm?dtl/28572/Recent_Developments_in_ Doklam_Area

6. Atul Aneja and Josy Joseph, "Rawat in Sikkim as China demands troop withdrawal," *The Hindu*, 30 June 2017, https://www.thehindu.com/news/national/sikkim-standoff-china-asks-army-chief-to-stop-clamouring-for-war/article19180321.ece

7. Foreign Ministry Spokesman Geng Shuang's regular press conference on 3 July 2017, *Ministry of Foreign Affairs of the People's Republic of China*, http://www.fmprc.gov.cn/mfa_eng/xwfw_665399/ s2510_665401/2511_665403/t1475054.shtml

8. "The facts and China's position concerning the Indian border troops' crossing of the China-India boundary in the Sikkim Sector into the Chinese territory," *The State Council, the People's Republic of China*, August 3, 2017 http://english.www.gov.cn/state_council/ministries/2017/08/03/content_281475768 664370.htm

9. "Video on China-India border issue sparks heated discussion among netizens," *Xinhua*, 3 August 2017, https://web.archive.org/web/20170806235153/http:/www.ecns.cn/military/2017/08-03/ 267855.shtml

10. Aijaz Hussain, "China, India soldiers hurl stones at one another in Kashmir," *Associated Press*, 16 August 2017, https://web.archive.org/web/20170806235153/http:/www.ecns.cn/military/2017/08-03/267855.shtml

11. "Road construction inside Bhutanese territory violates agreements: MFA," *Kuensel*, 30 June 2017, https://kuenselonline.com/road-construction-inside-bhutanese-territory-violates-agreements-mfa/

12. "India expresses concern over road construction in Doklam," *Kuensel*, 1 July 2017, https://kuensel-online.com/india-expresses-concern-over-road-construction-in-doklam/

13. Srinath Raghavan, "China is wrong on Sikkim-Tibet boundary," *Mint*, 7 August 2017, http://www.live-mint.com/Opinion/kfpkmisQLSnGho2e2oo2rO/China-is-wrong-on-SikkimTibet-boundary.html

14. M. Taylor Fravel, "Danger at Do(k)lam," *Indian Express*, 18 July 2017, https://indianexpress.com/ article/opinion/columns/danger-at-dolam-plateau-doklam-stand-off-india-china-4755269/

15. The maps can be seen in Manoj Joshi, "Doklam, Gipmochi, Gyemochen: It's hard making cartographic sense of a geopolitical quagmire," *The Wire*, 20 July 2017, https://thewire.in/159407/doklam-india-china-bhutan/

16. The names can be checked in National Geospatial Intelligence Agency Geonames Search website, http://geonames.nga.mil/namesgaz/. Till mid-July 2020, at least, the website showed only one location of Gipmochi/Gyemochen, which was near Elephant Lake. The new location has been added recently.

17. Nirupama Rao, *The Fractured Himalaya: India, Tibet, China 1949–1962* (New Delhi, Penguin/Viking, 2021), p. 128.

18. The developments there and the Indian intelligence angle is described candidly by G.B.S. Sidhu, *Sikkim, Dawn of Democracy: The truth behind the merger with India* (New Delhi, Penguin/Viking, 2018).

19. Translation of the Resolutions of the 85th Session of the National Assembly of Bhutan (June 15–July

7, 2006) Section VIII, Border Talks. A translated summary of the National Assembly resolutions are available via http://www.nab.gov.bt/en/business/resolutions

20. Medha Bisht, "Sino-Bhutan boundary negotiations: Complexities of the 'Package Deal,'" *IDSA Comment*, 19 January 2010, http://www.idsa.in/idsacomments/Sino-BhutanBoundaryNegotiations_ mbisht_190110

21. Proceedings and Resolutions of the 75th Session of the National Assembly held from 20 June to 16 July 1997 Section III, Bhutan–China Boundary Talks, https://www.nab.gov.bt/assets/uploads/docs/ resolution/2014/75th_Session.pdf

22. Translation of the Proceedings and Resolutions of the 73rd Session of the National Assembly of Bhutan held from 10 August to 2nd September 1995 Section VII, Bhutan–China Boundary Talks, https:// www.nab.gov.bt/assets/uploads/docs/resolution/2014/73rd_Session.pdf p. 82

23. Tsering Shakya, "Bhutan can resolve its problem with China—if India lets it," *South China Morning Post*, 22 July 2017 http://www.scmp.com/week-asia/geopolitics/article/2103601/bhutan-can-solve-its-border-problem-china-if-india-lets-it. In Shakya's view, Bhutan has a weak case on the border issue anyway.

24. Proceedings and Resolutions of the 75th Session 20 June- 16 July 1997.

25. Translation of the Proceedings and Resolutions of the 79th Session of the National Assembly of Bhutan, June 28, 2001, Section X, Border Talks, https://www.nab.gov.bt/assets/uploads/docs/ resolution/2014/79th_Session.pdf pp. 145–6.

26. Thierry Mathou, "Bhutan–China relations: Towards a new step in Himalayan politics," *The Spider and the Piglet: Proceedings of the First International Seminar on Bhutanese Studies* (Thimphu, Centre for Bhutan Studies, 2004), p. 402.

27. See report on the status of Bhutan–China border negotiations, in Proceedings and Resolutions of the 4th Session of the National Assembly, Section IX, 20 November 2009 pp. 17–33, https://www.nab. gov.bt/assets/uploads/docs/resolution/2014/4th_session_eng.pdf

28. "Motion on Bhutan–China border talk," in Proceedings and Resolutions of the 6th Session of the First Parliament of Bhutan, Section XVI, 19 November 2010 pp. 47–50. https://www.nab.gov.bt/assets/ uploads/docs/resolution/2015/EngGeneralResolution6thSession.pdf

29. Suhasini Haidar and Ananth Krishnan, "Bhutan–China officials meet, agree to schedule much delayed boundary talks soon," *The Hindu*, 9 April 2021, https://www.thehindu.com/news/international/ Bhutan–China-officials-meet-agree-to-schedule-much-delayed-boundary-talks-soon/article34283 724.ece

30. Foreign Ministry Spokesperson Hua Chunying's regular press conference on 28 August 2017, *Ministry of Foreign Affairs of the People's Republic of China*, https://www.fmprc.gov.cn/mfa_eng/xwfw_665399/ s2510_665401/t1487932.shtml

31. Anil Gupta, "End of Doklam crisis, big diplomatic victory for India," *The Quint*, 29 August 2017, https://www.thequint.com/voices/blogs/doklam-standoff-diplomatic-win-for-india#read-more#read-more; Arihant Pawariya, "Beyond Doklam: How India can tame the dragon by taking a leaf out of its own playbook," *Swarajaya*, 29 August 2017, https://swarajyamag.com/ideas/beyond-doklam-how-to-tame-the-dragon-by-taking-a-leaf-out-of-its-own-playbook; "Doklam is a diplomatic victory for India: Kanwal Sibal," interview on *Rajya Sabha TV*, 30 August 2017, https://rstv.nic.in/ doklam-diplomatic-victory-india-kanwal-sibal.html

32. M. Taylor Fravel, "Why India did not 'win' the standoff with China," *War on the Rocks*, 1 September 2017, https://warontherocks.com/2017/09/why-india-did-not-win-the-standoff-with-china/

33. Richard M. Rossow, Joseph S. Bermudez Jr and Kriti Upadhyaya, "A frozen line in the Himalayas," *CSIS Briefs*, August 2020, https://www.csis.org/analysis/frozen-line-himalayas

34. Vishnu Som, "Exclusive: Satellite images hint at renewed China threat in Doklam," *NDTV News*, 22 November 2022, https://www.ndtv.com/india-news/exclusive-satellite-images-hint-at-renewed-china-threat-in-doklam-2328660

35. Vishnu Som, "Chinese land grab on Bhutanese territory, 4 villages built in 1 year," *NDTV News*, 18 November 2021, https://www.ndtv.com/world-news/chinese-landgrab-on-bhutanese-territory-4-villages-built-in-1-year-2615065

36. Devjoyot Ghoshal and Anand Katakam, "China steps up construction along disputed Bhutan border, satellite images show," *Reuters*, 13 January 2022, https://www.reuters.com/world/china/china-steps-up-construction-along-disputed-bhutan-border-satellite-images-show-2022-01-12/

37. Robert Barnett, "China is building entire villages in another country's territory," *Foreign Policy*, 7 May 2021, https://foreignpolicy.com/2021/05/07/china-bhutan-border-villages-security-forces/

38. Vishnu Som, "Bhutan's Denial of China Incursion is 'Blatant Untruth': Global Observers," NDTV. Com   21 November 2020, https://www.ndtv.com/india-news/bhutan-denies-chinese-incursion-blatant-untruth-say-global-observers-2328012

39. "Highlights of the Council's discussions 58th GEF meeting June 2–3, 2020 virtual meeting," *Global Environment Facility*, 16 June 2020, https://www.thegef.org/sites/default/files/council-meeting-documents/HIGHLIGHTS_58th_Council_Meeting%20%28002%29.pdf

40. Suhasini Haidar, "China doubles down on claims on eastern Bhutan boundary," *The Hindu*, 5 July 2020, https://www.thehindu.com/news/international/days-after-demarche-china-doubles-down-on-claims-on-eastern-bhutan-boundary/article31993470.ece

41. Manoj Joshi, "Lost victory in Doklam," *Observer Research Foundation*, 4 December 2020, https://www.orfonline.org/expert-speak/lost-victory-doklam/

42. Tshering Palden, "Bhutan–China sign MoU to expedite boundary negotiations," *Kuensel*, 15 October 2021, https://kuenselonline.com/Bhutan–China-sign-mou-to-expedite-boundary-negotiations/

9. ILLUSORY RESET

1. "Strong PLA to better protect global peace," *China Military Online*, 24 October 2017, http://english.chinamil.com.cn/view/2017–10/24/content_7798169.htm

2. Ravi Rikhye, "China's troop buildup in Doklam means India cannot protect Bhutan," *The Print*, 18 January 2018, https://theprint.in/opinion/goodbye-doklam-accepting-china-as-its-new-overlord-is-in-bhutans-best-interest/30058/

3. Hitherto, the Indian posture across the Himalayas was defensive.

4. "India: A military buildup on the border with China," *Stratfor*, 22 July 2013, https://worldview.stratfor.com/article/india-military-buildup-border-china.

5. Colonel Vinayak Bhatt (retd), "New trouble for India: China occupies northern Doklam with armoured vehicles and 7 helipads," *The Print*, 17 January 2018, https://theprint.in/defence/new-trouble-for-india-as-china-fully-occupies-doklam/29561/

6. Zhou Bo, "Doklam stand-off with China: Will India learn the right lessons or pay as Nehru did?" *South China Morning Post*, 8 January 2018, https://www.scmp.com/comment/insight-opinion/article/2127282/doklam-stand-china-will-india-learn-right-lessons-or-pay

7. Devirupa Mitra, "In official testimony to MPs, government revealed full story of Doklam," *The Wire*, 15 August 2018, https://thewire.in/diplomacy/doklam-parliamentary-standing-committee-india-china. Not surprisingly, some of these nuances were expunged from the report itself when it was published next month in September 2018.

8. Media Center, "20th meeting of the Special Representatives of India and China (December 22, 2017)," *Ministry of External Affairs, Government of India*, https://www.mea.gov.in/press-releases.htm?dtl/29232/20th_Meeting_of_the_Special_Representatives_of_India_and_China_December_22_2017

9. Devirupa Mitra, "As Dalai Lama event is shifted from New Delhi, Modi's new line on Tibet remains a puzzle," *The Wire*, 6 March 2018, https://thewire.in/diplomacy/experts-unravel-the-puzzle-of-indian-govts-circular-on-distancing-from-dalai-lama-event

10. "India–China informal summit at Wuhan," *Ministry of External Affairs, Government of India*, 28 April 2018, http://mea.gov.in/outgoing-visit-detail.htm?29853/IndiaChina+Informal+Summit+at+Wuhan.

11. "China, India reach broad consensus in informal summit," *Ministry of Foreign Affairs of the People's Republic of China*, 30 April 2018, http://www.fmprc.gov.cn/mfa_eng/wjdt_665385/wshd_665389/t1555656.shtml.

12. Media Center, "Prime Minister's keynote address at Shangri-La Dialogue (June 1, 2018)," *Ministry of External Affairs, Government of India*, https://www.mea.gov.in/Speeches-Statements.htm?dtl/29943/Prime+Ministers+Keynote+Address+at+Shangri+La+Dialogue+June+01+2018

13. Sushant Singh, "India, China to have new defence MoU, check Doklam-like incidents," *Indian Express*, 24 August 2018, https://indianexpress.com/article/india/india-china-to-have-new-defence-mou-check-doklam-like-incidents-5322109/

14. Geeta Mohan, "PM Modi meets Xi Jinping, Vladimir Putin and Ashraf Ghani at Bishkek," *India Today*, 14 June 2019, https://www.indiatoday.in/world/story/pm-modi-meets-xi-jinping-vladimir-putin-ashraf-ghani-bishkek-1548521-2019-06-14

15. "Indian Vice-President Naidu meets Wang Yi," *Ministry of Foreign Affairs of the People's Republic of China*, 21 December 2019, https://www.fmprc.gov.cn/mfa_eng/zxxx_662805/t1726789.shtml

16. "22nd meeting of the Special Representatives of China and India held in New Delhi," *Ministry of Foreign Affairs of the People's Republic of China*, 21 December 2019 https://www.fmprc.gov.cn/mfa_eng/zxxx_662805/t1726791.shtml

10. THE FUTURE: WAR, COMPETITIVE CO-EXISTENCE, OR ANTAGONISTIC COOPERATION?

1. Indrani Bagchi interview with Shivshankar Menon, "China's rising support for Pakistan, and their collusion, may affect our interests," *The Times of India*, 25 April 2021.

2. M. Taylor Fravel, "Stability in a secondary strategic direction: China and the border dispute with India after 1962," in Kanti Bajpai, Selina Ho and Manjari Chatterjee Miller (eds), *Routledge Handbook of China-India Relations* (London, Routledge, 2020).

3. Ye Hailin, "The impact of identity bias on the prospects of Sino–Indian relations," *Indian Ocean Economy Research*, Issue 3, 30 July 2020, http://www.cssn.cn/gjgxx/gj_ytqy/202007/t20200730_5163496.html (Machine translation)

4. M. Duchatel, "The border clashes with India: In the shadow of the US," *China Trends*, February 2021.

5. Liu Zongyi, "India thinks it has gotten the better of China, so it can dare China," *Observer.com*, 21 September 2020. Translated by Prof. Hemant Adlakha, *Indian Defence Review*, net edition 28 September 2020, http://www.indiandefencereview.com/interviews/india-thinks-it-has-got-the-better-of-china-so-it-can-dare-china/

6. Zhang Jiadong, "Crisis and opportunities often co-exist for cooperation and development to China-India relations," *China Military Online*, 28 June 2020, http://eng.chinamil.com.cn/view/2020-06/28/content_9842314.htm?

7. "Deputy Secretary Biegun remarks at the US-India Strategic Partnership Forum, August 31, 2020," *US Department of State* archived content, 2017–2021, https://2017–2021.state.gov/deputy-secretary-biegun-remarks-at-the-u-s-india-strategic-partnership-forum/index.html

8. National Security Council, "United States strategic framework for the Indo-Pacific". This is a document that had guided the Trump administration policy and was declassified on 12 January 2021 on the eve of the inaugural of the Biden administration, https://trumpwhitehouse.archives.gov/wp-content/uploads/2021/01/IPS-Final-Declass.pdf

9. Press Trust of India, "US provided some info, equipment to India during its border crisis with China: Pentagon Commander," *The Times of India*, 10 March 2021, https://timesofindia.indiatimes.com/

india/us-provided-some-info-equipment-to-india-during-its-border-crisis-with-china-pentagon-com-mander/articleshow/81432002.cms

10. In Shyam Saran's view the action was counterproductive. See "India waving SFF and Tibet cards won't scare China. Can't pull levers you don't have," *The Print*, 14 September 2020, https://theprint.in/opinion/india-waving-sff-and-tibet-card-wont-scare-china/501826/?

11. Sam Van Schaik, *Tibet: A history* (New Delhi, Amaryllis, 2012), p. 153.

12. John W. Garver, *China's Quest: The history of foreign relations of the People's Republic of China* (New York, Oxford University Press, 2016), pp. 313–14.

13. Gyalo Thondup and Anne F. Thurston, *The Noodle Maker of Kalimpong: The untold story of my struggle for Tibet* (Gurgaon, Random House India, 2015), p. 258.

14. "His Holiness's middle way approach for resolving the issue of Tibet," https://www.dalailama.com/messages/tibet/middle-way-app.roach

15. Full text, "Tibet's path of development is driven by an irresistible historical tide," White Paper, 15 April 2015, *The State Council, The People's Republic of China*, http://english.www.gov.cn/archive/white_paper/2015/04/15/content_281475089444218.htm

16. The Dalai Lama, "Reincarnation," His Holiness the Dalai Lama of Tibet, 24 September 2011, https://www.dalailama.com/the-dalai-lama/biography-and-daily-life/reincarnation

17. "Freedom of religious belief in China: White Paper October 1997," *Embassy of the People's Republic of China in the United States of America*, http://www.china-embassy.org/eng/zt/zjxy/t36492.htm

18. Xinhua, "Reincarnation of living Buddha needs gov't approval," *China Daily*, 4 August 2007, http://www.chinadaily.com.cn/china/2007–08/04/content_5448242.htm

19. Ben Blanchard, "China's Xi vows unceasing fight against Tibet separatism," *Reuters*, 26 August 2015, https://www.reuters.com/article/us-china-tibet/chinas-xi-vows-unceasing-fight-against-tibet-separatism-idUSKCN0QV0AE20150826?feedType=RSS&feedName=worldNews&rpc=69

20. "China sets policy directions for developing Tibet," *CCTV.com*, 30 August 2020, https://english.cctv.com/2020/08/30/ARTIJIagljLuIGEITKepvLr1200830.shtml; Shyam Saran, "Xi Jinping's visit to Tibet," *The Tribune*, 11 August 2021, https://www.tribuneindia.com/news/comment/xi-jinpings-visit-to-tibet-295785

21. Zhang Minyan, "Xi Jinping elaborated on the strategy of governing Tibet in the new era, all the main points are here," *Xinhuanet*, 30 August 2020, http://www.xinhuanet.com/politics/xxjxs/202008/30/c_1126431397.htm (Google Translate)

22. Ananth Krishnan, "Xi Jinping visits Tibet border region, first by Chinese leader in years," *The Hindu*, 23 July 2021, https://www.thehindu.com/news/international/xi-jinping-visits-tibet-border-region-first-by-chinese-leader-in-years/article35481755.ece

23. Sudhi Ranjan Sen, "US, India step up fight with China over the next Dalai Lama," *Bloomberg News*, 15 April 2021, https://www.bloomberg.com/news/articles/2021–04–14/who-will-be-the-next-dalai-lama-u-s-india-china-try-to-control-process?sref=NDAgb47j

24. Manoj Joshi, "India–China border row: How depopulation in mountains helps Beijing," *The Quint*, 25 November 2021, https://www.thequint.com/voices/opinion/india-china-border-row-how-depopulation-in-mountains-helps-beijing

25. "Xi encourages Tibetan herders to safeguard territory," *Xinhua*, 29 October 2018, http://www.xinhuanet.com/english/2017–10/29/c_136713312.htm

26. Jayadeva Ranade, "China's Xiaokang (well off) border defence villages in the Tibet Autonomous Region," *Vivekananda International Foundation*, 24 September 2019, https://www.vifindia.org/article/2019/september/24/china-s-xiaokang-border-defence-villages-in-the-tibet-autonomous-region

27. Ye Hailin," The impact of identity bias"

28. Yun Sun, "The Ladakh clash: China's India dilemma," *Global Asia*, September 2020 vol. 15, No.3, https://www.globalasia.org/v15no3/debate/the-ladakh-clash-chinas-india-dilemma_sun-yun

29. Snehesh Alex Philip, "Army beefs up Leh-based 14 Corps to counter belligerent China as winter

approaches," *The Print*, 12 November 2021, https://theprint.in/defence/army-beefs-up-leh-based-14-corps-to-counter-belligerent-china-as-winter-app.roaches/765133/

30. Sushant Singh, "Squaring off again in the Himalayan heights," *The Hindu*, 22 October 2021, https://www.thehindu.com/opinion/op-ed/squaring-off-again-in-the-himalayan-heights/article37116226.ece

31. Manu Pubby, "Operational alert in place: From Chumbi valley to Kibithu, China ups tension in the East," *The Economic Times*, 31 October 2021, https://economictimes.indiatimes.com/news/defence/operational-alert-in-place-from-chumbi-valley-to-kibithu-china-ups-tension-in-the-east/articleshow/87405232.cms

32. Dinakar Peri, "Chinese buildup in RALP area matter of concern: Officers," *The Hindu*, 30 October 2021, https://www.thehindu.com/news/national/chinese-build-up-in-ralp-area-matter-of-concern-officers/article37254191.ece

33. Details of China's build up can be seen in Sim Tack, "A military drive spells out China's intent along the Indian border," *RealClear World*, 22 September 2020, https://www.realclearworld.com/articles/2020/09/22/a_military_drive_spells_out_chinas_intent_along_the_indian_border_578286.amp.html?

34. Detresfa_, Sim Tack, The Intel Lab, Tyler Rogoway, "Tracking China's sudden airpower expansion on its western border," *thedrive*, 16 June 2021, https://www.thedrive.com/the-war-zone/41065/tracking-chinas-sudden-airpower-expansion-along-its-western-border

35. Tara Kartha, "India's defence needs money. If budget cannot provide it, we need to change how we fight," *The Print*, 29 January 2021, https://theprint.in/opinion/indias-defence-needs-money-if-budget-cant-provide-it-we-need-to-change-how-we-fight/593651/

36. Daniel Darling, "Budgetary pressures induce Indian Navy rethink," *Defense & Security Monitor*, 23 January 2020, https://dsm.forecastinternational.com/wordpress/2020/01/23/budgetary-pressures-induce-indian-navy-rethink/

37. Cited in Michael Pillsbury, "Geopolitical power calculations," in M. Pillsbury, *China Debates the Future Security Environment* (National Defense University Press, 2000), https://fas.org/nuke/guide/china/doctrine/pills2/index.html

38. See Happymon Jacob's interview with M. Taylor Fravel, 5 April 2021, https://www.youtube.com/watch?v=fm8u—Fz5MM

39. Singh, "Squaring off again in the Himalayas...."

40. "China, India agree to further ease border tension: Defense spokesperson," *China Military Online*, 27 August 2020 http://eng.chinamil.com.cn/view/2020-08/27/content_9891337.htm

41. Foreign Ministry spokesperson Zhao Lijian's regular press conference on January 2, 2021," *Ministry of Foreign Affairs of the People's Republic of China* https://www.fmprc.gov.cn/mfa_eng/xwfw_665399/s2510_665401/2511_665403/t1849568.shtml

42. Some of Ambassador Sun Weidong's speeches can be seen on the Embassy of China's website, http://in.china-embassy.org/eng/dsxxs/dshdjjh/t1820728.htm

43. Author notes of Institute of Defence Studies and Analyses-Sichuan University virtual bilateral dialogue, 20–21 November 2020.

44. See question by the Press Trust of India in "State Councillor and Foreign Minister Wang Yi meets the press 8 March 2021", *Ministry of Foreign Affairs, People's Republic of China* https://www.fmprc.gov.cn/mfa_eng/wjb_663304/wjbz_663308/2461_663310/t1859138.shtml

45. "Wang Yi speaks with Indian Foreign Minister Jaishankar on the phone, February 26, 2021," *Ministry of Foreign Affairs, People's Republic of China*, https://www.fmprc.gov.cn/mfa_eng/wjb_663304/wjbz_663308/activities_663312/t1856910.shtml

46. The Wire staff, "Rajya Sabha Secretariat disallowed question on whethere Chinese crossed LAC: Subramaniam Swamy," *The Wire*, 1 December 2021, https://thewire.in/government/subramanian-swamy-rajya-sabha-secretariat-question-lac-china-disallowed

47. Media Center,"Keynote address by External Affairs Minister at the 13th All India Conference of China Studies, January 28, 2021," *Ministry of External Affairs, Government of India*, https://www.mea.gov.in/Speeches-Statements.htm?dtl/33419/Keynote+Address+by+External+Affairs+Minister+at+the+13th+All+India+Conference+of+China+Studies

48. Nayanima Basu, "Quad is not 'Asian NATO', India never had 'NATO mentality', Jaishankar says," *The Print*, 14 April 2021, https://theprint.in/diplomacy/quad-is-not-asian-nato-india-never-had-nato-mentality-jaishankar-says/639924/

49. Qian Feng, "View from China: From line to zone," *Force* (September 2020), http://forceindia.net/cover-story/from-line-to-zone/

50. Yun Sun, "China's Strategic Assessment of India," *War on the Rocks*, 25 March 2020, https://warontherocks.com/2020/03/chinas-strategic-assessment-of-india/?."

51. Geeta Mohan, "India calls for early resolution of remaining LAC issues with China," *India Today*, 17 September 2021, https://www.indiatoday.in/india/story/india-china-s-jaishankar-wang-yi-sco-summit-lac-ladakh-1854078-2021-09-17

52. Sutirtho Patranobis, "India, China should focus on 'normalised management' of the border: Wang Yi at SCO," *The Hindustan Times*, 17 December 2021, https://www.hindustantimes.com/world-news/india-china-should-focus-on-normalised-management-of-border-wang-yi-at-sco-101631871314992.html

53. Rajat Pandit, "Army ready to thwart any mischief by China, while talks underway to resolve remaining 'friction points': General M.M. Naravane," *The Times of India*, 29 May 2021, https://timesofindia.indiatimes.com/india/army-ready-to-thwart-any-mischief-by-china-while-talks-underway-to-resolve-remaining-friction-points-general-m-m-naravane/articleshow/83046308.cms

54. For the upgrade of Chinese forces facing India in Ladakh, see Wang Shichun, "Large-scale replacement of PLA's Sino–Indian border mechanized forces," *Sina.com*, 7 February 2021, https://mil.news.sina.com.cn/china/2021-02-07/doc-ikftpnny5561650.shtml (Machine translation)

55. Shivshankar Menon, "India–China ties: The future hold 'antagonistic cooperation', not war," *The Wire*, 7 December 2020, https://thewire.in/external-affairs/india-china-ties-expect-antagonistic-cooperation-future-not-war

SELECT BIBLIOGRAPHY

Bajpai, Kanti, Karim, Afsir and Mattoo, Amitabh (eds), *Kargil and After: Challenges for Indian policy* (New Delhi, Har Anand, 2001).

Bajpai, Kanti, Ho, Selina and Chatterjee Miller, Manjari (eds), *Routledge Handbook of China-India Relations* (London, Routledge, 2020).

Banerjee, P.K *My Peking Memoirs of the Chinese Invasion of India* (New Delhi, Clarion Books, 1990), with a foreword by Han Suyin.

A.S. Bhasin, *Nehru, Tibet and China* (New Delhi, Penguin/Viking, 2021).

Bhattacharji, Romesh, *Ladakh: Changing yet unchanged* (New Delhi, Rupa, 2012).

Conboy, Kenneth and Morrison, James, *The CIA's Secret War in Tibet* (Lawrence, KA, University Press of Kansas, 2002).

Bingguo, Dai, *Strategic Dialogues: The memoirs of Dai Bingguo* (Beijing, People's Publishing House, 2016).

Deepak, B.R., *India and China: A century of peace and conflict 1904–2004* (New Delhi, Manas, 2005).

Dikötter, Frank, *The Tragedy of Liberation: A history of the Chinese revolution, 1945–57* (New York, Bloomsbury, 2013).

M. Taylor Fravel, *Strong Borders, Secure Nation: Cooperation and Conflict in China's Territorial Disputes*, (Princeton, Princeton University Press, 2008).

John W. Garver, *Protracted Contest: Sino–Indian rivalry in the twentieth century* (New Delhi, Oxford University Press, 2001).

————, *China's Quest: The history of foreign relations of the People's Republic of China* (New York, Oxford University Press, 2016).

Gupta, Shishir, *The Himalayan Face-off: Chinese assertion and the Indian riposte* (New Delhi, Hachette, 2015).

Guyot-Réchard, Bérénice, *Shadow States: India, China and the Himalayas, 1910–1962* (New Delhi, Cambridge University Press, 2017).

Hoffman, Steven A., *India and the China crisis* (New Delhi, Oxford University Press, 1990).

Jaishankar, S., *The India Way: Strategies for an uncertain world* (New Delhi, Harper Collins, 2020).

Kalha, Ranjit Singh, *India–China Boundary Issues: Quest for a settlement* (New Delhi, Indian Council of World Affairs/Pentagon Press, 2014).

Knaus, John Kenneth, *Orphans of the Cold War: America and the Tibetan struggle for survival* (New York, Public Affairs, 1999).

Krishnan, Ananth, *India's China Challenge: A journey through China's rise and what it means for India* (New Delhi, Harper Collins, 2020).

Lintner, Bertil, *China's India War: Collison course on the roof of the world* (New Delhi, Oxford University Press, 2018).

Malik, V.P., *Kargil: From surprise to victory* (New Delhi, Harper Collins, 2006).

Mullik, B.N., *My Years with Nehru: The Chinese betrayal* (New Delhi, Allied, 1971).

Maxwell, Neville, *India's China War* (Dehra Dun, Natraj, 2013).

Mehta, Jagat S., *Negotiating for India: Resolving problems through diplomacy* (New Delhi, Manohar, 2006).

Menon, Shivshankar, *Choices: Inside the making of India's foreign policy* (New Delhi, Allen Lane, 2016).

———, *India and Asian Geopolitics: The past, present* (Washington, DC, Brookings Institution Press, 2021).

Noorani, A.G., *India–China Boundary Problem 1846–1947: History and diplomacy,* (New Delhi, Oxford University Press, 2011).

Palit, D.K., *War in the High Himalaya: The Indian Army in crisis*, 1962 (London, Hurst, 1991).

Prasad, S.N. et al., (eds), *History of the Conflict with China, 1962* (New Delhi, Ministry of Defence History Division, 1992). [This is a manuscript of the history as readied for publication. It has yet to be actually published.]

Phuntso, Karma, *The History of Bhutan* (Gurgaon, Random House, 2013).

Raghavan, Srinath, *War and Peace in Modern India: A strategic history of the Nehru years*, (Ranikhet, Permanent Black, 2010).

Rao, Nirupama, *The Fractured Himalayas: India, Tibet, China 1949–1962* (New Delhi, Penguin/Viking, 2021).

Riedel, Bruce, *JFK's Forgotten Crisis: Tibet, the CIA and the Sino–Indian war* (New Delhi, Harper Collins, 2016).

Sandhu, P.J.S., *1962: A view from the other side of the hill* (New Delhi, United Services Institution, 2015).

Saran, Shyam, *How India Sees the World: From Kautilya to the 21st century* (New Delhi, Juggernaut, 2017).

Schaffer, Howard B., *The Limits of Influence: America's role in Kashmir* (New Delhi, Penguin, 2009).

Seth, Vikram, *From Heaven Lake: Travels through Sinkiang and Tibet* (New Delhi, Penguin, 1990).

SELECT BIBLIOGRAPHY

Sidhu, G.B.S., *Sikkim, Dawn of Democracy: The truth behind the merger with India* (New Delhi, Penguin/Viking, 2018).

Singh, Jaswant, *A Call to Honour: In service of emergent India* (New Delhi, Rupa, 2006).

Singh, K. Natwar, *My China Diary: 1956–1988* (New Delhi, Rupa, 2009).

Singh, Zorawar Daulet, *Power Shift: India–China relations in a multipolar world* (New Delhi, Macmillan, 2020).

Small, Andrew, *The China Pakistan Axis: Asia's new geopolitics* (London, Hurst, 2015).

Talbott, Strobe, *Engaging India: Diplomacy, democracy and the bomb* (Washington DC, Brookings Institution Press, 2004).

Smith, Jeff M., *Cold Peace: China-India rivalry in the 21st century* (Lanham, MD, Lexington Books, 2014).

Thondup, Gyalo and Thurston, Anne F. *The Noodle-maker of Kalimpong: The untold story of my struggle for Tibet* (Gurgaon, Random House India, 2015).

Van Schaik, Sam, *Tibet: A history* (New Delhi, Amaryllis, 2012).

Shakya, Tsering, *The Dragon in the Land of Snows: A history of Tibet since 1947* (New York, Penguin, 1999).

Woodman, Dorothy, *Himalayan Frontiers: A political review of British, Chinese, Indian and Russian rivalries* (London, Barrie and Rockliff, 1969).

INDEX

INDEX

INDEX

Pakistan, 177, 217, 240
  BRI proposal of China, 179
  China military assistance, 105
  China intervention India-
    Pakistan war (1965), 71–2
  Ghauri missile, 95, 96
  Kargil war, 100–2
  LoC establishment of, 102–3
  Vajpayee visit (2004), 120
Panag, Lt. Gen. H. S., 19, 38
Panchen Lama, 236
Pangda (village), 205, 206
Pangong Tso, xiii, 2, 13, 190, 219, 224
  Chinese attack during 1962 war, 63, 64
  Chinese blocking of Indian patrols, 15, 17–18, 28–30
  Finger 8, 219
  PLA-KMT battle, 7
  See also Galwan/Galwan river valley
Parthasarathi, G., 74
Patranobis, Sutirtho, 41
Pawar, Sharad, 83
People's Daily (newspaper), 51, 97
Phobrang, 30
PLA (People's Liberation Army, China), 17, 18, 209–10, 226–7, 235
  Depsang issues, 155–60, 167
  15th Airborne Corps (PLA), 240
  Galwan clashes, 22–4
  signed Border Defence Cooperation Agreement, 162
  Border transgressions, 167–8
  and KMT battle, 7
Political Parameters Agreement (2005), 121–5, 127–8, 150–1
  suggestion of a swap of claims, 123
Pompeo, Mike, 228, 245

Pottinger, Matt, 228, 245
Pudong, 111–12
Pulwama, 217
Putin, Vladimir, 218

Qi Fabao, Senior Colonel 22–3
Qian Feng, 169, 248
Qian Qichen, 90
Qin Gang, 159–60
Quadrilateral Grouping (Quad), 215, 227, 229, 230–1
Quishi, 61
Qureshi, Shah Mehmood, 217

R&AW. *See* Research & Analysis Wing (R&AW)
Raghavan, Srinath, 61
Raisina Dialogue, 180, 231, 247
Rajan, D. S., 172–3
Rajya Sabha (India), 203, 247
Ranade, Jayadeva, 239
Rao, Narasimha, 81
Rao, Nirupama, 51, 58, 192–3
Rashtrapati Bhavan, 177, 238
Rawat, General Bipin, 188
RBA. *See* Royal Bhutan Army (RBA)
Regional Comprehensive Economic Partnership (RCEP), 12, 220, 246
Ren Guoqing Senior Colonel, 200
Research & Analysis Wing (R&AW), 232, 235
Rice, Condoleezza, 128
Rijiju, Kiren, 216
Rikhye, Ravi, 210
Royal Bhutan Army (RBA), 184, 187, 195, 200–1
Rudd, Kevin, 229
Russia—India—China (RIC) Grouping, 149, 174, 240

285